TOEFL PREP for Spanish Speakers

By Greg Britt

© Copyright 2009 by Greg Britt

All rights reserved.
No part of this book may be reproduced
in any form, by photostat, microfilm, xerography,
or any other means, or incorporated into any
information retrieval system, electronic or
mechanical, without the written permission
of the copyright owner.

All inquiries should be addressed to:
BSL Books, under the direction of
Britt Servicios Lingüísticos
Insurgentes Sur 56-4, Colonia Juarez,
06600 México D.F., México
Tel., (525) 546-6160, e-mail: britt.mx@gmail.com

Originally published in 2002.

TOEFL is a registered trademark of Educational Testing Service. This publication is
NOT endorsed nor approved by ETS. BSL Books bears sole responsibility for this book's
contents, and is not connected with ETS.

Reservados todos los derechos.

Registro Público del Derecho de Autor (Instituto Nacional del Derecho de Autor, Secretaria
de Educación Pública), Número de Registro: 03-1999-081312480500-01.

TOEFL PREP for Spanish Speakers

By Greg Britt

Table of Contents

PART ONE Introduction to Course — 1

PART TWO Introduction to Structure and Written Expression (Grammar) — 5
- STEP ONE
  - Main Clauses — 18
  - Subordination — 34
- STEP TWO
  - Subject-Verb Agreement — 58
  - Subject-Pronoun Agreement — 76
  - Verb Tense and Form — 86
  - Pronoun Form and Reference — 95
- STEP THREE
  - Verbals — 114
  - Word Form — 134
- STEP FOUR
  - Word Order — 158
  - Parallel Structure — 175
  - Unnecessary Repetition — 187
- STEP FIVE
  - Correct Usage — 194

PART THREE The Written Essay — 221

PART FOUR Listening Comprehension — 225

PART FIVE Reading Comprehension and Vocabulary — 232

APPENDICES — 236

To Mrs. Hall, my most inspiring teacher,
whom I might impersonate but could never imitate.

ACKNOWLEDGEMENTS

Many thanks to Rosa Aguilar Montes de Oca who first asked me
"Can you help me with the TOEFL exam?"

Thanks to Victor Hugo Ramos for use of his course notes in Spanish.

Thanks to Guadalupe Marcial for tirelessly working with me through rough drafts.

Thanks to Mónica Lobatón for helping me understand
some of the mysterious world of publishing in Mexico.

Thanks to the talented reviewers and teachers of pilot programs.

Most of all, thanks to my students, the hundreds who have worked through this program and
taught me more than I could have possibly taught them.

TOEFL PREP for Spanish Speakers

Introduction

PART ONE

This program, unlike any other TOEFL preparation method, was written especially for **Spanish-speaking students**. It addresses the particular needs that Spanish-speaking students, as opposed to, say Japanese-speaking students, have with English usage. Because Spanish and English are so similar, many problems in usage arise when things are different. Most Spanish speakers share the same problems. Here, we will examine those problems within the context of TOEFL preparation, often giving explanations in Spanish. While this will be of obvious benefit to the Spanish-speaking student, it will also help the teacher (especially the native-speaking English teacher) give useful explanations to his students in Spanish.

- This Program

Although this book can be used for self-study, its **work-text** style is particularly useful for group courses. You can also take an on-line, on-demand video course—the author has recorded over 25 hours of video that works through this book (visit the web site below for details). There's enough explanation to adequately address important points with enough exercises to provide practice. Frequent **Mini TOEFL practice exercises** help us see the material in the context of the TOEFL exam and get used to the pressure of being timed. Full length **practice exams**, not included in this edition but widely available, are also a valuable preparation aid.

- The TOEFL Exam

Before you begin this (or any) TOEFL preparation program, you should already have a fairly high level in English. If not, the program is difficult and your progress will be slow. This program is recommended for students who have a TOEFL level of at least 450 points and who need to score above 550. You might expect to improve your score from 35 to 50 points with careful study of this program. **Individual results vary, however**. Even a perfect program and the best teacher can't guarantee results if you don't also do your part with serious, consistent study.

- General Strategy

THIS PROGRAM

Those who start on a lower level will see quicker results, while those with a higher level will progress more slowly. It's much easier to improve a score of 500 points to 550 than it is to improve 550 points to 600. In fact, around 575 points, we enter a "red zone" where progress is much slower: it is necessary to study a great deal more for less improvement.

Before you actually begin the program, you might take some time to review the following **introductory material** on the TOEFL exam (including information on the updated computerized version) and general test strategy and study tips.

Have a question? You can e-mail the author at britt.mx@gmail.com. Interested in the **online-program?** Visit www.dfbritt.com for details. Good luck!

INTRODUCTION

The TOEFL Exam

GENERAL INFORMATION

The Test of English as a Foreign Language, or TOEFL, is a standardized proficiency exam. It is used to test and grade the English ability of non-native speakers. It is published by Educational Testing Service (ETS). The Institutional (ITP) and Paper-based (PBT) exams include multiple choice formats and are divided into three parts: Listening comprehension, Structure and Written Expression, and Reading and Vocabulary. The exams last about two hours.

Although there are other English proficiency tests, TOEFL has become the standard by which most measure English skills. The TOEFL tests American (not British) English. **Almost all universities will require the TOEFL exam for admission**. Usually between 550 and 600 points on PBT are required by better schools. You may also be required to take other tests, such as SAT, ACT, GMAT, or GRE to complete your admission requirements.

For complete information on the TOEFL exam and the registration process, you will need to obtain an official **TOEFL bulletin**. If you are unable to pick up one locally, you can contact **Educational Testing Service**. They can be reached by mail, e-mail, fax, or cable:. MAIL: TOEFL Services, Educational Testing Service, P.O. Box 6151, Princeton, N.J, 08541-6151, USA, E-MAIL: toefl@ets.org (their web site address is: http://www.toefl.org).
The bulletin is free.

10 FREQUENTLY ASKED QUESTIONS
1. What's the highest possible score on the TOEFL?

If you could take an ITP or PBT TOEFL exam with no error, the score would be around 667, although each test is graded separately taking into consideration various factors. However, for our purposes, anything over 620 should be considered quite exceptional. (The scores mentioned here have not been converted to the new computer testing scale.)

2. What is considered a good score?

That depends on your particular situation. There is no passing or failing grade. In general, any score below 400 on ITP/PBT is considered low, while any score above 600 is considered high. A score of 660 would rank you in the 99th percentile (99% of all test takers scored lower). Again, most schools ask for around 550. If your score falls just a few points lower than the college requests, don't panic. The admissions department may offer some flexibility.

3. Can I take the TOEFL more than one time?

Sure, you can take it as many times as you want although you should not repeat the same ITP format. ETS will report only the scores that you authorize them to report. However, taking real exams is an expensive way to practice. You should complete your preparation and take a few practice exams before taking the real test.

4. How long is my score valid?

2 Years for PBT. During a 2-year period you can request that ETS report your score to institutions. A separate fee is charged for this service if requested after your test date. There is no expiration date for ITP, though the date of application is included on the score report.

5. Do I have to take the Test of Written English?

No, this was a separate exam, with a separate registration—it is no longer administered. However, an essay in included on the PBT (not ITP).

6. When do I get my scores?

If you take the institutional TOEFL you should get your score almost immediately. For PBT, scores are available about 2 weeks after taking the test.

7. How is the TOEFL scored?

You will receive a section score for each of the three sections and an overall score. Based on the number of correct answers, each section is given a converted score. Once you have three converted scores, add them together, divide by 3, then multiply by 10 to get your overall score.

8. Can I change my testing date?

Yes, but you'll be charged a fee if you change your PBT testing date and it might be difficult to find an open date since fewer and fewer PBT tests are offered where the iBT (Internet-based) is available. Changing your ITP date depends on the policies of the institute where you plan to take the test.

9. How much does the exam cost?

You should check locally. The institution exam is around US $45., while the PBT version is around $100. Again, you should check locally as prices can vary depending on region.

10. Do I have to show identification to take the test?

Yes, in fact identification requirements are quite strict. You will need to present all required documents and identification (with photo). Check locally (or refer to the bulletin) for exact requirements. You will not be admitted to take the exam if you do not meet all identification requirements.

iBT, the official TOEFL

The iBT (Internet-based) TOEFL is now available in most parts of the world, although the official PBT is still widely available—dates might be limited where the iBT is available. The iBT now includes a speaking section and uses an "integrated skills" approach. Students will be asked to read, write, listen, and speak.

This book does not prepare students for the iBT, per se. It is intended for students planning to take the ITP or PBT. However, it does provide an excellent foundation course for those planning to take the iBT. Many students do not have the grammatical skills they need to even begin preparing for the iBT. Used as a pre-iBT course, this book will help improve the grammar skills you'll need for success on the iBT. Even though there is no longer a specific grammar section on the iBT, grammar skills are still an important part of the grading criteria. After you finish studying this book, you should then get some specific practice in the four sections of the iBT if you plan to take that version.

Also, the **scale for scoring** has changed. It is easy to compare your computer-based score with the paper-based score by checking a concordance table. The iBT has a 120 point range—a maximum of 30 points can be scored in each of the four sections.

So, again, this program is intended for students preparing to take the ITP or PBT versions, but works well as a pre-iBT program. It's also appropriate for an advanced grammar course and for English teacher training—especially good for Spanish-speaking English teachers or native English-speaking teacher who teach Spanish-speaking students.

TEST STRATEGY AND STUDY TIPS

Most importantly, allow **sufficient time** to complete this program—it is intended for use in a course of 40-50 hours, plus additional outside work. Try to work through all of the exercises and take the 3 **practice exams** before you take the actual test: one early in your program, one in the middle, and one at the end. Review the errors on these exams carefully—this is an excellent method of eliminating errors on future exams. Sometimes examine why the wrong answers are wrong, not just why the right answers are right.

We will discuss specific strategy as we study each individual section of the test. In general, follow these tips:

- Always guess if you don't know the answer—you only get credit for correct answers and there is no penalty for guessing.
- Establish and use the same "guessing letter"—assuming there is an equal distribution among the correct answers, this would give you a 25% chance of guessing correctly.
- Always use the "process of elimination" to eliminate answers you are sure are wrong.
- Be completely familiar with the directions for each part of the test. Be familiar with the answer sheet and the correct way to mark your answers.
- Make sure you know the exact place and time of the exam as well as everything you'll need on the day of the test.
- As you're taking the test, frequently check to make sure the number on your answer sheet corresponds to the number on your test book (this does not apply to the computer format).
- Just days before the exam, continually review the Common Usage Errors (Appendix F). This is a good way to pick up some quick extra points.
- On the night before the exam, a good night's rest is more beneficial than last minute "cramming".

TOEFL PREP for Spanish Speakers

GRAMMAR INTRO.

PART TWO   Structure and Written Expression

Most TOEFL programs begin with the first section of the exam itself—Listening Comprehension. Of course, there does seem to be logical reason for following the test order. This program, however, will begin with the second section of the TOEFL exam—**Structure and Written Expression**. It is recommended that you begin your TOEFL study with this section. The reason for this is twofold: first, this is the area where many students have the **greatest**

- Format of Section
- Strategies
- Grammar Terms
- Explanation of Five Step Program

Introduction

difficulty (and, naturally, the lowest score), and second, this section of the test can actually be **improved more easily** than the others. Which is not to say that the grammar section is easy, because it's not. But because listening and reading abilities, which are tested in the first and third TOEFL sections, are the results of many years of development, it is hard to improve these areas quickly. On the other hand, beginning your TOEFL preparation with the grammar section is **more time efficient**, producing immediate results—and points! In fact, actual point value given for correct answers is considerably higher for this section than for the other two on the pencil and paper version—it will also help **improve writing ability** for the writing tasks included on the PBT and IBT exams. This section of the TOEFL has very little to do with one's ability to speak or understand spoken English. Good writers will find this section easier. Those with writing deficiencies will hopefully notice marked improvement. Again, this section is also useful in preparing for the written essay, which is addressed specifically in Part Three of this book.

Many students may achieve their desired level on the exam without ever giving further attention to sections one or three (Listening Comprehension and Reading Comprehension). That depends entirely on the student's level (and study habits) when beginning the program. As you begin studying section two (Structure and Written Expression), however, it would be a good idea to begin **exposing yourself to as much English as possible**—listen to the radio, watch TV and movies, and **read as much as possible in English**. This will help you prepare for the first and last sections. Also, make an effort to **speak in English as often as possible** with friends, family, classmates, etc. who might speak English.

We might also note here that the TOEFL tests **formal written English**. This is important to consider because formal English can be very different from the English we speak with our friends, hear on TV and in movies, or hear in pop music. In fact, we are so constantly bombarded with informal English that it might surprise you how wrong the correct, formal structures can sound.

The Structure and Written Expression section of the TOEFL consists of two parts. Part A, **Sentence Completion**, requires that an incomplete sentence be correctly completed by choosing among four choices. Part B, **Error Identification**, requires that an error be identified. One of four underlined word(s) must be changed (or eliminated) in order to make the sentence correct.

GRAMMAR INTRO.

Let's look at an example question from each part:

PART A, Sentence Completion

_____ The reports _____ the newspaper prints are always accurate.

    A) of   B) and   C) which   D) in

PART B, Error Identification

_____ Of <u>all</u> the cars <u>in</u> this parking <u>lot</u>, mine is in the <u>worse</u> condition.
         A   B   C   D

    A couple of strategy tips: **Don't waste time in Part A trying to find an error among the answer choices**—all of the answers are grammatically correct when considered independently, while only one correctly completes the error. Also, in Part B, **it's your job only to identify the error, not to correct it.** Thinking of ways to correct it will waste valuable time. As you are working through this preparation program, however, *do* concentrate on correcting all errors, as it will improve your speed and efficiency for the actual exam.

    It should be noted here that when taking the **Institutional (or PBT) TOEFL** it is not necessary to begin with the first question and work in order. In fact, you are free to answer the section any way you choose. For some students, there might be advantages to beginning the section with Part B instead of Part A. You probably can't yet determine if this would be beneficial for you unless you have taken several practice exams already. Once you have taken a few exams, you might feel that one part is more difficult than the other. If Part A seems more difficult, you might try starting with Part B. The idea is to work rather quickly through the easier section to save extra time for the more difficult one.

And that brings up the subject of **time**. In the Structure and Written Expression Section, twenty five minutes are allowed to answer forty questions. Many students could take this section almost completely error free if given a couple of hours to do so. Unfortunately, timing is a crucial factor and during your preparation you should try to establish an **internal rhythm** that helps you know exactly when you've spent enough, but not too much time, on each question. You will have approximately 35 seconds for each question (that's 37.5 seconds to be exact). The timed **"Mini TOEFL" exercises** found in this section of your study program will help you establish an effective time strategy. If you encounter problems with time running out before you finish a section of the TOEFL (except for Listening Comprehension, which is controlled by an audio program) on practice exams, remember to work a little faster from the first question when you take your next practice exam. Avoid being stuck with several unanswered questions and no time to answer them. Above all, **never leave blanks**—at least put a guessing answer for which there is no penalty.

We will begin this section (Part Two, which covers the second part of the actual exam, Structure and Written Expression) with **an explanation of grammar terminology**. It seems even the most advanced student has occasional difficulty with this—for many it might take just a quick review, however. It is necessary, whether studying alone or with a teacher, to use a great deal of grammar terms in this section simply because the section tends to be a bit complex grammatically and we have no other way in which to identify the structures except by using their "official" grammatical names. This program is designed especially for Spanish speakers, and a full explanation of terms will be given with their **Spanish equivalents**. Often the grammar of Spanish is learned somewhat differently than that of English. But we will try to note as closely as possible the similarities.

After carefully reviewing the grammar terms, you should work systematically through the **five problem areas**. When taking practice exams, try to conscientiously categorize practice questions within the five categories. This will help you later when you may not immediately see an error and need to make a quick analysis.

Remember, hard work and careful attention to detail in this section will greatly reduce, if not nearly eliminate, the need for additional study of the first and last sections of the TOEFL.

GRAMMAR INTRO.

EXPLANATION OF GRAMMAR TERMINOLOGY

We'll base our explanation of grammar terminology on the **PARTS OF SPEECH** which will be used frequently throughout this program. Other grammar terminology will be explained as we go along. Remember that any given word might function in a number of different ways within a sentence. The function that a word serves in one sentence might be different from the function of the same word in another sentence. Understanding the different PARTS OF SPEECH along with careful analysis of the sentence structure will help you determine which function the word is serving. Refer to the following "Quick Check" and then give careful attention to any parts of speech that you're not sure about in the detailed explanations that follow.

QUICK CHECK

PART OF SPEECH	FUNCTION	EXAMPLES
A. NOUN	A person, place, thing, or idea	boy, Carl, Paris, book, love
B. PRONOUN	A substitute for a noun	it, her, me, them, I, that
C. ADJECTIVE	Describes a noun or pronoun	big, blue, loud, fast
D. VERB	Expresses action	eat, arrive, dance
E. ADVERB	Modifies a verb, adjective, or adverb	fast, quickly, newly
F. PREPOSITION	Shows the relationship between a noun or pronoun and another	to, during, around, at, with, up

PARTS OF SPEECH

A. NOUN *Sustantivo* — activity

The noun is a word that describes a person, place, thing, or abstract idea. For example: girl, pencil, Madrid, love, Mary. In Spanish this is called a "sustantivo". Nouns are considered to have gender, number, and case. In English, the gender is not particularly important. All nouns are considered neutral except when the word refers to something specifically masculine or feminine (such as girl, tigress, man, and lady).

On the contrary, there are no neutral nouns in Spanish—all are either masculine or feminine. The gender of nouns in Spanish is very important because it determines the gender of accompanying determiners (such as *un, la, el*) and adjectives.

The number of a noun, both in Spanish and English, refers to its singular or plural form. Although many irregular plurals are formed in English (such as *teeth* for *tooth*), most are formed by adding "s" or "es".

Feet Foot

Only one extra "case" exists in English—the possessive, which is formed by adding " 's " to singular nouns. The case never changes for Spanish nouns (the possessive being formed with the article "de"). Daniella's travel

In both Spanish and English, the three most common uses of nouns are as subjects, objects, or complements. For example:

Subject

Mr. Contreras is Mexican. El señor Contreras es mexicano.

Direct Object (of a verb)

She has a book. Ella tiene un libro.

Indirect Object (of a verb)

He gave the book to <u>Mary</u>.   El le dio el libro a <u>María</u>.

Object (of a preposition)

We are in the <u>school</u>.   Estamos en la <u>escuela</u>.

Complement

This is a pretty <u>book</u>.   Este es un <u>libro</u> bonito.

(*) Review countable / uncountable Noun's list

Nouns can be both countable (nouns which have a plural form and can be counted) or uncountable (those without plural forms) in both Spanish and English. <u>Uncountable nouns</u> (air, love, weather) do not have plural forms. There are some differences between Spanish and English in respect to what is countable or not. For example, the word "furniture" is considered uncountable, but its Spanish equivalent, "mueble", is countable (un mueble, los muebles). The Spanish word "mobiliario" is uncountable and closer to the English "furnishings"—both are uncountable.

Nouns often act as adjectives (see **Adjectives**) to describe other nouns. <u>Since there are no plural adjectives in English,</u> avoid the common error that many Spanish speakers make by making nouns which are acting as adjectives plural (or otherwise "conjugated"). For example, "un edificio de tres pisos" becomes "a three <u>floor</u> building", not "a three <u>floors</u> building". The mouse has "a three <u>inch</u> tail", not "a three <u>inched</u> tail".

B. <u>PRONOUN</u> *substitute the noun.*

Like nouns, pronouns have <u>gender</u>, <u>number</u>, and <u>case, but more distinctions are made.</u> Care must be taken when choosing the correct form—pronouns also change depending on the person. In Point Two of this program, we will give careful attention to choosing the correct pronoun form and assuring that we have correct agreement and reference.

Pronouns are generally used and defined the same in Spanish as in English. It is important to note that <u>you</u> has several Spanish forms: *tú, usted, ustedes*, and in some Spanish speaking regions, *vosotros and vosotras*.

It is interesting that while in Spanish more emphasis is normally put on the masculine or feminine aspect of words, in the case of the possessive adjective more emphasis is given in English to this aspect. For example, *the book is <u>his</u>* or *this is <u>his</u> book*. In Spanish we use <u>su</u> without placing importance on the gender, *este es <u>su</u> libro*.

It seems that demonstrative pronouns are much easier to learn in English than in Spanish. In English there are only four forms:

SINGULAR	PLURAL
this	these
that	those

here/there.

NOTE: "one" and "ones" are sometimes substituted.

In English, the demonstrative pronouns refer simply to singular or plural nouns that are either "here" or "there". It is a bit more complicated in Spanish. For example, instead of choosing between "this" or "that", we must choose among "éste, ése, ésta, ésa, ésto, éso, aquello". These are only the singular forms—corresponding plural forms also exist.

C. ADJECTIVE

The adjective is a word that describes a noun or a pronoun. For example, *large, eager, happy, blue, sophisticated*. Adjectives have three forms: absolute, comparative, and superlative. Adjectives in English do not agree in gender or number as they do in Spanish.

Word order is also important in respect to the correct use of adjectives. In Spanish, the adjective generally comes after the noun it describes (un libro <u>azul</u>), while in English it comes before the noun (the <u>blue</u> book).

Nouns often function as adjectives, but are never plural or otherwise changed from their simple form.

D. VERB

In both English and Spanish, verbs tell the action or activity being performed. Helping verbs, or auxiliary verbs, are often used with main verbs to show the tense (present, past, etc.) and to show meaning that can not be expressed by the main verb alone. The second step of this section will address common verb problems. We will examine in detail problems in areas of verb tense, form, and agreement. It is vital that you be familiar with the irregular past and participle forms of verbs. You might review the list found in Appendix A of this book.

E. ADVERB

Adverbs are words that modify verbs, adjectives, or other adverbs by telling how, when, where, or how much: Please come <u>quickly</u>. It's <u>really</u> pretty. They perform <u>extremely</u> well. Adverbs also include words that can show comparison between verbs, just as adjectives do for nouns: quickly, more quickly, most quickly; fast, faster, fastest.

In Spanish, adverbs are normally presented in eight categories:

Lugar: cerca, abajo, arriba

Tiempo: hoy, ayer, temprano

Modo: bien, quedo, buenamente

Cantidad: mucho, nada, bastante

Orden: antes, luego, primeramente

Afirmación: cierto, ciertamente, seguro

Negación: no, nunca, tampoco

Duda: tal vez, a lo mejor, quizás

F. PREPOSITIONS

Prepositions are words that express place, time, and other circumstances and show the relationship between two parts of a sentence: *at, for, in, on, of, to*. They are often part of prepositional phrases when used with a noun or pronoun as their object. (Refer to list of prepositions in Appendix B.)

Examples of Spanish prepositions (to help you make a comparison): *a, ante, bajo, cabe, con, contra, de, desde, en, entre, hacia, para, hasta, por, sin.*

Prepositions can create special problems for Spanish speakers because they rarely translate literally from one language to the other. In English, for example, "I think *of* you", while in Spanish, "pienso <u>en</u> ti". If you translate the latter, you might get something like "I think *in* you", which is incorrect. In English, we often change the meaning of verbs by adding a preposition. In Spanish, we often change the verb completely. Compare the following English-Spanish equivalents: to look *for*—buscar, to look *at*—mirar, to look *into*—investigar. In addition to reviewing the list of phrasal verbs and idiomatic expressions in the Appendices, you might need to consult a more complete dictionary of phrasal verbs or American English idioms.

If you have at least a working knowledge of the grammar terms explained above, you should now be ready to start the program. This section of the program, which covers the second part of the actual exam, Structure and Written Expression, is organized in five general points, as follows:

I Identification of the subject and verb of the main clause (while avoiding repetition) and a study of subordination.

II Subject-verb agreement (and a review of verb tense and form), pronoun-subject agreement (and a review of pronoun form and reference).

III Verbals (active and passive verbal adjectives) and word form.

IV Word order (subject-verb inversion), parallel structure, unnecessary repetition.

V Problematic verbs, count and non-count nouns and modifiers, *make* vs. *do*, *a* vs. *an*, idiomatic and usage problems.

NOTE: The Appendices at the end of this book contain the following reference information, much of which might be useful as you complete this section of the program: reference lists of irregular verb forms, prepositions, phrasal verbs, verbs that take gerunds or infinitives, idiomatic expressions, common usage errors, false cognates (English-Spanish), and verb tense modals.

Become familiar (memorize, if possible) with the following abbreviations that will be used to indicate specific problems within each of the five points, or *steps*. Think of these as *steps* because they provide the most logical, step-by-step order for quickly analyzing TOEFL questions.

STEP ONE

MC   explanation: Problem with **Main Clause**; check subject and verb, avoid repetition.

example error: That girl *she* is always complaining.

SC   explanation: Problem with **Subordinate Clause**; check subject, verb, subordinating signal.

example error: Carl learned to speak Spanish *while was living in Mexico.*

GRAMMAR INTRO.

STEP TWO

S=V explanation: Error in **Subject-Verb Agreement**

example of error: The teacher along with his twenty students *are* going to visit the museum.

S=P explanation: Error in **Subject-Pronoun Agreement**

example error: Everyone should do *their* best on the exam.

VTF explanation: Error in **Verb Tense or Form**

example error: Last Saturday Rafael *catched* two fish at the lake.

PFR explanation: Error in **Pronoun Form or Reference**

example error: If you were *me*, would you buy a new car?

STEP THREE

VBL explanation: Error in **Verbal** usage

example error: John Grisham's latest novel has to be one of the most *interested* books I've read.

WF explanation: Error in **Word Form**

example error: His *resigning* from the company came as a shock.

STEP FOUR

WO   explanation: Error in **Word Order**

example error: Never *we have* studied so hard before.

PS   explanation: Error in **Parallel Structure**

example error: Ulises enjoys swimming, playing football, and *to ride* horses.

UR   explanation: **Unnecessary Repetition**

example error: Our professor has asked that our research topics be *concise* and *succinct.*

STEP FIVE

CU   explanation: **Correct Usage** (a variety of idiomatic and structural errors)

example error: Diet cola has *less* calories than normal cola.

Do not feel frustrated because you do not understand at this point all of the errors that are listed above. Each grammar point will be studied individually. Try now to simply become familiar with the general concept of each type of error and its corresponding abbreviation. To help you become comfortable in analyzing errors using this five step method, we will present several exercises, which, like the following one, will give you an opportunity to practice. The classification of the error may be very difficult (if not impossible) at first. Don't worry. The classification of the error will become easier as you progress in the program and study each type of error in detail. Concentrate more for the moment on recognizing and correcting the errors. That's why the answers to these exercises have been included. As you work through the program, try to cover the answers and see if you can improve your accuracy classifying the errors.

TOEFL PREP for Spanish Speakers

MC

STEP ONE

QUICK CHECK   Grammar Problem Areas

STEP ONE

> MC   (Main Clause)

  SC   (Subordinate Clause)

STEP TWO

  S=V   (Subject-Verb Agreement)

  S=P   (Subject-Pronoun Agreement)

  VTF   (Verb Tense or Form)

  PFR   (Pronoun Form or Reference)

STEP THREE

  VBL   (Verbal)

  WF   (Word Form)

STEP FOUR

  WO   (Word Order)

  PS   (Parallel Structure)

  UR   (Unnecessary Repetition)

STEP FIVE

  CU   (Correct Usage)

- Structures that Function as Subjects

- Gerunds vs. Verbs

- Repeated Subjects and Omitted Verbs

Main Clauses

MAIN CLAUSES

EXERCISE SWE-1

Directions: Using the abbreviations that identify each type of error, classify the following twelve (one of each type) errors, then try to correct the errors. In future exercises like this one, try to cover the answers and practice classifying the errors based on the twelve we've reviewed.

__MC__ 1. A subject it must not be repeated within a clause.

__VBL__ 2. *To Kill a Mockingbird*, which was written by Harper Lee, is a very interested book.

__WO__ 3. The child was just barely enough tall to reach the sink.

__PS__ 4. Among his many hobbies, he enjoys to cook, swimming, and reading.

__UR__ 5. Although he worked many hours on his document, the final draft was concise and succinct.

__SC__ 6. The new restaurant is quite popular, although is very expensive.

__S=V__ 7. The swimming instructor, along with his 30 students, are learning the breast stroke.

__WF__ 8. The use of drugs among teenagers is sometimes a result of an emotion problem.

__CU__ 9. Diet sodas have less calories than normal ones.

__VTF__ 10. The little boy could not reach the coins that had fell behind the sofa.

__S=P__ 11. Everybody in the class will give their oral report today.

__PFR__ 12. The lifeguard doesn't allow us running around the pool.

Remember that in English adjectives always come before the word *enough*. Be careful because in Spanish sentence number 3 would read correctly: *suficientemente alto* in English is *tall enough*.

NOTE: The 🔑 symbol, as found before question number 3 of the previous exercise, should be given special attention. When you see this symbol, always check the bottom of the page for an important explanation of a grammatical or idiomatic element (or perhaps a problematic vocabulary word) that can cause special problems for Spanish speakers.

By definition, every complex sentence contains a *main clause* and at least one *subordinate clause*. Both main clauses and subordinate clauses have a subject and a verb, but only the main clause can function independently as a sentence. The subordinate clause depends upon the main clause for meaning and can not function alone. It is possible to have a main clause with no subordination, but you can not correctly have a subordinate clause without first having a main clause to support it.

We will begin with a study of main clauses. When you have a **MC** error it will usually involve a repeated subject or an omitted verb. In rare occasions, you might find a repeated verb or a missing subject. In order to help identify such errors with the subject and verb of the main clause, we will review the five types of structures that function as subjects in English, followed by a review of verb identification.

Una oración (principal o subordinada) debe tener sujeto y verbo, y no debe omitirse ni repetirse ningún elemento.

There are five structures that can function as **subjects** in English. They are: the noun, pronoun, gerund, infinitive, and noun clause. Let's look at an example of each.

1. **Noun**   The <u>teacher</u> is very nice.
2. **Pronoun**   <u>He</u> is very nice.
3. **Gerund**   <u>Learning</u> is fun.
4. **Infinitive**   <u>To learn</u> is fun.
5. **Noun Clause** <u>That we attend class</u> is important.

Notice that the pronoun is used to replace a simple noun subject. Also notice that the gerund and infinitive are interchangeable as subjects. This can be confusing to Spanish speakers, however, because in Spanish we use infinitive subjects, but not gerund subjects. You can say "Aprender es divertido", but not "Aprendiendo es divertido".

Try not to confuse gerunds for verbs. Remember: *A gerund is a gerund, a verb is a verb. A gerund is never a verb.* The problem is that we often conveniently call everything with "ing" a *gerund*. That is not the case. By definition, a gerund is not a verb and must have some form of the verb *to be* before it to "activate" it as a verb. Compare the following: **Gerunds:** swimming, playing, reading. **Verbs:** is swimming, were playing, have been reading. Also keep in mind that an infinitive needs to be joined with a conjugated verb to function as a verb.

Be careful with the verb *attend*. Don't substitute it for *assist*. *Assist* is what we call a "false cognate". That is a word that looks the same in Spanish and English but has a different meaning. In Spanish we use *asistir* for attend, but in English *assist* means to help. Avoid saying "I will *assist* the meeting". Refer to Appendix G for a more complete list of false cognates.

MAIN CLAUSES

Perhaps the most difficult of the five subject structures is the noun clause. The noun clause is a type of subordinate clause and has its own subject and verb. If you are confused, go to the verb and ask yourself, "what?" *What is important?* **That we attend class.** The answer will lead you to the noun clause. In fact, anytime you have trouble locating your subject, always go to the verb which should lead you to the source of its action—the subject.

EXERCISE SWE-2

Directions: Find and underline the subject in the main clause in each sentence. Then classify it, putting the number of the corresponding subject form in the blank. 1. Noun, 2. Pronoun, 3. Gerund, 4. Infinitive, 5. Noun Clause.

  __2__ 1. <u>She</u> will attend college at an American university.

  _____ 2. Fishing is a popular sport in Ixtapa.

  _____ 3. This is my sister's book.

  _____ 4. Breathing contaminated air causes respiratory problems.

  _____ 5. Whoever finds the lost puppy will be rewarded.

  _____ 6. Tornadoes arise when conditions that cause ordinary thunderstorms are unusually violent.

  _____ 7. To drive a bus requires special training.

  _____ 8. Mumps is a contagious disease in which the salivary glands swell up.

  _____ 9. Papyrus is a reed-like plant belonging to the family of sedges.

  _____ 10. Falling down stairs might result in serious injury.

  _____ 11. That pigeons can find their way home is an amazing ability.

  _____ 12. Subjects should not be repeated within a clause.

  _____ 13. To study for long periods of time is not recommended.

  _____ 14. Silk is the thread or cloth made from the fine web of the silkworm.

  _____ 15. Advertising is considered a science as well as an art.

Now we will practice identifying the verb(s) of main and subordinate clauses.

EXERCISE SWE-3

Directions: Find all the verbs and all parts of each verb in the main and subordinate clauses. Draw a line under each part, as in the example.

1. El Palacio de Bellas Artes <u>is located</u> in the historical district of Mexico City.
2. The lilies will begin blooming around Easter.
3. There should have been more discussion before a decision was reached.
4. Unlimited information is available on the Internet.
5. Several months are sometimes necessary to adequately prepare for the TOEFL exam.
6. Spanish is not widely spoken in Brazil.
7. The doctor was sued on malpractice charges due to gross negligence.
8. Although it was the world's most popular language, Latin is now considered rather unimportant.
9. Housework, including washing dishes, vacuuming carpet, and cleaning floors, is no longer done exclusively by women.
10. There will be a short delay before the start of the movie.
11. The Mexican political system has seen sweeping changes in recent history.
12. The introduction of longer tennis rackets has given players more powerful serves.
13. Citizens of the United States are discouraged from traveling to certain countries.
14. David Letterman is considered by many to be the funniest talk show host.
15. Many scholarships are available to international students who score above 550 on the TOEFL.

MAIN CLAUSES

Before we continue our study of **MC** errors, we'll take a short break to do a **MINI TOEFL** practice exercise. These exercises are designed exactly like Parts A and B of the actual TOEFL. They are also timed to help simulate the actual exam.

MINI TOEFL-1

Directions: In questions 1-5, choose the one word or phrase that best completes the sentence. In questions 6-10, identify the underlined word(s) that should be changed to make the sentence correct. **TIME: 6 minutes**

_____1. Shivering is automatically activated by the temperature of the blood dropping too _____.

(A) high   (B) lowly   (C) low   (D) soon

_____ 2. The color of a human being's skin _____ on three pigments which are found in the body.

(A) designed to be (B) depends (C) belonging (D) arrives

_____ 3. _____ 1,040 species of amphibians have been identified.

(A) As many as (B) As many (C) As much as (D) Much as

_____ 4. A twelve-year-old is not _____ to buy alcoholic beverages.

(A) as old enough (B) old enough (C) enough old (D) old as

_____5. Researchers are studying many drugs to discover if _____ cancer.

(A) can they cure (B) it can cure (C) they can cure (D) curing

24

MAIN CLAUSES

_____6. The congressman which introduced the bill has been criticized for his questionable
                           A   B   C   D
judgment.

_____7. Among the many activities at the kindergarten, the children most enjoy painting,
          A   B   C
singing, and to play games.
              D

_____8. Because Chop Suey is served in nearly all Chinese restaurants, it is not Chinese at all.
          A   B   C   D

_____9. Not until around 1900 watches did appear on bands to
                  A   B
be worn around the wrist.
   C   D

_____10. The butterfly has a long, lengthy tube, called a proboscis, through which it can
                       A   B   C
suck the nectar from flowers.
         D

Remember that **MC** errors normally involve repeated subjects or missing verbs. We've practiced identifying subjects and verbs, and that brings us to a special problem. Many words in English function in many ways—they can function as a verb and another part of speech. If you don't know, for example, that *book* can function as a verb, it could cause problems.

25

MAIN CLAUSES

Suppose you're analyzing a sentence—trying to find the subject and verb. You might come across a word like *book* and not recognize it as a verb. After concluding that the sentence has no verb it is easy to begin "inventing" errors that don't really exist.

The following exercise will help you recognize many problematic words that typically function as verbs or as other parts of speech. It is important that you understand their verbal and non-verbal meaning.

EXERCISE SWE-4

Directions: Many of the following words can function in different ways. In the blank, write **AV** if the word *always* functions as a verb, **NV** if it *never* functions as a verb, and **B** if it can function *both* as a verb and another part of speech. Consider the word only as it is written—with no changes.

__B__	1. sleep	____	11. clean
____	2. need	____	12. paint
____	3. window	____	13. close
____	4. might	____	14. hope
____	5. open	____	15. can
____	6. 🔍 trip	____	16. cure
____	7. observe	____	17. house
____	8. warm	____	18. will
____	9. advice	____	19. elevate
____	10. laugh	____	20. smoke

🔍 Extra careful with this word! *Trip* in Spanish has related verbal and non-verbal meaings: *viaje* and *viajar*. Its English equivalent is not so logical. *Trip* as a noun means *viaje*, but *trip* as a verb means *tropezar*. Avoid using *trip* when you mean *travel*.

Can you think of other words that can function as verbs and other parts of speech? If you're studying alone, try to make a short list. If you're working with a group, try playing a word game—take turns naming a "tricky" word.

Three words can function as auxiliary verbs and should be given special attention. They are: *might, can,* and *will.* Let's take a closer look at their function.

QUICK CHECK

	AUXILIARY VERB	**NOUN**
MIGHT	EXPRESSES POSSIBILITY I might go to Acapulco this weekend.	power, strength, fuerza, poder
CAN	EXPRESSES ABILITY I can speak English.	lata or bote una lata de frijoles.
WILL	EXPRESSES FUTURE I will take the TOEFL soon.	testamento, the legal document

Again, make sure you understand the verbal and non-verbal meanings of all of the above "tricky" words (as well as any you might have added). We'll continue in the next exercise reviewing "tricky" words—words that can function as a verb and another part of speech. Pay attention to the function of the word in each particular sentence—watch out for new words that are not included in the above exercise.

MAIN CLAUSES

EXERCISE SWE-5

Directions: Carefully read the following sentences. Based on the sentence structure, if the underlined word is a verb, write **V** in the blank. If it functions as another part of speech, write **X** in the blank.

__X__ 1. After Alma received the telegram, all <u>hope</u> of resolving the difficult situation disappeared.

_____ 2. Experienced travelers who desire nothing more than to relax and read <u>book</u> travel on Amtrak trains.

_____ 3. It seems every Easter Sunday is beautiful and sunny and the kids always <u>spring</u> from their beds at the crack of dawn to find their Easter baskets full of goodies.

_____ 4. With my left eye closed, I can view <u>close</u> images with my right eye.

_____ 5. The executives met for several hours in the meeting room and finally decided to <u>table</u> the motion.

_____ 6. Although Miguel remained in bed for hours, he wasn't able to get much <u>sleep</u>.

_____ 7. With the idea of lots of money dancing around in his head, he was able to <u>bank</u> a shot and win the pool tournament.

The word *spring* has four distinct definitions: 1) the season, *la primavera*, 2) the verb, to jump, *brincar, saltar*, 3) the natural source of water, *manantial*, and 4) the coiled wire that is resistant to force, *resorte*. You might have heard the "Espanglish" expression "*un boxespring*", which is literally, "caja de resortes".

MAIN CLAUSES

_____8. Due to carelessness, one 🔍 can fell on the floor.

_____9. While in the airport newsstand reading a book, Ana heard the page and ran for the departing flight.

_____10. Tomorrow morning the will of the deceased is scheduled to be reviewed by the family attorney.

_____11. The small raft suddenly hit a reef and began to rock.

_____12. Wearing his new suit, Emilio misspelled the last word and had to settle for a tie.

_____13. With tears of desperation rolling down her cheeks, the woman sent out a shrill cry for help.

_____14. Don't trip on the wet deck of the boat.

_____15. Like many animals, the raccoon mothers its babies until they can survive on their own.

_____16. The convention hotel can house all of the members of the association, but you're welcome to stay in our home.

_____17. Check your watches so that we can time this exercise.

_____18. Even if they never become reality, dreams are an important source of inspiration.

_____19. In Edgar Allen Poe's "The Raven", there is frequent reference to a knocking at his chamber door.

_____20. While Guadalupe was gathering flowers from the garden, the sun rose.

🔍 Compare *one can fell on the floor* and *one can fall on the floor*. We can often tell if an auxiliary verb is functioning as a verb or noun by examining the verb that follows—if that verb is conjugated, it is functioning as a noun. If it is not, it is functioning as an auxiliary verb.

Before we be begin our study of **SC** (Subordinate Clause) errors, it will be useful to review the difference between clauses and phrases. A clause has a subject and verb, but a phrase is simply a group of words without both a subject and active verb.

The following exercise will give you practice distinguishing between **clauses** and **phrases**. In order to do this you will need to pay attention to gerund and infinitive subjects—try not to confuse them for verbs. Remember a gerund does not function as a verb without being connected with some form of the verb *to be* and an infinitive needs to be connected with a conjugated verb to function as an active verb.

EXERCISE SWE-6

Directions: Examine the function of each word in the following sentences to determine if it is a **clause** or a **phrase**. In the blank, put **C** for clauses and **P** for phrases.

__C__ 1. waiting is annoying

_____ 2. the child walking down the street

_____ 3. to study Japanese every day

_____ 4. money makes the world go 'round

_____ 5. seeing is believing

_____ 6. reservations are necessary

_____ 7. predicting the weather is tricky

_____ 8. smoking is not always socially acceptable

_____ 9. pronouncing the alphabet

_____ 10. waiting a long time for the bus

_____ 11. winning is not everything

_____ 12. baking chocolate chip cookies

_____ 13. arriving after the closing of the shop

_____ 14. painting is a form of artistic expression

_____ 15. dams generate electricity

Remember, **MC** errors normally have a repeated subject or missing verb in the main clause. In rare instances you might find a repeated verb or missing subject. You should now be able to easily identify subjects and verbs (while avoiding confusions with words that function in different ways), gerunds, and infinitives. An important point to keep in mind: repeated subjects are the easiest errors to identify on the TOEFL exam. These will be the *regalos* that you can't afford to miss!

EXERCISE SWE-7

Directions: The following sentences are supposed to be correct main clauses. Some of them are correct, but some of them repeat the subject or do not have a verb. In the blank write **check** (√) if the sentence is correct, **minus** (−) if the verb is missing, and **plus** (+) if the subject is repeated.

__+__ 1. The world's first subway it opened in London.

_____ 2. The bears dancing in the circus.

_____ 3. Ivory comes from the tusks of elephants.

_____ 4. Penicillin it is one of the most important medical discoveries of our time.

_____ 5. All of the students with their teacher.

_____ 6. Exercising is good for the heart.

_____ 7. The lioness with its three cubs.

_____ 8. Forms of reading and writing in nearly all civilizations.

_____ 9. Capital punishment it is very controversial in the U.S.

_____ 10. The amount of blood in a person's body depends on his size.

_____ 11. The bus full of passengers crashed.

_____ 12. The test taken by the students.

_____ 13. The Pope he heads Vatican City.

_____ 14. No two fingerprints exactly alike.

_____ 15. The little girl practicing the violin.

MAIN CLAUSES

In the **MINI TOEFL** that follows, try to find **MC** errors—usually repeated subjects or missing verbs. However, all of the errors in this practice exercise and those that follow will not be directly related to the specific point you're studying. There will be a few unrelated errors. This is because it is important to recognize errors, but also important to recognize correct structures. If you know in advance that all of the errors are related to a specific point, you might not get the practice you need recognizing correct structures and might begin "inventing" errors that don't really exist.

MINI TOEFL-2

Directions: In questions 1-5, choose the one word or phrase that best completes the sentence. In questions 6-10, identify the underlined word(s) that should be changed to correct the sentence. **TIME: 6 minutes**

_____1. The unicorn _____ a mythical animal that never actually existed.
(A) it was   (B) was   (C) believed   (D) only

_____2. Asparagus _____ a member of the lily family and has many varieties.
(A) belonging to   (B) it is   (C) is   (D) grows

_____3. Erosion _____ the action whereby land is slowly diminished by water.
(A) it is   (B) is that   (C) being   (D) is

_____4. _____ that the world's first postage stamp appeared in England.
(A) It was in 1847   (B) Because in 1847
(C) That is 1847   (D) In 1847 that it was

MAIN CLAUSES

_____ 5. The hamburger _____ name from its place of origin, Hamburg, Germany.

(A) and its   (B) got its   (C) along with its   (D) it got its

_____ 6. Atlanta, home of the 1996 Olympic Games, it is the capital of Georgia and the
                                                    A   B   C
largest city in the southeastern U.S.
                    D

_____ 7. The Boeing 747, which was first flown in 1969, it is the biggest jetliner in the
                         A   B   C   D
world.

_____ 8. Although Delaware the second smallest state in the Union, it is the first state of
                           A   B   C   D
the U.S.

_____ 9. Based on population, Mexico City it is the largest city in the world.
                  A   B   C   D

_____ 10. The Great Wall of China, constructed completely by hand, it runs a length of
          A   B   C D
1500 miles.

33

TOEFL PREP for Spanish Speakers

SC

STEP ONE

QUICK CHECK   Grammar Problem Areas

STEP ONE

    MC   (Main Clause)

    >SC   (Subordinate Clause)

STEP TWO

    S=V   (Subject-Verb Agreement)

    S=P   (Subject-Pronoun Agreement)

    VTF   (Verb Tense or Form)

    PFR   (Pronoun Form or Reference)

STEP THREE

    VBL   (Verbal)

    WF   (Word Form)

- Subordinate Clauses
- Noun Clauses
- Adjective Clauses
- Adverb Clauses

Subordination

STEP FOUR

    WO   (Word Order)

    PS   (Parallel Structure)

    UR   (Unnecessary Repetition)

STEP FIVE

    CU   (Correct Usage)

SUBORDINATION

EXERCISE SWE-8

Directions: Using the abbreviations that identify each type of error, classify the following ten errors, then try to correct the errors. Only ten of the twelve types of errors are listed in order to minimize "elimination" guessing.

PFR 1. The young man who Claudia wants to marry lives in California.

_WO_ 2. It would be an understatement to say that Cinderella met interesting someone at the gala event.

VBL 3. After buying groceries at the market, dinner was prepared.

_PS_ 4. This year our football team is expected to be strong, talented, and know that it takes hard work to win.

_UR_ 5. Aside from the fact that Carolina is opposed to the use of real animal fur, she found the coat far too expensive and costly.

_WF_ 6. Styles may come and go, but traditionally tailoring like cuffed pants and button down shirts will always be in fashion for men.

_MC_ 7. Although he had always been a clown, Bozo he wanted to learn the flying trapeze.

_S=P_ 8. Everyone in the class hopes to achieve a high score on their TOEFL exam.

_S=V_ 9. Neither the director nor the choir members likes the lyrics.

_SC_ 10. Alcohol is actually a narcotic stimulates the brain.

SUBORDINATION

By definition, every complex sentence contains at least two elements: a **main clause** and at least one **subordinate clause**. It might contain several subordinate clauses and phrases, but as a minimum it must contain a main clause and a subordinate clause. Can you remember the main difference and similarity between a main and subordinate clause?

QUICK CHECK

SUBORDINATE CLAUSE	DESCRIPTION	EXAMPLE
NOUN	Functions as subject or object of main clause	*What the teacher said* surprised the class.
ADJECTIVE	Always follows and describes a noun.	The book *which I am reading* is interesting.
ADVERB	Always begins with an adverbial conjunction.	*Although it is very dangerous*, many people like hang gliding.

Una oración compleja es aquella que tiene dos enunciados, uno principal, y uno subordinado. Un enunciado principal es aquel que tiene sujeto y predicado y puede funcionar independientemente como una oraciòn. Un enunciado subordinado es aquel que depende del enunciado principal para su significado. Puede funcionar en una oración como adjetivo, adverbio, o sustantivo. Sin embargo, un enunciado subordinado tiene sujeto y predicado, una frase no tiene ambos, aunque los dos dependen de un enunciado principal.

As we begin our study of **SC** errors keep in mind that **focusing on the main clause will help you identify the subordinate clause.** It's also useful to identify **phrases** so that they can be "thrown away". Phrases (with the exception of verbal phrases, which we will study in the VBL section) rarely play an important grammatical role in the sentence and usually have nothing to do with the error. They only cause confusion. Again, focus your attention on identifying the main and subordinate clauses, while eliminating phrases from consideration.

Understanding Subordination is vitally important to your success on the TOEFL. We must learn to quickly analyze sentences to find errors. A good understanding of subordination will provide you with the foundation you need to analyze many other types of errors. You will see that many of the problem areas that we will study require that we first separate our sentence, finding the main ans subordinate clauses. For example, we can't really know if we have a repeated subject if we don't first know which subject goes with which clause. What at first might seem like an error may actually be correct because every clause must have a subject.

We will study three types of subordinate clauses: the **noun**, **adjective**, and the **adverb** clauses.

Noun clauses as we saw in the **MC** point, can function as subjects (along with nouns, pronouns, gerunds, and infinitives). They can also function as objects of a main clause. The noun clause is perhaps the most difficult of all clauses to understand because it can not be completely separated from the main clause (the adjective and adverb clauses can). The noun clause becomes an integral part of the main clause, functioning as subject or object.

Noun clauses are typically *marked* with introductory words, or subordinating signals, such as: that, why, what, how, or where. We will learn to recognize noun clauses using these words. But do not become too dependent on them because we will also see *unmarked* noun clauses that have no introductory words. Try to focus more on the sentence structure. Remember the noun clause functions as a noun (in meaning) but has its own subject and verb. It will serve as the subject or object of the main clause.

Let's examine a few examples of each:

NOUN CLAUSE SUBJECTS

<u>That Eric arrived two hours late</u> made his mother angry.

<u>What the boy said</u> made his friend sad.

<u>How he can afford to buy a new car</u> is a mystery to me.

NOUN CLAUSE OBJECTS

We didn't hear <u>what the teacher said</u>.

The university catalog explains <u>how students can apply for scholarships</u>.

I know <u>where my pet snake is hiding</u>.

Subordinate **Adjective** clauses are fairly easy to recognize because they *always* follow the noun (or possibly pronoun) that they describe. Obviously, it would be impossible to begin a sentence with an adjective clause. In fact, adjective clauses are often found in the middle of the main clause. They begin with subordinating signals such as: who, that, which, where, or when. Again, do not focus entirely on introductory words—the adjective clause can also be *unmarked*.

ADJECTIVE CLAUSES

Baseball, <u>which is America's favorite pastime</u>, is actually a British invention.

Acupuncture is an ancient Chinese treatment <u>which is still used in many parts of the world</u>.

None of the students know the teacher <u>who is substituting for their English class</u>.

This verb, *afford*, does not really have a Spanish counterpart. Its closest translation would be "tener dinero para comprar", "permitirse el lujo".

Subordinate **Adverb** clauses are usually found in the beginning or end of a sentence. They *always* begin with subordinating signals (they are never *unmarked*). They begin with what we call *adverbial conjunctions*. These are words such as: although, as soon as, before, and since.

ADVERB CLAUSES

We decided not to swim in the sea <u>because the water looked dirty</u>.

<u>Although it is very long</u>, *Gone with the Wind* remains a favorite movie.

<u>While they were walking down the beach</u>, the couple enjoyed the sunset.

We will begin our study of **SC** errors by distinguishing between main clauses and subordinate clauses. Remember, they both have a subject and a verb, but the main clause can function independently while the subordinate clause can't. The following exercise will help you distinguish between the two.

EXERCISE SWE-9

Directions: Decide if the following sentences are **main clauses** or **subordinate clauses**. In the blanks, write **MC** for main clauses and **SC** for subordinate clauses.

<u> SC </u> 1. if we are able to arrive two hours before the opening

_____ 2. singing is an important element of the church service

_____ 3. since we arrived home from our Cancun vacation

_____ 4. hard study is necessary to pass the course

_____ 5. 🔍 that oranges are a great source of vitamin C

🔍 The word *that* has two meanings in English: *que* and *esta*. Here we have the *que* meaning. To make a main clause in this sentence, you'd need the plural form of *that*: *those*.

SUBORDINATION

_____6. "surfing the web" is popular among teenagers

_____7. even though Guatemala is located south of Mexico

_____8. as soon as the rainy season is over

_____9. as if the car were newly painted

_____10. jumping rope increases the heart rate

_____11. the little boy is pretending to be asleep

_____12. when you called me on the phone from Caracas

_____13. that we would experience severe flooding

_____14. that diamonds are more valuable than gold

_____15. if they could see me now

Now we'll distinguish between subordinate clauses and phrases. Remember that a subordinate clause has a subject and verb. A phrase is a group of words that does not contain a subject and an active verb. Again, phrases should usually be "thrown away" when analyzing sentences to find errors. In the following exercise, we will distinguish between subordinate clauses and phrases by checking the sentence for a subject and verb. Be careful with infinitive and gerund subjects—try not to confuse them for verbs.

EXERCISE SWE-10

Directions: Examine the following sentences and write **SC** in the blank for **subordinate clauses**. Mark an **(X)** for **phrases**.

__X__1. after returning home from the movie

_____2. a self-cleaning oven

_____3. because the flight had been canceled

_____4. that he knew the answer to the question

_____5. the most sophisticated system available

SUBORDINATION

_____ 6. which he knew nothing about

_____ 7. although he later changed his mind

_____ 8. speaking Spanish like a native speaker

_____ 9. to study everyday for the TOEFL exam

_____ 10. since he graduated from college

_____ 11. what he did on vacation

_____ 12. to see the animals in the zoo

_____ 13. whom he wants to marry

_____ 14. as soon as tickets go on sale

_____ 15. unless he improves his study habits

Now we'll combine the material studied in the last two exercises and try to distinguish among main clauses, subordinate clauses, and phrases.

EXERCISE SWE-11

Directions: Examine the following sentences and in the blanks write **MC** for **main clauses**, **SC** for **subordinate clauses**, and **(X)** for **phrases**.

_X_ 1. looking at the snow through the small window

_____ 2. his wishes for a better job

_____ 3. 🔍 because of the severe freeze

_____ 4. because the children were beginning to get tired

_____ 5. to play a musical instrument

🔍 Note that *because of* introduces a phrase, while *because* introduces a subordinate clause.

_____6. the tulips bloom in the spring

_____7. an elderly couple strolling down the street

_____8. in one ear and out the other

_____9. the coconut is the fruit of the palm tree

_____10. who came to the New World with Columbus

_____11. about the size of a boulder

_____12. as soon as the clock strikes twelve

_____13. pronouncing words in French

_____14. to taste fine wines by the glass

_____15. after the director's talk is over

When analyzing a TOEFL question, you should first divide your sentence. Find your main clause, subordinate clause(s), and phrase(s). Ask yourself two key questions: 1) *what do I have?* and 2) *what do I need?* First try to find the main clause. If you don't have a main clause, determine what you need to make one. Without exception, **every TOEFL question must have a main clau**se (and never more than one).

Sometimes it is necessary to eliminate a word or words to create a main clause. It is typical on the TOEFL to find a sentence that starts with a main clause subject and continues with two or more subordinate clauses. The subject is left "suspended" with no support of a main clause and the subordinate clauses are also left unsupported. *The solution to this type of error is to eliminate a subordinating signal, which will create a main clause.* Examine the following sample question.

Oliver Twist <u>which</u> was written by Charles Dickens who <u>also wrote</u>

          A   B

<u>numerous other</u> novels before dying <u>on</u> June 9, 1870.

          C   D

In this sentence, the error is A. Notice that if you eliminate the subordinating signal "which" you create a main clause that supports the subject "Charles Dickens" as well as the other subordinate clauses.

If you determine that you have a complete main clause (*what do I have?*) you should next try to complete the sentence (*what do I need?*) with 1) a subordinate clause, 2) a phrase, or 3) a connecting word such as "and" and another verb to extend the main clause.

Before we study the different types of subordinate clauses individually, try to apply these principals of subordination to the TOEFL context. The following TOEFL practice contains several typical subordination (**SC**) errors, as well as some unrelated errors.

MINI TOEFL-3

Directions: In questions 1-5, choose the one word or phrase that best completes the sentence. In questions 6-10, identify the underlined word(s) that should be changed to correct the sentence.

TIME: 6 minutes

_____1. Hong Kong, which has returned to Chinese rule, _____ a British territory.

    (A) that   (B) with   (C) was   (D) being

_____2. Teotihuacan, _____ home to two pyramids, is located in Mexico.

    (A) which is   (B) who is   (C) is   (D) it's

_____3. Vincent Van Gogh _____ for his post-impressionist paintings.

    (A) who is known   (B) is renowned   (C) being   (D) known

_____4. Many people can not believe _____ has actually walked on the moon.

    (A) which he   (B) men   (C) really   (D) that man

_____5. When a muscle contracts _____ lactic acid which causes tiredness.

    (A) they produce   (B) producing   (C) it produces   (D) causes

_____6. The Tower of London which was built by William the Conqueror who played an important role
                        A   B   C

in British history.
   D

_____7. At the start of a piece of music is found the key signature tells how many sharps and flats are to
           A   B   C   D

be played.

_____8. Elizabeth Taylor, who growing up in the U.S., was English by birth.
                          A   B   C   D

_____9. New York City, who is nicknamed the "Big Apple", has many skyscrapers.
                       A   B   C   D

_____10. Oprah Winfrey who hosts a famous talk show who is said to be the richest woman in the U.S.
                            A   B   C   D

Because subordination is so important when analyzing TOEFL questions, we will give further attention to the **three types of subordinate clauses**. Of course, it will never be necessary for you to actually classify subordinate clauses on the TOEFL exam. Careful study of the various types of clauses and sentence structures, however, will give you the knowledge and skills necessary for making a quick analysis of a sentence.

SUBORDINATION

We'll begin with **noun clauses** which can function as the subject or object of the main clause. A marked noun clause will begin with the word *that* or an interrogative such as *what*, *why*, or *how*.

EXERCISE SWE-12

Directions: Some of the following sentences contain noun clauses (which will function as the subject or object of the main clause and begin with the word *that* or an interrogative). If the sentence contains a noun clause write **NC** in the blank. If the sentence does not contain a noun clause write (**X**) in the blank. Underline the noun clauses.

__NC__ 1. <u>That there is life in outer space</u> has not been proven.

_____2. Jaime gave an oral presentation to the group.

_____3. I heard that we won the game.

_____4. The book explains how children acquire a second language.

_____5. Where we shop for fresh vegetables is right around the corner.

_____6. Only children believe that the Tooth Fairy really exists.

_____7. That it infrequently rains in the desert does not prevent some specially adapted animals from existing.

_____8. The association is made up of only English teachers.

_____9. The melted rock inside a volcano is called magma.

_____10. How much money the politician spent on his campaign remains a mystery.

_____11. That cigarettes cause cancer makes them a serious health threat.

_____12. Researchers have discovered that about 95% of the population is right handed.

_____13. In 1892 an English scientist named Sir Francis Galton discovered that no two fingerprints are the same.

_____14. The instruction booklet explains how the microwave oven is operated.

_____15. How twins interact during childhood is the subject of her new book.

SUBORDINATION

_____16. It is unfortunate for sports fans that the game had to be canceled because of bad weather.

_____17. That student feels that his project is the best.

_____18. Scientists believe that dogs and cats are color blind.

_____19. How the brain functions is being studied by medical students.

_____20. Delaware is sometimes called "The Diamond State" because of its great value in proportion to its size.

When a noun clause functions as the object of a main clause, it can be **unmarked**, which means the subordinating signal has been eliminated. Compare the following:

marked noun clause: The teacher felt <u>that</u> her students were improving.
unmarked noun clause: The teacher felt her students were improving.

Both sentences are grammatically correct and both have the same meaning. Can you identify the unmarked noun clauses in the following sentences?

EXERCISE SWE-13

Directions: Underline the **unmarked noun clauses** in the following sentences. If you find it helpful, try replacing the omitted *that*.

1. We all hope <u>the weather report is accurate.</u>

2. The little boy said he wanted to be a fireman.

3. The policeman said the man had run a red light.

4. It is obvious the congressman will lose the election.

5. The doctor reported the patient was in stable condition.

6. Some believe crystals have healing powers.

7. The journalist reported the new law had been passed.

8. We all hope we will score above 500 on the TOEFL.

9. The school principal said we will have a fire drill today.

10. The diet plan suggests carbohydrates be limited.

We'll work now with **adjective clauses**—remember an adjective clause always follows a noun (or pronoun) and gives us a description of that noun *Marked* adjective clauses begin with words such as: *that, when, where, which, who,* etc. Remember, adjective clauses often appear in the *middle* of the main clause.

EXERCISE SWE-14

Directions: Identify and underline all of the **adjective clauses** in the following sentences. The clauses in sentences 1-5 are **marked**. In sentences 6-10 they are **unmarked** (no subordinating signal).

1. The bad smelling odor of skunks is contained in a liquid <u>that the animal produces</u>.

2. The liquid which the skunk discharges is called musk.

3. Musk is produced by two glands which are located near the base of the skunk's tail.

4. Only a small amount of liquid, which can be smelled from half a mile away, is discharged.

5. The musk, which can also sting the eyes, can be sprayed up to 12 feet.

6. Insects skunks eat include beetles, crickets, and grasshoppers.

7. Two kinds of skunks scientists have classified are the striped and hog-nosed.

8. The size skunks typically reach is 14 to 19 inches.

9. The bobcat is one of the few enemies the skunk must avoid.

10. Hog-nosed skunks are the only skunks scientists have found in South America.

When subordinate noun and adjective clauses follow words such as *fact, dream, proof, theory, hope,* etc. they can both begin with *that*. Adjective clauses, but not noun clauses, can also begin with *which*. Starting a noun clause with *which* would be considered an error.

It should sound wrong to begin a noun clause with *which*. If you're not sure, try inserting a form of the verb *to be* between the noun and the clause. Compare:

noun clause: the news (is) that the president resigned.
adjective clause: the news that was reported this morning.

It should sound wrong to say "the news **is** that was reported this morning". You can also look at this from a more logical point of view: the noun clause specifically **states** the news (it answers the question "what is the news?"), while the adjective clause only **describes** it.

The following **strategic tip** might save you some confusion on this rather delicate point: if you have determined that your sentence must be completed with *that* or *which* (in the Sentence Completion section) always choose *that*. The TOEFL never offers two correct choices. More analysis could be required if this type of structure is tested in the Error Identification section. Watch for this type of error while you're focusing on **SC** errors in the following TOEFL practice exercise. Remember to find the main clause first--it will help you identify **SC** errors.

SUBORDINATION

MINI TOEFL-4

Directions: In questions 1-5, choose the one word or phrase that best completes the sentence. In questions 6-10, identify the underlined word(s) that should be changed to correct the sentence.

TIME: 6 minutes

_____1. The media publicized the president's decision _____ would seek reelection.

    (A) was that he   (B) which he   (C) and it   (D) that he

_____2. _____ hopeful that a cure will be found for the HIV virus.

    (A) That is   (B) It is   (C) To be   (D) That it is

_____3. Houdini once claimed _____ could escape from within any locked container.

    (A) which he   (B) that he   (C) always   (D) to

_____4. _____ a book that contains definitions of thousands of words.

    (A) An dictionary   (B) That a dictionary is   (C) A dictionary is   (D) It

_____5. The fact that the ozone is disappearing _____ many environmentalists.

    (A) disturbs   (B) disturbing to   (C) disturbance of   (D) disturbing

_____6. <u>Many</u> people <u>that</u> bullfighting is not a sport <u>at all</u>, but torture of an <u>innocent animal</u>.
      A   B   C   D

_____7. Financial <u>advisors</u> know <u>that</u> the best investment is for <u>first time</u> stock market <u>investors</u>.
                 A   B   C   D

SUBORDINATION

_____8. <u>Raised</u> in Monroeville, Alabama, Truman Capote <u>was</u> an author <u>wrote about</u> American
            A   B   C

life <u>in the</u> Deep South.
     D

_____9. The event was not really <u>success</u> <u>because</u> the rain <u>started</u> early <u>in the afternoon</u>.
                                  A   B   C   D

_____10. Dr. Morrison's office <u>is located</u> on the <u>second floor</u> of the <u>administrative</u> building, a three
                                A   B   C

<u>floors</u> building.
  D

Subordinate **adverb clauses** always begin with *adverbial conjunctions*. They are never unmarked. Check the following list to become familiar with some of the most common adverbial conjunctions.

ADVERBIAL CONJUNCTIONS

after, although, as, as far as, as if, as long as, as soon as, as though, because, before, by the time, even if, even though, except that, if, in case, in the event, in order that, now that, once, provided, rather than, 🔍 since, so, so that, sooner than, though, till, until, when, where, while

🔍 Remember that *since* has two meanings: *desde* and *porque*.

SUBORDINATION

EXERCISE SWE-15

Directions: Find and underline the **adverb clauses** in the following sentences (some sentences have more than one). Put parenthesis ( ) around the **main clauses.**

1. (Nielson ratings are used by television networks) <u>so that they know about a show's popularity</u>.

2. García is the most common Latin last name, although Chang is the most popular last name in the world.

3. Even though no one knows the exact birth date of Jesus Christ, Christmas is celebrated around the world on December 25.

4. Since it was invented in 1886 the secret formula for making Coca Cola has been known to only seven men.

5. Because the ostrich is an extremely large bird, it can not fly, although it can run at speeds of nearly 60 miles per hour.

6. Unless Roberto repairs his bicycle he will have to take the bus to school, even though it will take him twice as much time.

7. Although Holland is the world's biggest producer of tulips, the flower actually came from Asia.

8. Until computers were invented, writers had to rely on typewriters even though their work was rather tedious.

9. The university bookstore will be closed this week so that inventory can be taken before the new semester begins.

10. Tickets for Broadway musicals are very expensive although half priced tickets are sometimes available if you wait until the last minute.

11. Please advise the front desk staff as soon as you know if you will be departing earlier than previously planned.

12. Unless our television is repaired by Saturday we won't be able to watch the football game.

13. If you book your flight early you can qualify for discounts although any changes will be penalized.

14. When his alarm clock rang Antonio turned it off and continued sleeping although it was time for him to wake up.

15. The light of the moon can create a lunar rainbow, although its colors are weaker than those created by the sun.

We've now studied each type of subordinate clause individually and should be ready to work with them all together in complete sentences. In the following exercise we will practice distinguishing among **main clauses, subordinate clauses, and phrases**. We'll further classify the subordinate clauses as *noun, adjective,* or *adverb*.

Of course on the actual TOEFL exam you will not have to actually classify sentences in this way. But understanding these grammatical elements will improve your skills at identifying and correcting errors on the exam.

SUBORDINATION

EXERCISE SWE-16

Directions: Examine the following sentences. If the underlined part is a **main clause**, write **MC** in the blank. Write **(X)** for **phrases**, and **SC** for **subordinate clauses**. Further classify subordinate clauses by writing **(N)** for *noun,* **(ADJ)** for *adjective,* or **(ADV)** for *adverb* above each one.

__X__ 1. Venezuela is located in the northeast corner of South America, <u>just above the equator.</u>

_____ 2. Venezuela does not really experience changes in weather, <u>although the months of July and August are hotter than usual.</u>

_____ 3. <u>A rainy season is experienced</u> from May to November.

_____ 4. <u>Although many creeds are represented</u>, the majority of Venezuelans are Roman Catholic.

_____ 5. Angel Falls, <u>which is the highest waterfall in the world</u>, is located in Venezuela.

_____ 6. <u>Spanish is spoken in Venezuela</u>, although English is taught in the public school system.

_____ 7. Nearly 50% of Venezuelans are under 18 years of age, <u>while 70% are under 30.</u>

_____ 8. Like many Latin American countries, <u>Venezuela's police forces are generally undertrained, poorly paid, and understaffed.</u>

_____ 9. What changed Venezuela was the discovery of oil <u>which made it rich overnight.</u>

_____ 10. <u>Like Mexico City and Tokyo,</u> Caracas has incredible traffic jams.

_____ 11. Venezuela has 144 miles of tropical beaches <u>which includes 72 small islands.</u>

_____ 12. <u>That the Caracas subway system opened in 1983</u> has helped ease congestion in some parts of the city.

_____ 13. <u>Until the bolivar was devalued in 1983,</u> Caracas was one of the most expensive cities in the world.

_____ 14. <u>That 75% of the population lives in an urban environment</u> causes problems of overcrowded conditions.

_____ 15. <u>Venezuela's Caribbean location makes it a paradise for many water sports</u>, although some of the beaches near Caracas are polluted.

53

SUBORDINATION

If you feel that you still need more practice in distinguishing among main clauses, subordinate clauses, and phrases, just pick up any English book, magazine, or newspaper. You'll find an endless supply of sentences just waiting to be studied.

Don't forget to ask yourself "what do I have?" and "what do I need?" when analyzing a TOEFL error. The following exercise will help you do just that. It contains sentences with a missing word. By looking at the structure of the sentence, try to decide what that missing word must be: **main subject** (subject of the main clause), **main verb** (verb of the main clause), **subordinating signal** (introductory word of the subordinate clause), or **subordinate verb** (verb of the subordinate clause). If you can work through this exercise with a clear understanding and few errors, you have successfully completed Step One and are ready to take your next step in the program.

EXERCISE SWE-17

Directions: One word has been omitted from the following sentences. In the blank, write the number that corresponds to the missing word: **1. main subject   2. main verb   3. subordinating signal   4. subordinate verb**.

___2___ 1. Argentina ---------- the second largest country in South America.

_____ 2. Argentina's capital is Buenos Aires, ---------- is one of the largest cities in South America.

_____ 3. Many ---------- visit Argentina, especially Buenos Aires.

_____ 4. People from many countries settled in Argentina, --------- most came from Spain and Italy.

_____ 5. Argentina's Constitution provides a government which ---------- somewhat similar to that of the United States.

_____ 6. Unlike most other Latin American countries, ... has relatively few Indians.

_____ 7. Argentine customs ---------- the influence of immigrants from European countries.

_____ 8. Argentina has four main land regions, which ---------- the Pampa, a grassy plain that extends 300 miles.

54

SUBORDINATION

_____9. ---------- enjoys four distinct seasons, much like those of the United States.

_____10. Buenos Aires has one of the busiest airports in Latin America, ---------- some 200 other airports are located throughout the country.

_____11. Isabel Perón, ---------- was the first woman to become president of a nation in the Western Hemisphere, was the wife of Juan Perón.

_____12. Argentina's economy ---------- largely on agricultural products.

_____13. The nation ---------- the world's leading exporter of beef.

_____14. The tango, which ---------- in Buenos Aires, is an adaptation of a Spanish folk dance.

_____15. Many Argentines ---------- Madonna's portrayal of Evita Perón in the movie adaptation of Andrew Lloyd Webber's Broadway hit.

MINI TOEFL-5

Directions: In questions 1-5, choose the one word or phrase that best completes the sentence. In questions 6-10, identify the underlined word(s) that should be changed to correct the sentence. **TIME: 6 minutes**

_____1. Ducks have webbed feet that enable _____ swim fast, even in rough waters.

    (A) them to   (B) to their   (C) its   (D) they

_____2. _____ the ozone layer is completely destroyed, nearly all living creatures will die.

    (A) For   (B) So   (C) Although   (D) If

_____3. Although there is no cure for the common cold, sleeping, resting, _____ can be helpful.

    (A) and to drink juice   (B) and drinking fluids

    (C) and that drinking fluids   (D) which drank fluids

Note that in conditional sentences *is* is used with *will*, while *were* is used with *would*.

SUBORDINATION

_____ 4. _____ turns copper green is its patina, a green film.

   (A) That   (B) What   (C) How   (D) What is

_____ 5. Crying _____ stress, although it may irritate the eyes.

  (A) is relieving (B) what they relieve (C) relieves (D) relieves it which is

_____ 6. New York City, _____ one of the world's largest cities, is larger than any other cities in
                              A   B   C   D

the United States.

_____ 7. Although testing water samples, correct levels of chlorine can be maintained in swimming
               A   B   C   D

pools.

_____ 8. After they became extinct, dinosaurs lived on the earth for nearly 150 million years.
            A   B   C   D

_____ 9. Since Eduardo was afraid of highs, he didn't join his friends
         A   B   C   D

on the roller coaster ride.

_____ 10. Although was defeated for the presidency several times, Cuauhtémoc Cárdenas was finally
            A   B   C

elected mayor of Mexico City.

    D

POP QUIZ

Can you name the four definitions of the word *spring*?

In Spanish, what does *to trip* mean as a verb?

What is the difference between a main and subordinate clause?

What are the three types of subordinate clauses?

What are the five structures that function as subjects in English?

TOEFL PREP for Spanish Speakers

STEP TWO

QUICK CHECK   Grammar Problem Areas

STEP ONE

    MC (Main Clause)

    SC (Subordinate Clause)

STEP TWO

    > S=V (Subject-Verb Agreement)

    S=P (Subject-Pronoun Agreement)

    VTF (Verb Tense or Form)

    PFR (Pronoun Form or Reference)

STEP THREE

VERBS and PRONOUNS, Agreement, Tense, Form, Reference

    VBL (Verbal)

    WF (Word Form)

STEP FOUR

    WO (Word Order)

    PS (Parallel Structure)

    UR (Unnecessary Repetition)

STEP FIVE

    CU (Correct Usage)

Rules for Subject-Verb Agreement

SUBJECT-VERB AGREEMENT

EXERCISE SWE-18

Directions: Using the abbreviations that identify each type of error, classify the following ten errors, then try to correct the errors. Only ten of the twelve types of errors are listed.

__PFR__ 1. We must remember to make us reservations early in order to secure accommodations during the holiday weekend.

__VTF__ 2. Marco learned many new things by the time he finishes his TOEFL program.

__CU__ 3. The French horn does a mellow tone that blends well with woodwind instruments.

__UR__ 4. Simultaneously, both telephones rang at the same time.

__MC__ 5. The boat floating down the river all afternoon.

__S=V__ 6. The furniture in the apartment belong to the owner.

__PS__ 7. The little boy aspires to be a race car driver, an astronaut, or a member of the fire department.

__SC__ 8. The children remained sad, even though tried to cheer them up.

__VBL__ 9. Although I am not a big fan of science fiction, the movie was quite interested.

__WF__ 10. The lovely flowers at the wedding ceremony smelled sweetly and the candles softly glowed.

We begin **Step Two** with a study of subject-verb agreement. The concept of subject-verb agreement is quite simple: singular subjects take singular verbs; plural subjects take plural verbs. Subject-verb agreement errors are fairly common on the TOEFL exam.

If you don't see an error immediately when taking Section Two of the TOEFL, first apply the information learned in Step One: divide the sentence, separating phrases, subordinate clauses, and the main clause (while checking for **MC** or **SC** errors). Then find the subject and verb in each clause and check for correct agreement.

Subject-verb agreement often works differently in English and Spanish. Translating to Spanish is not usually a good idea and will often lead to an incorrect answer.

59

SUBJECT-VERB AGREEMENT

We will examine several cases where the verb can be in either singular or plural form (depending on various factors), must always be in singular form, or must always be in plural form.

SINGULAR OR PLURAL VERBS

In the following cases, a singular or plural verb might be used depending on the structure of the sentence and the subject which the verb refers to.

1. As you begin studying subject-verb agreement, concentrate on isolating the verb from phrases or clauses that might separate the subject and verb. Prepositional phrases can be especially tricky. Remember that words separating a subject and verb have no effect on its singularity or plurality. Notice the following example with prepositional phrases.

	accompanied by		
	together with		
The **teacher**	*as well as*	his students	**is visiting** the museum.
	in addition to		
	along with		

You can see in this example that *the teacher* is **singular** and the verb must also be **singular**. This is good subject-verb agreement. Again, the phrase separating the subject and verb **has no effect**. Often on the TOEFL exam a singular subject is presented--followed by phrases containing many plural words. By the time you get to the verb it sounds OK to put a plural verb. Avoid this trap by isolating the subject.

2. Collective nouns are words that refer to a group of people. These words are almost always used in a singular form. In fact, it sounds a bit rare to use them in a plural form. However, for the TOEFL exam we must learn that it is indeed possible to use such words in a plural form if it is considered that *the individual members of the group are acting independently*. Some of these collective nouns include: *family, team, police, class, audience, faculty, etc.*

SUBJECT-VERB AGREEMENT

How do we know if one of these words should take a singular or a plural verb? Simply check the sentence for a **pronoun** or **modifier** to give you a reference. Compare the following sentences:

The *committee* **are** in the process of making **their** decisions.

The *committee* **is** in the process of making **its** decision.

3. An easy rule to remember: nouns that refer to a language are singular but are plural when referring to a nationality. Compare the following:

🔑 *Chinese* **is** a difficult language to speak. The *Chinese* **include** a great deal of rice in their diets.

4. English includes some words that have Latin and Greek origins. These often have confusing singular and plural forms. Check the following list.

SINGULAR	PLURAL
appendix	appendices
alumnus	alumni
basis	bases
criterion	criteria
datum	data
index	indices
medium	media
phenomenon	phenomena

5. A few words in English do not change in form—they're the same in singular and plural. Some words always end in *s*, such as *series* and *species*. Other words, especially those referring to animals, never end in *s*, such as *sheep, deer, fish,* and *shrimp* (*fishes* and *shrimps* are alternative plural forms used in British English).

🔑 Notice that the article *the* precedes the noun indicating a nationality. Careful! In Spanish the article *el* proceeds the noun meaning language: *el inglés*.

61

Check modifiers and pronouns for singular or plural reference. Compare the following:

Those shrimp **smell** delicious.   *This* **is** the last shrimp I can eat.

6. Words such as *none, all, some, half, majority, any, etc.* can be singular or plural, depending on what they refer to. If a prepositional phrase follows one of these words, check the object of the phrase to determine if it has a singular or plural reference. Compare the following:

None of the **money** <u>is</u> mine.   *None* of the **guests** <u>have</u> arrived.

7. In their normal meanings, the words *there, here,* and *where* do not function as subjects. Sentences beginning with these words require an inversion of the subject and verb (see **WO** in Step Four). If your sentence begins with one of these words make sure the verb agrees with the subject, which is found *after* the verb. For example:

There **are** not enough <u>books</u> in this library.

Here **is** the <u>message</u> that was left for you this morning.

8. *Either...or, neither....nor,* and *not only...but also* are correlative conjunctions that introduce two subjects. The verb always agrees with the closest (second) subject. Examine the following:

Neither the children *nor* the **baby-sitter** <u>likes</u> the TV program.

Either the cats *or* the **dog** <u>has</u> destroyed the flower garden.

Not only the players *but also* the **coach** <u>hopes</u> for a victory.

Try this: Read the sentences again changing the position of the subjects (put the second subject first and the first one second) and change the verb to agree.

NOTE: these structures are also important when studying errors in pronoun-subject agreement (**S=P**, Step Two) and parallel structure (**PS**, Step four). These simple structures can cause a wide variety of errors, but they're quite easy to learn. Learn them well—they could be worth several points on the TOEFL exam!

SUBJECT-VERB AGREEMENT

If you understand the above cases where a verb might be in a singular or plural form, try the next exercise for practice.

EXERCISE SWE-19

Directions: Identify and underline the subjects of the following sentences. If the subject is *singular*, write **is** in the blank. If the subject is *plural*, write **are**.

1. <u>Cotton</u>, as well as wool and silk, __is__ produced from non-synthetic material.

2. The team _____ making plans for their big game.

3. The Japanese _____ known for technological advances.

4. The data _____ now available for your reference.

5. Deer _____ sometimes cruelly hunted for their antlers.

6. All of the rooms in the hotel _____ reserved.

7. Here _____ the candles for the birthday cake.

8. Not only the flight attendants but also the pilots _____ planning to go on strike.

9. Alumni of the university _____ asked to make financial donations.

10. Ana, along with her sister and three brothers, _____ hoping to travel to Disney World.

11. English _____ spoken in nearly all parts of the world.

12. Here _____ the results of the medical tests.

13. Some of the tickets _____ still unsold.

14. The police _____ planning its annual fund-raising event.

15. All of the creeks _____ becoming polluted by the oil spill.

Cotton is an example of an uncountable noun (just like *wool, silk, polyester*, etc.) Remember that uncountable nouns, by definition, have no plural form—they couldn't possibly take a plural verb.

SINGULAR VERBS

Now we'll examine cases where a singular verb is always used.

1. Titles of books, newspapers, magazines, etc. always take a singular verb (even if plural in form). Examine the following:

The Mexico City Times **is** one of two English newspapers in Mexico.

Star Wars **has** been released again after many years.

2. Academic subjects are always singular (even if plural in form). For example: *mathematics, physics, statistics*. The same applies to certain sports activities such as *gymnastics*. Examine the following: *Mathematics* **is** Roberto's favorite subject. *Gymnastics* **is** one of the most popular Olympic sports.

3. Some abstract nouns such as *politics, news, ethics,* and *information* take singular verbs (even when plural in form). Examine the following:

Ethics **is** a branch of philosophy.

The *news* of the results **is** important to scientists.

Words like *news* can be tricky. While always plural in form, *news* is considered singular (and uncountable). However, in Spanish we have singular and plural forms—*la noticia, las noticias.*

4. Nouns indicating specific amounts or measurements of money, time, degree, or quantity take singular verbs. Examine the following:

Two hundred dollars **is** required to open a checking account.

Thirty minutes **isn't** enough time to finish my homework.

Can you think of similar sentences with this type of subject? Try now to formulate a few using various kinds of measurements.

Careful with this word. The word *mathematic* does not exist (it must end in *s* unless the shortened form *math* is used). Like all academic subjects, it is always singular in form, but in Spanish it's considered plural—*las matemáticas.*

Be careful with amounts of money. They can be expressed in a singular or plural form in Spanish: *los doscientos pesos son...doscientos pesos es....*

5. Names of diseases always take a singular verb (even when plural in form).

For example, *measles, mumps, herpes, AIDS*. Examine the following:

AIDS **is** preventable although proper education is necessary.

Measles **is** a serious disease for adult victims.

6. The expression *the number of* takes a singular verb (*a number of* is plural). For example: *The number of students* **is** increasing.

7. Two subjects joined by *and* take a plural verb, but if preceeded by *each* or *every* a singular verb is used. Examine the following: *Each* boy and girl **was** given a small gift at the party. *Every* employee and visitor **wears** an identification tag.

8. If the words *each, either,* or *neither* function as subjects, they take singular verbs. For example: *Each* of those cars **has** been checked for mechanical problems.

9. Words which end in "one", "body", or "thing" take singular verbs (even though they may be plural in meaning). These include words such as: *everyone, nothing, anybody, everything, nothing, someone, etc.* For example:

Everybody at the conference **receives** a certificate.

Nothing **is** more important to a person's health than a proper diet.

Perhaps some difficult vocabulary here--*Measles* means *sarampión*, *mumps* means *paperas*, *AIDS*, which stands for Acquired Immune Deficiency Syndrome, means *SIDA*.

10. The introductory *it* takes a singular verb. For example: 🔍 *It* **is** his lack of experience that makes him nervous about the new job.

Before we complete this **S=V** section, we'll take a break to complete a **MINI TOEFL** practice exercise. This will help you see how **S=V** errors might be tested in the TOEFL context. As always, some unrelated errors will be included.

🔍 The introductory *it* (sometimes referred to as the *impersonal, existential,* or *anticipatory it*) can be confusing to Spanish speakers. English teachers and grammar books often say that the *it* refers to "the fact". *It* really refers to nothing, but in English a verb must have a subject and if there is no subject we use *it* (avoid using *that* in its place). While in Spanish you can say *es posible,* in English we must say *it is possible.*

SUBJECT-VERB AGREEMENT

MINI TOEFL-6

Directions: In questions 1-5, choose the one word or phrase that best completes the sentence. In questions 6-10, identify the underlined word(s) that should be changed to make the sentence correct.

TIME: 6 minutes

_____1. Every partner and associate _____ invited to the seminar in order to become familiar with the latest advancements.

        (A) has been   (B) were   (C) have been   (D) already

_____2. Mrs. Hall, along with her students and teaching assistants, _____ a trip to Europe this Summer.

        (A) will be   (B) are planning (C) were organizing (D) is planning

_____3. Not only the crime rate, but also the percentage of unemployment _____ taken into consideration when rating cities.

        (A) are   (B) had   (C) is   (D) were

_____4. The criteria for accepting students in the new doctoral program _____ been established yet.

        (A) have not   (B) have   (C) hasn't   (D) has also

_____5. A number of Mexican citizens _____ expressed outrage over the proposed U.S. immigration laws.

        (A) has   (B) was   (C) have   (D) did

_____6. The information <u>on</u> the various exam dates and <u>registration deadlines</u> <u>were</u> useful to <u>many</u> aspir-
                        A   B   C   D
ing university students.

67

SUBJECT-VERB AGREEMENT

_____7. One of the <u>most famous</u> alumni of our university <u>he</u> <u>was</u> asked <u>to speak</u> at the graduation.
                           A   B C   D

_____8. Manuel, along with his twenty classmates, <u>are planning</u> a <u>trip</u> to Cancun <u>to celebrate</u> graduating
                                                        A   B   C

<u>from</u> medical school.
D

_____9. For decades, <u>studies</u> of cigarette smoking <u>have shown</u> that smoking is <u>extreme dangerous</u> and
                         A   B   C

<u>causes</u> cancer.
D

_____10 Although the researchers 🔍 <u>are needing</u> additional funds to complete their project, the rector
                                            A

<u>has no</u> authority <u>to approve</u> <u>them</u>.
  B   C   D

🔍 Avoid using certain verbs in continuous tenses. These verbs include "emotion" verbs such as *like, need, want, love,* etc. It is correct to say *I need money*, not *I am needing money*.

SUBJECT-VERB AGREEMENT

PLURAL VERBS

In the following cases, a plural verb is always used.

1. The expression *a number of* takes a plural verb (remember that *the number of* takes a singular verb). For example: *A number of* books **are** missing from the library.

2. Two subjects joined by *and* take a plural verb (unless preceded by *each* or *every*). Examine the following:

Both the Ritz Hotel *and* the Plaza **are** completely booked this week.

A little boy *and* his mother **were** waiting for the school to open.

3. *Several, many, both,* and *few* take plural verbs. Examine the following:

A *few* of the classes **have** been relocated to other classrooms.

Both **are** hoping to qualify for scholarships that cover tuition.

4. Many words that indicate articles of clothing or accessories take plural verbs. Such words include: *shorts, pants, jeans, trousers, glasses, etc.* They would take a singular verb, however, if the subject is changed to *pair*. Compare the following:

My sunglasses **are** black.   This *pair* of sunglasses **is** black.

Sometimes it is useful to make a mental association to help you remember rules and details needed for the TOEFL exam. These can be made in English or Spanish—use your imagination. To remember these four words, for example, you might remember something like, "**S**unday **M**orning **B**reak**F**ast" to give you the starting letters of **S**everal, **M**any, **B**oth, and **F**ew. Then imagine a picture that helps you relate your trigger words to the actual words you need to remember. In this case, you might imagine eggs for breakfast--several plates of eggs, one plate with many eggs, another with only a few, etc. It doesn't matter how ridiculous your mental picture is. In fact, the more unusual the idea, the more effective it is!

5. Many words describing tools take plural verbs. Such words include: *tongs, scissors, pliers, tweezers, clippers,* etc. Again, if you change the subject to *pair*, they take a singular verb.

Pliers and *tweezers* can be tricky for Spanish speakers, because both are expressed as *pinzas* in Spanish. Compare these drawings:

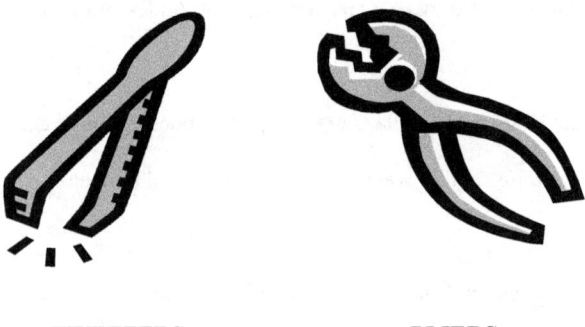

TWEEZERS   **PLIERS**

6. Some words such as *riches, thanks,* and *means* always take plural verbs unless the subject is changed with expressions such as *a word of, a note of, a world of,* etc.

We have now finished reviewing cases where a singular or plural verb is used, only a singular verb is used, or only a plural verb is used. Before we finish our study of **S=V** errors, we'll do some exercises that combine all of the above situations.

SUBJECT-VERB AGREEMENT

EXERCISE SWE-20

Directions: Identify the subjects in the following sentences. Then fill in the blank with **is** if the subject is singular or **are** if the subject is plural.

1. That species of bird __is__ common in Nebraska.

2. The baby deer in the zoo _____ playing with its mother.

3. The media _____ invited to cover the event.

4. Japanese _____ rarely studied by American students.

5. A number of teachers _____ attending the conference.

6. Mathematics _____ useful to engineers.

7. The faculty _____ discussing the parking problem among themselves .

8. Most of the money _____ mine.

9. Not only the tulips but also the lilies _____ blooming.

10. The towels and bed spreads _____ drying in the sun.

11. Every car and truck _____ inspected to verify emissions.

12. Here _____ the data you requested.

13. It _____ the librarian who purchases the books.

14. Everyone in the cast _____ an experienced singer or actor.

15. The national news as well as local reports _____ disturbing.

Blooming comes from the verb *to bloom* and means *florecer*.

SUBJECT-VERB AGREEMENT

EXERCISE SWE-21

Directions: Identify and underline the subject which the verb must agree with. Then fill in the blank with the correct verb from the choices given at the end of the sentence.

1. In its verdict, the <u>jury</u> _is_ finding the defendant innocent of all charges. (*is, are*)

2. The history of indigenous languages _____ being studied by the students in the comparative linguistics course. (*is, are*)

3. Because of insufficient water treatment, cholera _____ still a threat to those who don't consume only purified water. (*is, are*)

4. For English speakers living in Latin America, *Essential Spanish for Tourists* _____ phrases which are useful in daily communication. (*provides, provide*)

5. Everyone in this group of musicians _____ a chance to be selected to perform in the concert. (*has, have*)

6. Neither the sales manager nor the secretaries _____ received their paychecks. (*has, have*)

7. Soccer players and referees _____ protected from fans by a seven foot moat which encircles the stadium in Rio de Janeiro. (*is, are*)

8. There _____ a check for $300. in the envelope. (*was, were*)

9. A blue and white van _____ waiting to take the executives from the hotel to the airport. (*is, are*)

SUBJECT-VERB AGREEMENT

10. Some of the movie _____ been cut to shorten its length to two hours. (*has, have*)

11. Every parking attendant and usher _____ given free admission to the event in exchange for their volunteer work. (*is, are*)

12. The number of crimes committed by juveniles _____ decreased substantially. (*has, have*)

13. A good pair of sunglasses _____ essential for lifeguards. (*is, are*)

14. A school of tropical fish _____ seen by the scuba diver. (*was, were*)

15. It _____ his athletic ability and his academic achievement that impressed the admissions officer. (*was, were*)

MINI TOEFL-7

Directions: In questions 1-5, choose the one word or phrase that best completes the sentence. In questions 6-10, identify the underlined word(s) that should be changed to correct the sentence.

Time: 6 minutes

_____1. Every fruit and vegetable served by the restaurant _____ grown.

    (A) are organically   (B) were organically

    (C) have been organically   (D) is organically

_____2. Everyone, including the clerical staff, _____ to attend the staff meeting scheduled for tomorrow morning.

    (A) has   (B) will   (C) have   (D) had

SUBJECT-VERB AGREEMENT

_____3. He was accepted by the university _____ .

   (A) when he had seventeen years   (B) at the age of seventeen

   (C) when seventeen were his age   (D) with seventeen years

_____4. Many students in Mexico City as well as Tokyo _____ English classes and the TOEFL exam.

      (A) assist   (B) takes   (C) take   (D) assists

_____5. My new screwdriver as well as a pair of pliers _____ found in the drawer

      (A) were   (B) had   (C) was   (D) also

_____6. All of the money which <u>were</u> discovered <u>in the</u> thief's house <u>was believed</u> to be <u>counterfeit</u>.
                                    A   B   C   D

_____7. These dangerous bacteria <u>is sometimes</u> found in the food supply but <u>can be</u> killed by <u>cooking</u> at
                                                    A   B   C

a very <u>high temperature</u>.
        D

_____8. <u>The</u> Department of Foreign Languages <u>are requesting</u> <u>more funds</u> in order <u>to install</u> a sophisti-
       A   B   C   D

cated laboratory.

Counterfeit means *falsificado*.

_____ 9. The president, <u>accompanied by</u> several secret service agents and assistants <u>are planning</u> <u>to arrive</u>
                                        A   B   C

to the press conference <u>within</u> minutes.
                         D

_____ 10. Not only the washer and dryer <u>but also</u> half of the furniture <u>have already</u> been <u>loaded</u> onto the
                                       A   B   C

<u>moving truck</u>.
    D

POP QUIZ

How do you say *measles* and *mumps* in Spanish?

Is the word *furniture* singular or plural in form?

What is the singular form of the word *data*?

TOEFL PREP for Spanish Speakers

STEP TWO

QUICK CHECK   Grammar Problem Areas

STEP ONE

    MC   (Main Clause)

    SC   (Subordinate Clause)

STEP TWO

    S=V   (Subject-Verb Agreement)

    >S=P   (Subject-Pronoun Agreement)

    VTF   (Verb Tense or Form)

    PFR   (Pronoun Form or Reference)

STEP THREE

    VBL   (Verbal)

    WF   (Word Form)

Rules for Subject-Pronoun Agreement

VERBS and PRONOUNS, Agreement, Tense, and Form

STEP FOUR

    WO   (Word Order)

    PS   (Parallel Structure)

    UR   (Unnecessary Repetition)

STEP FIVE

    CU   (Correct Usage)

SUBJECT-PRONOUN AGREEMENT

EXERCISE SWE-22

Directions: Using the abbreviations that identify each type of error, classify the following ten errors, then try to correct the errors. Only ten of the twelve types of errors are listed.

  __WO__ 1. Rarely we do cook at home because we prefer eating out.

  __MC__ 2. German Shepherds, which make lovable pets, they are frequently trained to assist the blind.

  __PFR__ 3. The hair stylist whom does her hair is quite expensive.

  __S=V__ 4. Not only the teachers but also the principal have decided to play in the annual basketball game.

  __PS__ 5. When visiting New York, I enjoy shopping in SoHo, attending Broadway plays, and to eat in China Town.

  __WF__ 6. *Titanic* was the expensivest movie ever produced.

  __VBL__ 7. Power surges aren't harmful to electrical appliances left unplugging.

  __S=P__ 8. Everyone leaving the concert must have their hand stamped in order to be readmitted.

  __UR__ 9. The brief, short report highlighted the most important events of the annual meeting of stockholders.

  __CU__ 10. Setting in the sun for long periods of time without any kind of protection can be harmful to the skin and could even cause cancer.

This program has been designed so that students can begin at any point, or skip around through the material as desired. However, if you've just finished studying the **S=V** (subject-verb agreement) point, the following **S=P** (subject-pronoun agreement) point will be easy. There are fewer rules, and the rules are the same as the previous **S=V** rules. Subordination is still important when analyzing **S=P** errors; separate your clauses to correctly identify which pronoun refers to which subject, then check the agreement.

SUBJECT-PRONOUN AGREEMENT

Before we begin our study of **S=P** errors, let's take a look at the various forms of pronouns. The following chart classifies all of the pronouns in English by their form (only the demonstrative pronouns, *this, that, these,* and *those* are not included) Refer often to this chart until the pronouns become familiar. This will also be important for the following **PFR** (pronoun form or reference) point.

QUICK CHECK

SUBJECT	OBJECT	POSSESSIVE ADJECTIVE	POSSESSIVE PRONOUN	REFLEXIVE
I	ME	MY	MINE	MYSELF
YOU (SINGULAR)	YOU	YOUR	YOURS	YOURSELF
HE	HIM	HIS	HIS	HIMSELF
SHE	HER	HER	HERS	HERSELF
IT	IT	ITS	-----	ITSELF
WE	US	OUR	OURS	OURSELVES
YOU (PLURAL)	YOU	YOUR	YOURS	YOURSELVES
THEY	THEM	THEIR	THEIRS	THEMSELVES
ONE	ONE	ONE'S	-----	ONESELF
WHO	WHOM	WHOSE	WHOSE	-----

SUBJECT-PRONOUN AGREEMENT

The concept of subject-pronoun agreement is the same as that of subject-verb agreement. As mentioned, the rules are the same, but fewer. However, **S=P** errors can still be somewhat more difficult than **S=V** errors for one important reason: when checking the subject-verb agreement, there is only one singular or plural verb form from which to choose. But, when checking the subject-pronoun agreement, there are several singular choices from which to choose. We must think not only in number, but also gender, form, and reference. Let's begin with a few examples of **S=P** errors. Try to find the subject-pronoun agreement errors in the following five sentences.

1. Neither of the girls in my school has their own car.
2. The coach as well as the players is in their office.
3. Either Fernando or Eduardo should have brought their watch.
4. Each of the students has their credential.
5. All of the library books have its own identification number.

RULES FOR SUBJECT-PRONOUN AGREEMENT

1. Words which end in "one", "body", or "thing", even though plural in meaning, take singular verbs (see rule number ten under "Singular Verbs"). Singular pronouns are also used to refer to these words.

For example:

Everybody at the conference receives **his** certificate today.

Everything should be put in **its** proper place.

Remember, in Spanish you don't distinguish between masculine and feminine gender when choosing a possessive pronoun; in English you must. For example, the pronoun *su* could be translated to *his* or *her,* depending on the appropriate gender.

79

SUBJECT-PRONOUN AGREEMENT

2. When two subjects are joined by *and* (unless preceded by *each* or *every*), a plural verb is required (see rule two under "Plural Verbs"). Plural pronouns are also used in this case.

For example:

Both Cristal *and* Edna are doing **their** homework.

Pedro *and* I are taking **our** cars.

Let's test our understanding of these two rules before continuing with the last two.

EXERCISE SWE-23

Directions: Identify the subjects and complete the sentences with an appropriate pronoun. Make sure to read the complete sentence and maintain logical reference.

1. Everyone who dines in this restaurant will have __his__ parking ticket validated.

2. Both the cheerleaders and the football players will be issued _____ uniforms tomorrow.

3. Everyone is invited to bring _____ husband to the dinner.

4. Someone left _____ umbrella.

5. My cousin and I will spend _____ vacations in Ixtapa.

6. It is disturbing to the teacher that no one completed _____ final project on time.

7. Everyone should remain seated until _____ name is called.

8. Both snakes and iguanas shed _____ skin.

9. My sister and I are saving _____ money to buy a new computer.

10. Anyone who studies hard can improve _____ TOEFL score.

S=P RULES CONTINUED

3. *Either…or, neither…nor,* and *not only…but also* are correlative conjunctions that introduce two subjects. The verb (see rule eight under "Singular or Plural Verb") and the pronoun agree with the closest (second) subject.

For example:

Either my mom *or* my **dad** left <u>his</u> keys on the table.

Not only the senators *but also* the **president** will give <u>his</u> speech tonight.

4. Collective nouns (such as *family, team, police, class, audience, faculty,* etc.) can be used in a plural or singular form. If the verb is singular, use a singular pronoun. If the verb is plural, use a plural pronoun (see rule two under "Singular or Plural Verb").

For example:

The *committee* **are** in the process of making **their** decisions.

The *committee* **is** in the process of making **its** decision.

Let's test our understanding of the final two rules by completing the following exercise.

EXERCISE SWE-24

Directions: Identify the subjects and complete the sentences with an appropriate pronoun.

1. The crew is going to dock <u>its</u> ship tonight.

2. Our team is trying to tie _____ previous record.

3. Not only the captain but also the soldiers are in _____ camp.

4. The family has moved to _____ new apartment.

5. Either Janet or her sisters will take _____ turn next.

6. The committee is going to present _____ report tomorrow.

7. Neither the students nor the teachers have _____ class schedules.

8. The faculty are preparing _____ recommendations.

9. Neither the cats nor the dog is in _____ house.

10. Not only my brother but also my sister is finishing _____ degree.

Now let's combine all the rules for **S=V** and **S=P** and test our understanding with further practice. The following exercise is an excellent review of both subject-verb agreement and subject-pronoun agreement.

EXERCISE SWE-25

Directions: All of the following sentences are wrong because they have errors in subject-verb agreement and/or subject-pronoun agreement. Rewrite the sentences, correcting the errors.

1. Neither the reporters nor the photographer have received their assignment.

   <u>Neither the reporters nor the photographer **has** received **his** assignment.</u>

2. Everyone have to present their identification in order to receive a discount.

   _____

3. The English department, along with the other departments, are going to order their new computer equipment soon.

   _____

SUBJECT-PRONOUN AGREEMENT

4. The one million dollars were given to the lucky winner who won them in the raffle.

   _____

5. Both Puerto Vallarta and Cozumel is popular in the winter because of its warm climates.

   _____

6. The catalog listing U.S. universities are available at the library because many students request them.

   _____

7. Anyone who abuses their pet should be criminally charged for their actions.

   _____

8. Everyone need to take their final exam today.

   _____

9. Many a man have tried to discover the fountain of youth.

   _____

10. Contrary to speculation, books has actually increased in popularity in our computer age; many thought it would disappear.

    _____

SUBJECT-PRONOUN AGREEMENT

Before we continue our study of other verb and pronoun errors, let's end this section with a **MINI TOEFL** practice exercise.

MINI TOEFL-8

Directions: In questions 1-5, choose the one word or phrase that best completes the sentence. In questions 6-10, identify the underlined word(s) that should be changed to correct the sentence.

Time: 6 minutes

_____1. *The New York Times*, famous for _____ Sunday edition, features critiques of Broadway musicals.

    (A) their   (B) it's   (C) his   (D) its

_____2. Unlike any other U.S. president, President Clinton believed it to be in the best interest of _____ country to fight the tobacco companies.

    (A) their   (B) her   (C) his   (D) its

_____3. That chain of fast food restaurants will go out of business if it doesn't find a way to improve _____.

    (A) its hamburgers   (B) it's hamburgers

    (C) their hamburgers   (D) ours hamburgers

_____4. Not only the doctor but also the nurses are attending _____ patients in the emergency room.

    (A) his   (B) her   (C) them   (D) their

_____5. Everyone must bring _____ final project to class today.

    (A) its   (B) his   (C) my   (D) their

SUBJECT-PRONOUN AGREEMENT

_____6. Both the lawyer and <u>his</u> clients <u>are required</u> by law to present <u>his</u> case before the <u>grand jury</u> on
                                A   B   C   D

Wednesday.

_____7. <u>Although</u> it is <u>illegal</u>, some people <u>still throw</u> <u>his</u> trash out of the car window.
               A   B   C   D

_____8. Everyone <u>have</u> to report to <u>his</u> job no later <u>than</u> 8:00 <u>tomorrow morning</u>.
                 A   B   C   D

_____9. The <u>Mexican</u> soccer team <u>is preparing</u> for <u>their</u> important World Cup game <u>against</u> the unde-
                 A   B   C   D

feated Brazilian team.

_____10. <u>Not only</u> the panda but also the polar bears <u>will be</u> moved from <u>its</u> homes in the zoo to a <u>warmer</u>
                A   B   C   D

climate.

TOEFL PREP for Spanish Speakers

VTF

STEP TWO

QUICK CHECK   Grammar Problem Areas

STEP ONE

    MC   (Main Clause)

    SC   (Subordinate Clause)

STEP TWO

    S=V   (Subject-Verb Agreement)

    S=P   (Subject-Pronoun Agreement)

    >VTF   (Verb Tense or Form)

· Time Markers

· Irregular Verbs

VERBS and PRONOUNS, Agreement, Tense, and Form

    PFR   (Pronoun Form or Reference)

STEP THREE

    VBL   (Verbal)

    WF   (Word Form)

STEP FOUR

    WO   (Word Order)

    PS   (Parallel Structure)

    UR   (Unnecessary Repetition)

STEP FIVE

    CU   (Correct Usage)

VERB TENSE OR FORM

EXERCISE SWE-26

Directions: Using the abbreviations that identify each type of error, classify the following ten errors, then try to correct the errors. Only ten of the twelve types of errors are listed.

_S=P_ 1. Both Horacio and Gilberto are doing his homework.

VTF 2. The club president will led tonight's discussion on upcoming community projects.

_CU_ 3. The team doctor has all ready rushed to the sidelines to examine the injured player.

_WO_ 4. Under the table three boxes of books are.

_SC_ 5. Mexico City has been testing an alarm system will alert residents of earthquakes approaching from the Pacific coast.

_UR_ 6. Due to the rising cost of paper, the prices of books have increased by nearly 25% more.

VBL 7. Juan and I are very interested in the apartment advertising in today's paper.

_S=V_ 8. Either the Amazon or the Nile are the world's longest river.

_PS_ 9. *Carmen, The Barber of Seville*, and the music of *The Marriage of Figaro* are popular among opera fans.

_MC_ 10. Playing Ping-Pong it is good exercise for violinists.

While subject-verb agreement is important, it is also useful to spend a little time reviewing the **tense** and **form** of verbs (**VTF** errors). It might be useful to also review the reference lists in **A. Irregular Verbs** and **H. Verb Tense Modals** in the Appendices.

We'll begin with tense errors. Tense errors involve **time markers** which control the verb tense. A time marker can be one word or a phrase that specifies the time—the verb should be in logical agreement with the time marker. This is grammatical, but also logical. You would not want to say that you *did* something *tomorrow*, or that you're *going to do* something *yesterday*.

 This works the same in Spanish. You wouldn't say that *mañana hizo algo*, or *ayer voy a hacer algo*.

If your **time marker** clearly indicates *past activity*, make sure your verb is in the past tense. If your time marker indicates *future activity*, make sure your verb is in a future tense. If your time marker indicates that the subject of the sentence is *dead*, make sure your verb is *"dead"*. In other words, don't use an active verb with a dead subject.

Most students do not have great difficulty in using correct tenses with time markers. There are, however, two groups of **"special" time markers** that might cause confusion. The first group includes time markers such as: *up until now..., for some time now..., since..., so far...* All of these time markers have the same basic meaning: "until this moment in time", *hasta ahora*. They indicate that an activity has started in the past, continued into the present, but without completion—the activity continues.

When you have a time marker indicating this type of activity you'll need to use the **present perfect or present perfect continuous tense**. The formula for constructing the **present perfect** tense is:

has / have + participle.

The formula for constructing the **present perfect continuous** tense is:

has / have + been + present participle.

For example: Ana has been studying the TOEFL *since last month*.

The time marker in this sentence is *since last month*, which indicates present perfect activity. Notice *has* is used because *Ana* is singular (*have* is used for plural subjects.)

 This equates in Spanish to *Ana ha estado estudiando desde...*

The second group includes time markers that begin with *by*, such as: *by the end of this year* and *by this time next year*. These time markers mark a specified time in the future in order to speculate about completed activity *by* a certain time. *A fin de año, por estos dias en el próximo año.*

These types of time markers are used to speculate about past, completed activity in the future. The activity has not been completed at this moment in time, but will be completed *by* a certain time. *From a point of view in the **present*** you're speculating about ***completed*** activity in the ***future***.

When you have a time marker indicating this type of activity you'll need to use the **future perfect or future perfect continuous tense**. The formula for constructing the **future perfect** tense is:

will + have + past participle.

The formula for constructing the **future perfect continuous** tense is:

will + have + been + present participle.

For example: Ana will have learned many things *by the end of the class*.

The time marker in this sentence is *by the end of the class*, which indicates future perfect activity. Notice there is no distinction between singular and plural; *have* is always used, not *has*. Also, only the *past participle* (not the present participle) is used.

This equates in Spanish to *Ana habrá aprendido muchas cosas nuevas antes que termine su clase.*

VERB TENSE OR FORM

EXERCISE SWE-27

Directions: Underline the time markers and put parenthesis ( ) around the verbs in the following sentences. If the verb is in the correct tense put a check (√) in the blank. If the verb is in the wrong tense put an **X**.

__√__ 1. <u>From time to</u> time every car (needs) a tune up.

_____ 2. The government is planning for some time now to devalue its currency.

_____ 3. The stadium is under reconstruction since the end of the football season.

_____ 4. So far no decisions have been reached concerning the proposal.

_____ 5. No cure for Aids has been found up until now.

_____ 6. When she died, Princess Diana has been in her thirties.

_____ 7. By the end of the class most students will had finished the assignment.

_____ 8. In the early seventies, Donna Summer is recording numerous disco hits.

_____ 9. The temperature has been dropping quickly since this morning.

_____ 10. By the time we get home the guests will had arrive for the birthday party.

That concludes our work on verb tense. Now we'll continue our **VTF** study by working with verb form errors. As you know, many verbs in English have irregular past and past participle forms (again, it might be useful to refer to Appendix A.) It is necessary that you have a good working knowledge of these irregular verb forms.

It will be useful to begin reviewing these if you don't know them well. Besides reviewing lists, it might be helpful to make flash cards or listen to recorded cassettes with irregular forms. This is, unfortunately, a question of rote memorization. There is no magical way to learn them. Some grammar books categorize these verbs into groups that follow certain spellings. This might only make matters more confusing, however. It is also not recommended to write them over and over (sometimes called *planas* in Spanish) in an attempt to learn them.

VERB TENSE OR FORM

EXERCISE SWE-28

Directions: All of the following sentences are incorrect. Circle the verb that is in the wrong tense and write the correct verb in the blank.

made 1. Global communications have been (make) easier thanks to e-mail.

_____ 2. The first triathlon was hold in Hawaii in February, 1978.

_____ 3. Dick Francis has wrote many books with a horse racing theme.

_____ 4. In general, cats will lived longer than dogs.

_____ 5. Tattoos, while offensive to some, have became quite popular.

_____ 6. It was recently discovering that there are ice formations on the moon.

_____ 7. The longest symphony, Number Three in D Minor, was wrote by Gustav Mahler.

_____ 8. A good upholsterer can made an old couch just like new.

_____ 9. The development of electric cars has gave new hope for reducing air pollution.

_____ 10. This pocket watch was give to me by my great grandfather.

_____ 11. Only 1,116 Stradivarius violins were make of which some 700 can be accounted for today.

_____ 12. The mosaic on the UNAM campus library in Mexico City is know as the largest mosaic in the world.

_____ 13. The postman was bit by the ferocious dog.

_____ 14. At the trial, the defendant sworn to tell the truth.

_____ 15. For several hours, no one knew what had became of the lost child.

Before we continue our study of other pronoun errors, let's end this section with a **MINI TOEFL** practice exercise.

VERB TENSE OR FORM

MINI TOEFL-9

Directions: In questions 1-5, choose the one word or phrase that best completes the sentence. In questions 6-10, identify the underlined word(s) that should be changed to correct the sentence.

Time: 6 minutes

_____1. For some time now, cigarette advertising _____ tightly controlled by the United States government.

    (A) has been (B) have been (C) was (D) is

_____2. Emilio _____ his doctorate by the end of next year.

    (A) will have finished (B) will has finished (C) has finished (D) finished

_____3. The book club _____ a new book during the first week of each month.

    (A) always sending (B) always send (C) always (D) always sends

_____4. The choir director will _____ the presentation of Handel's *Messiah*.

    (A) led (B) lead (C) leads (D) have lead

_____5. My sister has _____ quite fluent in Spanish while living in Chile.

    (A) become (B) became (C) becoming (D) having become

_____6. <u>Many</u> of the passengers that <u>were killed</u> in the airplane crash <u>are flying</u> to
       A   B   C

Tokyo <u>to attend</u> a conference on business administration.
      D

VERB TENSE OR FORM

_____7. After the mischievous little boy had threw a rock through the neighbor's
       A   B   C

window he was severely punished by his parents.
       D

_____8. Steven Spielberg has became one of the most popular film
        A   B

directors after directing the widely successful movie *ET*.
 C   D

_____9. Although the development of the artificial language Esperanto was an
            A   B

extreme important achievement, it no longer remains very popular.
 C   D

_____10. The incredibly advance of English across the face of the globe is a
     A   B

phenomenon without parallel in the history of language.
 C   D

 **POP QUIZ**

Can you translate the following sentences into English?

Juan ha estado estudiando el TOEFL por tres semanas.

María habrá aprendido muchas cosas nuevas antes que termine la clase.

Do you know the past and past participle forms of the these verbs?

Become

Swing

Swear

Begin

Lose

Feel

Fall

TOEFL PREP for Spanish Speakers

STEP TWO

QUICK CHECK   Grammar Problem Areas

STEP ONE

    MC   (Main Clause)

    SC   (Subordinate Clause)

STEP TWO

    S=V   (Subject-Verb Agreement)

    S=P   (Subject-Pronoun Agreement)

    VTF   (Verb Tense or Form)

    >PFR   (Pronoun Form or Reference)

STEP THREE

    VBL   (Verbal)

    WF   (Word Form)

- Pronoun Forms

- Correct Pronoun Reference

VERBS and PRONOUNS, Agreement, Tense, and Form

STEP FOUR

    WO   (Word Order)

    PS   (Parallel Structure)

    UR   (Unnecessary Repetition)

STEP FIVE

    CU   (Correct Usage)

PRONOUN FORM OR REFERENCE

EXERCISE SWE-29

Directions: Using the abbreviations that identify each type of error, classify the following ten errors, then try to correct the errors. Only ten of the twelve types of errors are listed.

__PS__ 1. Among the qualities desired of the new director are patience, reliability, and to be punctual.

__CU__ 2. Beside a Corvette, Daniel also owns a Mercedes and a Ferrari.

__PFR__ 3. The teacher doesn't approve of us speaking Spanish in our English class.

__S=P__ 4. Carmen and I will spend my weekend at the beach.

__WF__ 5. The teacher kept the student's attention with a real interesting story.

__S=V__ 6. Mathematics are difficult for me, although I enjoy studying algebra.

__SC__ 7. The Howrah bridge which is located in Calcutta, India which is the world's busiest bridge.

__VTF__ 8. By the end of the day the box office will sold all of the tickets for the Erasure concert.

__WO__ 9. Only once I have been to Disneyland.

__VBL__ 10. The press was extremely interested in the president's interested news conference.

Now we return to the pronouns to complete STEP TWO with a study of errors in pronoun form and reference (**PFR** errors). Hopefully you're already familiar with the various forms of pronouns after reviewing the chart at the start of the **S=P** section. Let's review the chart again, this time as an exercise to test your memory. If you haven't studied the **S=P** section, take a quick look at the pronoun chart before continuing.

PRONOUN FORM OR REFERENCE

EXERCISE SWE-30

Directions: Some blanks have been left in the following chart of pronoun forms. Fill in the blanks with the correct pronoun form. Check your work with the complete chart on page 78.

SUBJECT	OBJECT	POSSESSIVE ADJECTIVE	POSSESSIVE PRONOUN	REFLEXIVE
I	ME	_____	MINE	MYSELF
YOU (SINGULAR)	YOU	YOUR	YOURS	_____
HE	HIM	HIS	_____	HIMSELF
SHE	_____	HER	HERS	HERSELF
IT	IT	_____	-----	ITSELF
WE	US	_____	OURS	OURSELVES
YOU (PLURAL)	YOU	YOUR	_____	YOURSELVES
THEY	_____	THEIR	THEIRS	THEMSELVES
ONE	ONE	ONE'S	-----	_____
_____	WHOM	WHOSE	WHOSE	-----

Be careful with a few confusing elements of the pronoun organization. Notice that the possessive adjective and pronoun for *he* are the same: *his*. However, the object and possessive adjective for *she* are the same: *her,* while the possessive pronoun is different. Also be careful with the possessive adjective *its*. Notice there is no apostrophe. Adding the apostrophe completely changes the meaning of the word: *it's* is the contraction of the verb *to be,* "it is".

In informal English you might hear some incorrect pronoun forms. Avoid using incorrect forms such as *hisself* or *theirselves*.

🔍 Should you have difficulty keeping the various forms straight, it might be useful to remember a simple sentence as an example of each form.

Note the following example sentences (abbreviations for the respective forms are used):

I (S) sing a song.

She sings a song to **me** (O).

This is **my** (PA) book.

This book is **mine** (PP).

I cooked dinner **myself** (R).

🔍 To make sure you understand the meaning of the above sample sentences, here they are in Spanish. Careful, however! Pronouns work quite differently in Spanish than in English and translating is not always a good idea.

Yo canto una canción.

Ella me canta una canción a **mí**.

Este es **mi** libro.

Este libro es **mío**.

Cociné la cena **yo mismo**.

Let's practice with the various pronoun forms. Continue referring to your chart of pronoun forms until you are confident of using them correctly. Substitute forms using your example sentences if necessary. Also remember that subordination is important here—you must identify clauses in order to correctly identify pronoun forms.

EXERCISE SWE-31

Directions: Using the abbreviations for the pronoun forms (S, O, PA, PP, R), identify the underlined pronoun forms in the following sentences by putting the correct abbreviation in the blank.

__S__ 1. <u>He</u> is the owner of that beautiful new home.

_____ 2. That beautiful new home belongs to <u>him</u>.

_____ 3. That is <u>his</u> beautiful new home.

_____ 4. That beautiful new home is <u>his</u>.

_____ 5. He bought the beautiful new home <u>himself</u>.

_____ 6. It was <u>she</u> who made the decision.

_____ 7. This is a photograph of Angélica and one of <u>her</u> friends.

_____ 8. Your TOEFL score is much higher than <u>mine</u>.

_____ 9. <u>Your</u> singing is hurting my ears!

_____ 10. <u>Whom</u> did you visit on your trip to Costa Rica?

_____ 11. The girl <u>who</u> came to my party was beautiful.

_____ 12. The cat is in <u>its</u> house.

_____ 13. We must send <u>our</u> college admission applications this week.

_____ 14. Miguel taught <u>himself</u> to speak Portuguese.

_____ 15. <u>It</u> was the biggest birthday cake I had ever seen.

Before we begin our study of the rules for each pronoun form, let's stop and do a **MINI TOEFL** practice exercise. NOTE: In this exercise, unlike other similar exercises, *all* of the errors are related to pronoun form. We'll repeat this exercise after reviewing the pronoun form rules, so don't worry if you have a few errors the first time.

MINI TOEFL-10

Directions: In questions 1-5, choose the one word or phrase that best completes the sentence. In questions 6-10, identify the underlined word(s) that should be changed to make the sentence correct.

TIME: 6 minutes

_____1. Although the voice sounds familiar, I'm not completely sure _____ is on the phone.

    (A) who (B) whose (C) whom (D) it's

_____2. Everyone except _____ was invited to the party.

    (A) hers (B) she (C) her (D) herself

_____3. If you were _____, would you allow Terri to go to the concert?

    (A) me (B) her (C) my (D) I

_____4. Our parents don't approve of _____ staying out past midnight.

    (A) our (B) we (C) us (D) ours

_____5. Instead of spending money on a hotel room, I think I'll stay with some friends of _____ when I go to visit Lima.

    (A) me (B) I (C) our (D) mine

_____ 6. The man whom lives above my apartment disturbs me with his extremely loud music.
                    A   B   C   D

_____ 7. After asking it residents to conserve water during the 🔍 drought, the
                      A   B

Mexico City government was finally forced to shut off the water for 24 hours.
                         C   D

_____ 8. Because the play required several quick costume changes, the actors
          A   B

had to dress theirselves very quickly between acts.
              C   D

_____ 9. Between you and I, I think Patricia is gaining weight because she has
                  A   B

little time for exercise with her full schedule of classes.
C   D

_____ 10. I don't mind sharing me lunch with you, but I only brought peanut butter crackers.
              A   B   C   D

Note: In the above questions number 3 and 9, you'll find two very common errors. In informal speech, even native speakers will say "between you and *I*" and "if you were *me*". The correct forms are: "between you and *me*" and "if you were *I*". The rules that follow will explain why.

🔍 **Drought** means *sequía* while **flood** means *inundacion*. It's interesting that *drought* is a non-count noun while *flood* is a countable noun.

101

RULES FOR PRONOUN FORM

Remember, when you have an error in pronoun form it's because you're using the *incorrect* form. If you apply the following rules for the five forms of pronouns, you should be able to avoid such errors.

SUBJECT PRONOUNS

Subject pronouns include *I, you, he, she, we,* etc. Keep referring to your pronoun form chart until you can remember them. Also keep in mind that the following three subject pronoun rules apply to the correct use of *who*.

1. Our first rule is quite logical. Use a subject pronoun if the pronoun is functioning as a subject. It could be the subject of the main or subordinate clause. *El pronombre en forma de sujeto está usado como el sujeto de una oración principal o subordinada.* Notice the subject pronouns in the following examples:

   He watched a movie on TV after his parents went to bed.

   After *he* went to bed, his parents watched a movie.

2. Use a subject pronoun form immediately following any form of the verb *to be*. *El pronombre en forma de sujeto es usado cuando sigue del verbo **to be***. Notice the subject pronouns in the following examples:

   It was **he** at the door.

   It must have been **they** who called last night.

Many people, even native speakers of English, have trouble with the use of *who* and *whom*. Remember that *who* is the subject form, and its use follows the subject pronoun rules, while *whom* is an object form and its use follows the object pronoun rules. Some English grammar books might give you special rules for the use of *who* and *whom*. This is really not necessary, however. You probably don't have much trouble with other subject or object forms such as *I* and *me* or *he* and *him*. If you get confused with *who* or *whom* try substituting it with a pronoun that is easier for you (if you would use *I*, use *who*, if you would use *me*, use *whom*, for example).

3. Use a subject pronoun form when comparing two subjects (avoid mixing subject and object forms)

El pronombre en forma de sujeto es usado cuando dos sujetos están siendo comparados. Notice the subject pronouns in the following examples:

They studied for their exam more than **we** did.

She is much taller than **I**.

EXERCISE SWE-32

Directions: Examine the subject pronouns in the following sentences. If the sentences are correct, put a check (√) in the blank. If they are incorrect, put an (**X**).

__X__ 1. If you were me, would you wear a coat and tie to the party?

_____ 2. The neighbors whom live across the street are very nice.

_____ 3. It might have been she who wrote you the secret letter.

_____ 4. Enrique has more computer experience than I.

_____ 5. Y'all must be quiet in the library.

_____ 6. They have practiced more for the game than us.

_____ 7. The criminal whom the police arrested was recently convicted.

_____ 8. If I were you, I would try to get more rest.

_____ 9. She has saved more money for the trip than I.

_____ 10. When she first moved her didn't know anyone.

OBJECT PRONOUNS

Object pronouns include: *me, her, him, us, them, etc.* These rules apply to the correct use of *whom*.

1. This rule is like the first rule for the subject form. If the pronoun functions as the object (direct or indirect) of a clause (main or subordinate), use an object pronoun. *El pronombre en forma de objeto es usado cuando funciona como objeto directo o indirecto en una oración principal o subordinada.*

Notice the object pronouns in the following examples:

If I buy **him** a drink, he will be very happy.

That woman is staring at **me**.

2. Use an object pronoun when the pronoun functions as the object of a preposition. A list of prepositions is found in the Appendices. Prepositions include words such as: *between, among, with, but, except.* *El pronombre en forma de objeto es usado cuando funciona como objeto de una preposición.*

Notice the object pronouns in the following examples:

Everyone except **her** was invited to the party.

The girl with **whom** I live is my sister.

3. This rule is similar to the third rule for the subject form. Use an object pronoun when comparing two objects. *El pronombre en forma de objeto es usado cuando los objetos de dos oraciones están siendo comparados.* Notice the object pronouns in the following examples:

The teacher likes **you** better than she likes **me**.

The puppy plays more with **me** than with **her**.

EXERCISE SWE-33

Directions: Examine the object pronouns in the following sentences. If the sentences are correct, put a check (√) in the blank. If they are incorrect, put an (**X**).

__X__ 1. This secret must be kept strictly confidential between you and I.

_____ 2. Our guests, whom are visiting from Puerto Rico, will leave tomorrow.

_____ 3. If I see her at the party tonight I'll tell her to call you.

_____ 4. I'll be mad if you go to the movie without me.

_____ 5. No one except the teacher knows whom passed the test.

_____ 6. If you want to go with I, you'd better get ready fast.

_____ 7. The doctor is more concerned about my sister than me.

_____ 8. If you buy him the CD, he will be happy.

_____ 9. The friend whom I called was not at home.

_____ 10. The baby-sitter seems to like my sister more than I.

POSSESSIVE ADJECTIVES

Possessive adjectives include: *my, your, his, her, our, their,* etc. We have only two rules for this form.

1. Use the possessive adjective form to modify a noun and indicate possession. *El pronombre en forma de adjectivo posesivo es usado para modificar un sustantivo e indicar posesión.* Notice the object pronouns in the following examples:

This is **my** book. This is **your** book. These are **our** books.

2. The possessive adjective form is used to modify a gerund. Careful here! It might sound good to put an object form in this position and you will often hear it incorrectly spoken. *El pronombre en forma de adjectivo posesivo es usado para modificar a un gerundio.* Notice the possessive adjectives in the following examples:

She appreciates **my** helping her.

My child loves **my** reading bedtime stories to him.

EXERCISE SWE-34

Directions: Examine the possessive adjectives in the following sentences. If the sentences are correct, put a check (√) in the blank. If they are incorrect, put an (**X**).

__√__ 1. That dog seems to have lost its way home.

_____ 2. Does my violin playing bother you?

_____ 3. Anne Rice demonstrates a great deal of imagination in her novels.

_____ 4. This is not mine book.

_____ 5. The preacher is bothered by us speaking during the church service.

_____ 6. Your problem should be checked by a medical professional.

_____ 7. My brother is jealous of my winning the scholarship.

_____ 8. You selling the car so quickly comes as a surprise.

_____ 9. Her dog bit her three times on her leg.

_____ 10. Please write your names on your answer sheets.

POSSESSIVE PRONOUNS

Possessive pronouns include: *mine, yours, hers, his, ours, theirs*, etc. We have three rules for the use of this form.

1. The possessive pronoun form is used to avoid repeating a noun which functions as the subject or object of a main clause or to avoid repeating the second noun in a comparison (a comparison of similar things with different owners). *El pronombre en forma de pronombre posesivo es usado para evitar repetir un sustantivo que funcione como sujeto u objeto de la oración principal y también para evitar repetir el segundo sustantivo en una comparación (una comparación entre cosas similares con dueños diferentes).*

This rule might seem somewhat complicated, but should be easier after examining the following examples:

He forgot his book so he borrowed **mine**.

My girlfriend is prettier than **yours**.

Your test grade is high but **hers** isn't.

My sister's car is larger than **mine**.

2. You can use the possessive pronoun form with the verb *to be* to show possession. *El pronombre en forma de pronombre posesivo es usado con el verbo* to be *para indicar posesión.*

Notice the possessive pronouns in the following examples:

This sweater is **his**.

These flowers are **hers**.

3. You can also use the possessive pronoun form with the preposition *of* to show possession. *El pronombre en forma de pronombre posesivo es usado con la preposicón* **of** *para indicar posesión.*

Notice the possessive pronouns in the following examples:

This is an old book *of* **mine**.

I would like you to meet some friends *of* **ours**.

EXERCISE SWE-35

Directions: Examine the possessive pronouns in the following sentences. If the sentences are correct, put a check (√) in the blank. If they are incorrect, put an (**X**).

__X__ 1. Marcela and a friend of her will meet us at the airport.

_____ 2. Your grades are good but mine are not.

_____ 3. Your collection of compact disks is much bigger than my.

_____ 4. The clothes in the dryer are ours.

_____ 5. I found an old composition of her in the box in the attic.

_____ 6. Raul's ideas are very different from mine.

_____ 7. I think this umbrella is your because that one is mine.

_____ 8. These books are not ours; they are property of the library.

_____ 9. Your car is much faster than his.

_____ 10. Your apartment is perfectly clean while mine is a disaster.

PRONOUN FORM OR REFERENCE

REFLEXIVE PRONOUNS

The last group of pronouns that we will study is the reflexive from. This is probably the easiest group to learn. Reflexive pronouns include: *myself, himself, ourselves,* etc. Study the following three rules.

1. The reflexive form is used (optionally) to emphasize a noun or pronoun which refers to people. *El pronombre en forma reflexiva es usado para enfatizar un sustantivo o pronombre el cual se refiere a personas.*

Notice the reflexive pronouns in the following examples:
Michael Jordan **himself** autographed my basketball.
Since I live alone, I do all the housecleaning **myself**.

2. The reflexive form is used with the preposition *by* to indicate that someone or something does an activity alone or without help. *El pronombre en forma reflexiva es usado como el objeto de la preposición* by *para significar que alguien or algo hace una actividad solo o sin ayuda.* For example:
The timid girl prefers to be *by* **herself**.
Octavio learned to play the violin *by* **himself**.

The reflexive form is used much more frequently in Spanish than in English. In fact, in Spanish there are many verbs that are always used reflexively. Avoid literal translations or you might create some silly sentences in English. For example, in Spanish you would say, "*Voy a bañarme*" or "*Me voy a bañar*". If you translate this into English you might get "*I am going to bathe me*". Of course, in English you don't need the *me*. It is implicit that you intend to bathe yourself unless you specify that you plan to bathe someone else!

3. The reflexive form is used to refer to the subject of the sentence. *El pronombre en forma reflexiva es usado para referirse al sujeto de la oración.* Here the reflexive is used, as it is in Spanish, to describe activities which cause pain to the body. You *hurt, cut,* or *burn* **yourself.** For example:

Don't burn **yourself** with those matches!

Carmela hurt **herself** while skating down the steep hill.

EXERCISE SWE-36

Directions: Examine the reflexive pronouns in the following sentences. If the sentences are correct, put a check (√) in the blank. If they are incorrect, put an (**X**).

__X__ 1. My brother always gets hisself in difficult situations.

_____ 2. The president itself will give the commencement address.

_____ 3. We enjoy making home improvements ourselves.

_____ 4. Enrique taught himself to play tennis.

_____ 5. Our daughter is too young to stay home by herself.

_____ 6. Be careful not to cut yourself on the broken glass.

_____ 7. The students themselves planned the homecoming parade.

_____ 8. I enjoy traveling by yourself.

_____ 9. I painted the bedroom myself.

_____ 10. Jack and Jill are enjoying theirselves on vacation.

Before we complete the **PFR** section with a short study of pronoun reference, let's repeat the Mini TOEFL practice exercise that we did before we studied the individual rules for pronoun form. Remember, *all* of the errors are related to pronoun form. This time, you should be able to complete the exercise without any errors.

MINI TOEFL-11

Directions: In questions 1-5, choose the one word or phrase that best completes the sentence. In questions 6-10, identify the underlined word(s) that should be changed to make the sentence correct.

TIME: 6 minutes

_____1. Although the voice sounds familiar, I'm not completely sure _____ is on the phone.

    (A) who   (B) whose   (C) whom   (D) it's

_____2. Everyone except _____ was invited to the party.

    (A) hers   (B) she   (C) her   (D) herself

_____3. If you were _____, would you allow Terri to go to the concert?

    (A) me   (B) her   (C) my   (D) I

_____4. Our parents don't approve of _____ staying out past midnight.

    (A) our   (B) we   (C) us   (D) ours

_____5. Instead of spending money on a hotel room, I think I'll stay with some friends of _____ when I go to visit Lima.

    (A) me   (B) I   (C) our   (D) mine

_____6. The man <u>whom</u> lives above <u>my</u> apartment disturbs <u>me</u> with <u>his</u> extremely loud music.
              A   B   C   D

_____7. After asking <u>it residents</u> to conserve water <u>during the</u> drought, the
                   A   B

Mexico City government <u>was finally</u> forced to <u>shut off</u> the water for 24 hours.
                          C   D

PRONOUN FORM OR REFERENCE

_____8. Because the play required several quick costume changes, the actors
        A   B

had to dress theirselves very quickly between acts.
            C   D

_____9. Between you and I, I think Patricia is gaining weight because she has
          A   B

little time for exercise with her full schedule of classes.
  C   D

_____10. I don't mind sharing me lunch with you, but I only brought peanut butter crackers.
       A   B   C   D

Let's finish the **PFR** section by examining errors in **pronoun reference.** You might call this the *logical* use of pronouns; certain pronouns are used to refer to certain types of nouns and should be used correctly to avoid illogical reference. *Diferentes pronombres son usados para referirse a distintos tipos de sustantivos.* Obviously, you wouldn't want to use *he* if referring to a girl or *they* if referring to an apple. But some other reference errors may not be so obviously incorrect.

You can use **that** or **whose** for all types of nouns. But use **which** for only things, collective nouns, and animals (in general). **Who** and **whom** can be used only with people and pets.

Notice the distinction between animals in general and pets. The way we refer to an animal depends upon our relationship with that particular animal. If it is a pet, if you know the animal's name, you can refer to it like a person. The dog walking down the street that you don't know personally is an **it**, while your dog at home named Snoopy is **he**!

111

PRONOUN FORM OR REFERENCE

EXERCISE SWE-37

Directions: Examine the pronoun reference in the following sentences. If the sentences are correct, put a check (√) in the blank. If they are incorrect, put an (**X**).

__X__ 1. The river who separates the U.S. and Mexico is called the Rio Grande.

_____ 2. The dentist that I go to is from Argentina.

_____ 3. The arrival who was expected at noon will be half an hour late.

_____ 4. The musician whom I hired is a classical violinist.

_____ 5. The newspaper that he writes for is published in English.

_____ 6. Has anyone seen the stack of papers which I left on my desk?

_____ 7. The professor that teaches my class is a very nice person.

_____ 8. The surgeon which performed the operation is quite young.

_____ 9. The artist who painted this picture is well known.

_____ 10. The furniture who the couple selected was on sale.

_____ 11. The books which I found on the subject are extremely useful.

_____ 12. Animals that work in the circus are often mistreated.

_____ 13. I think it was our dog who dug up the roses.

_____ 14. The mother whose son won the race must be very proud.

_____ 15. The computer who I want to buy has a fax modem and sound system.

Just one more note about pronoun reference. Pronouns which begin adjective clauses (such as *who, which, that*) should refer only to nouns or pronouns. Normally, they will immediately follow the noun or pronoun and should not follow verbs, adjectives, or other parts of speech. *Los pronombres que comienzan un enunciado adjetivo subordinado sólo se pueden referir a sustantivos o pronombres y generalmente se encuentran después del sustantivo que describen. No se pueden referir a verbos, adjetivos, etc.*

PRONOUN FORM OR REFERENCE

Notice the incorrect reference in the following sentences:

wrong: The weather was <u>rainy which</u> made the football field muddy.

right: It was the rainy weather which made the football field muddy.

wrong: The test was <u>difficult which</u> the students were not prepared for.

right: The students were not prepared for the difficult test.

 **POP QUIZ**

Can you translate *sequía* and *inundación* into English? Which word is a count noun and which one is a non-count noun?

Try to correct the following pronoun errors and explain why they are wrong:

If you were me....Between you and I...

TOEFL PREP for Spanish Speakers

VBL

STEP THREE

QUICK CHECK   Grammar Problem Areas

STEP ONE

    MC   (Main Clause)

    SC   (Subordinate Clause)

STEP TWO

    S=V   (Subject-Verb Agreement)

    S=P   (Subject-Pronoun Agreement)

    VTF   (Verb Tense or Form)

    PFR   (Pronoun Form or Reference)

STEP THREE

    >VBL   (Verbal)

    WF   (Word Form)

· Active & Passive Verbal Adjectives

· Verbal Phrases

VERBALS

STEP FOUR

    WO   (Word Order)

    PS   (Parallel Structure)

    UR   (Unnecessary Repetition)

STEP FIVE

    CU   (Correct Usage)

EXERCISE SWE-38

Directions: Using the abbreviations that identify each type of error, classify the following ten errors, then try to correct the errors. Only ten of the twelve types of errors are listed.

_CU_ 1. An university degree is required of all teaching assistants.

_S=P_ 2. One of my five brothers will complete their college degree this year.

_WF_ 3. It is extremely danger to use electrical appliances near water.

_MC_ 4. The Room it was painted by Van Gogh, who is considered to be one of the most important impressionist artists.

_WO_ 5. Only after completing her degree in comparative linguistics Mari Carmen began studying Japanese.

_SC_ 6. Although it is strong, aluminum has many industrial uses.

VTF 7. The test had already began when Jaime arrived.

PFR 8. Although he is hardly ever used by many people, the metric system is the official system of measurement in the United States.

VBL 9. A lack of rain and the burned sun caused the plants to slowly die.

_UR_ 10. It is hoped that the jury will reach a just and fair decision.

We begin STEP THREE with a study of verbals. In this section (**VBL**) we will examine the use of verbals, or words that are derived from verbs but do not function as verbs. As mentioned in the introduction of the Structure and Written Expression section, any given word might function in a number of different ways within a sentence. You will learn that verbals do not function as verbs. In this section we will review the function of infinitives and gerunds (this is detailed in the **MC** section) and study verbal adjectives and verbal adjective phrases.

VERBALS

In the following example, notice how the word *playing* could be used as a gerund, a verb (with the verb *to be*), or a verbal adjective.

Playing football is good exercise. (**Gerund Subject**)

Carlos **is playing** football with his friends. (**Verb**)

The boy **playing** football is my brother.   (Verbal adjective)

Some students confuse infinitives and prepositional phrases that begin with *to*. Notice the difference in the following example:

prepositional phrases: to the dance, to church, to Puerto Rico

infinitives: to dance, to play, to sing

Un infinitivo es una forma verbal formado por la palabra to *y el verbo en forma simple. La palabra* to *tambien puede iniciar frases preposicionales.*

EXERCISE SWE-39

Directions: In the blanks, write **PREP** for prepositional phrases and **INF** for infinitives.

INF 1. to cry

_____ 2. to the park

_____ 3. to dance

_____ 4. to park

_____ 5. to benefit

_____ 6. to peace

_____ 7. to disqualify

_____ 8. to disturb

_____ 9. to happiness

_____ 10. to meditate

_____ 11. to sing

_____ 12. to reach

_____ 13. to swim

_____ 14. to stand

_____ 15. to pursue

_____ 16. to good health

_____ 17. to encounter

_____ 18. to the market

_____ 19. to reality

_____ 20. to prosperity

Now that you can distinguish between prepositional phrases and infinitives, let's practice more with infinitives. Remember an infinitive (as well as a gerund, noun, pronoun, or noun clause) can function as the subject of a sentence.

EXERCISE SWE-40

Directions: Examine the following sentences and underline and label the subject with (**S**), the verb with (**V**), and the infinitive with (**I**). In some of the sentences you will find an infinitive subject. Identify them with (**IS**).

      S   V   I
1. <u>Children</u> <u>love</u> <u>to paint</u>.

2. We go to school to learn.

3. To drive under the influence of alcohol is illegal.

4. Jesús wants to drive to New York.

5. Doctors need to keep themselves updated on new medical reports.

6. She went to the bakery to buy a cake.

7. To control insects spray the garden with an insecticide.

8. Researchers hope to find a cure for AIDS.

9. To eat only one meal per day is not healthy.

10. I want to see the new movie this weekend.

11. The marching band is going to perform at the football game.

12. Giovanna likes to cook lasagna and other Italian dishes.

13. We plan to put up the Christmas tree tomorrow.

14. We need to plan the party this week.

15. I hope to make a high score on my TOEFL exam.

Now we'll do the same thing with gerunds. Remember, a gerund does not function as a verb. It needs a verb *to be* to activate it into a verb. No verb *to be*, no verb! *El gerundio es una forma verbal que se forma añadiendo* ing *a un verbo en su forma simple. Un gerundio nunca funciona como verbo.*

EXERCISE SWE-41

Directions: Examine the following sentences and underline and label the subject with (**S**), the verb with (**V**), and the gerund with (**G**). In some of the sentences you will find a gerund subject. Identify these with (**GS**). In some of the sentences there is no gerund.

    GS   V

1. <u>Smoking</u> <u>causes</u> cancer.

2. My grandmother is arriving this afternoon.
3. They enjoy playing soccer on Sundays.
4. Backpacking in mountainous regions requires special equipment.
5. The orchestra is practicing a Vivaldi concerto.
6. Learning a new language is both difficult and fun.
7. He is becoming skillful at playing tennis.
8. 🔍 Flooding was caused by the breaking of the dam.

🔍 A couple of words in this sentence might be difficult (although some of these words were reviewed in the **PFR** section). *Flooding* comes from *flood*, which means *inundación* (*sequía* means *drought*). *Dam* means *presa*, the wall that holds water, not the animals killed by other animals, which is *prey*. *Prey* has the same pronunciation as *pray*, which means *orar*.

VERBALS

9. Mailing early insures delivery before the holidays.

10. The players are obviously becoming tired.

11. She thanked me for baby-sitting her children.

12. Swimming is a very complete exercise.

13. The family is going on vacation next week.

14. Roller blading without knee pads is risky.

15. Greg Louganis perfected the art of diving.

Before we complete the **VBL** section with a study of verbal adjectives and verbal adjective phrases, let's do a **Mini TOEFL** practice exercise.

MINI TOEFL-12

Directions: In questions 1-5, choose the one word or phrase that best completes the sentence. In questions 6-10, identify the underlined word(s) that should be changed to make the sentence correct.

TIME: 6 minutes

_____ 1. The students _____ working on their exams for nearly two hours.

    (A) which are (B) is (C) have been (D) who have been

_____ 2. Many retirees move to Florida _____.

    (A) for to live (B) to live (C) for living (D) living

_____ 3. We enjoy _____ in the ocean more than in a pool.

    (A) to swim (B) are swimming (C) swim (D) swimming

Note that after the verb *enjoy* a gerund is used. Other verbs require only gerunds. Refer to the Appendix D at the end of the book.

VERBALS

_____ 4. Your backhand _____ day by day.

    (A) is improving   (B) improving   (C) are improving   (D) to improve

_____ 5. The students _____ to complete their final projects before Friday.

    (A) is trying   (B) has been trying   (C) trying   (D) are trying

_____ 6. <u>Painting it</u> is one of <u>many ways</u> <u>to express</u> <u>oneself</u> artistically.

         A   B   C   D

_____ 7. <u>Donating money</u> to the orphanage <u>one</u> of the <u>kindest</u> things the rich man <u>ever did</u>.

         A   B   C   D

_____ 8. <u>Nearly all</u> of my classmates <u>have been studying</u> English <u>since</u> more

         A   B   C

<u>than</u> five years.

 D

_____ 9. <u>Studying</u> Japanese <u>is probably</u> one of the most <u>difficult thing</u> I have

        A   B   C

<u>ever done</u> .   night

             early last

 D

_____ 10. The kids <u>to sleep</u> <u>early</u> <u>because</u> tomorrow they <u>must</u> wake up very early in the morning.

                A   B   C   D

Every verb in English has two **verbal adjective** forms. They function like ordinary adjectives, but they are derived from verbs. A verbal adjective can be in the form of the present participle (which ends in *ing*) or the past participle (which ends in *d, t,* or *n*).

For example, the verb **to eat** has two verbal adjective forms: **eating** and **eaten**. From the verb **to surprise** we have **surprising** and **surprised**. *Los adjetivos verbales al igual que los gerundios e infinitivos están formados de verbos pero no funcionan como verbos. Existen dos formas de adjetivos verbales: el presente participio y el pasado participio.*

EXERCISE SWE-42

Directions: Examine the following sentences. Find and put parenthesis ( ) around the verbal adjectives.

1. The (burning) forest has made the people (living) around the area very nervous.
2. Of the many varieties of plants grown in hanging baskets, ferns are the most popular.
3. Football players recruited by the coach should report to practice three months before the first scheduled game.
4. The bubbling soup must be left to cool before it is served to the hungry children.
5. The film showing at the cinema was directed by an aspiring actor.
6. The music playing now on the radio reminds me of the music that was popular fifteen years ago.
7. Folding chairs were set up around the pool to accommodate the exhausted guests.
8. The girls swimming in the lake are spending their summer vacation here with their parents.
9. The accused defendant is scheduled to make a court appearance during the coming week.
10. The man selling ice cream in the park is sometimes frightened by the barking dogs.
11. The torn pillows can be easily mended by an experienced upholsterer.
12. Neglected and abused children are sometimes removed from the custody of their parents.
13. The air circulating through this building is much cleaner than the polluted air outside.
14. The rooms reserved at the hotel will be available after noon.
15. A tossed salad usually includes shredded lettuce, sliced tomatoes, grated cheese, and a dressing.

VERBALS

Do you think you can distinguish between verbal adjectives and active verbs? The next exercise will give you some practice.

EXERCISE SWE-43

Directions: Examine the following words. Decide if they are active verbs or verbal adjectives and write them in the appropriate column below.

is walking	eating	looking	drank
are playing	looks	will call	jumping
selling	acting	have been fed	crying
speaking	was put	remembering	are studying
were helping	participating	reviewing	is cooking

ACTIVE VERBS   **VERBAL ADJECTIVES**

As discussed, a verbal adjective can take the form of the present participle (ing) or the past participle (d,n, t). It is necessary to consider the noun that your verbal adjective is describing to choose the correct form. If the noun is actively *doing* the action, use the present participle form. If the noun is passively *receiving* the action, use the past participle form. *Un adjetivo verbal puede tomar la forma en presente (ing) o en pasado (d,n,t) participio. Cuando el sustantivo que esta siendo descrito está activamente haciendo la acción se necesita en presente, y cuando el sustantivo esta recibiendo la acción se usa en pasado participio.*

Examine the following examples:

 The **excited** children. The **exciting** movie. If you have confusion, think of the following drawing, which should make it clear.

Using the verb **to threaten** (*amenazar*), notice that the snake is actively **threatening**, while the mouse is passively **threatened**.

 This can be confusing for Spanish speakers because sometimes the distinction between active and passive verbal adjectives is made, and sometimes it is not. For example, in Spanish you say that a book is *interesante*, not *interesado*, just like in English where a book is *interesting* not *interested*. However, in English you say the *bored* audience, but the *boring* speech. In Spanish it's the same: *un discurso **aburrido**, el publico **aburrido**.*

123

Let's practice forming active and passive verbal adjectives.

EXERCISE SWE-44

Directions: In this exercise, you'll be given a verb and two nouns. Using the (1) verb, describe the (2) first noun actively and the (3) second noun passively.

1. (1) to burn (2) sun (3) dinner

      burning sun   burned dinner

2. (1) to convince (2) argument (3) students

3. (1) to surprise (2) present (3) child

4. (1) to annoy (2) noise (3) parents

5. (1) to exhaust (2) exam (3) test takers

6. (1) to entertain (2) actors (3) audience

7. (1) to frighten (2) story (3) kids

    _____   _____

8. (1) to amuse (2) joke (3) guests

    _____   _____

9. (1) to entertain (2) clowns (3) public

    _____   _____

10. (1) to excite (2) soccer match (3) fans

    _____   _____

Now let's get a little closer to the TOEFL format. In the following exercise you'll be given a choice of two verbal adjectives. Try to find the incorrect one.

EXERCISE SWE-45

Directions: In the following sentences there are two underlined verbal adjectives. Try to find the incorrect one and write the corresponding letter (A or B) in the blank.

___A___ 1. The <u>boring</u> students nearly fell asleep during the <u>boring</u> class.

               A   B

_____ 2. The <u>excited</u> movie was enjoyed by the <u>excited</u> children.

               A   B

VERBALS

_____3. The required reading is found in that book advertising by the bookstore.

                  A   B

_____4. The thought-provoked question was examined by the interested lawyer.

                  A   B

_____5. An experienced technician needs to examine the malfunctioned computer.

                  A   B

_____6. María and her friends were amazed by the astounded magician.

                                    A   B

_____7. The freshly painting wall makes the unpainted wall look drab.

                      A   B

_____8. The artist contracting to paint the portrait is known for his inspired

                         A   B

works of art.

_____9. A penny saved is a penny earning.

                      A   B

_____10. The freezing weather killed the flowers planting by the mailbox.

                  A   B

VERBALS

For just a little more practice with verbal adjectives, before we move on to verbal adjective phrases, let's do another short exercise.

EXERCISE SWE-46

Directions: Notice the verbal adjectives in the following sentences. If the sentences are correct, write OK in the blank. If they are incorrect, put an (**X**).

__X__ 1. Steamed broccoli is much healthier than boiling broccoli.

_____ 2. The speeding car was eventually stopped by pursued police.

_____ 3. Crying children should be taken to the nursery located on the first floor.

_____ 4. The TOEFL exam is now administered in a computerizing format.

_____ 5. Your thesis topics must be approved by your counselor if they are not among the specifically assigned topics listed in this memorandum.

_____ 6. The struggling student found the course material too advancing.

_____ 7. The new Volkswagen Beetle is produced in Mexico and exported to the United States.

_____ 8. The uniformed guard kept a close eye on the suspecting shoplifter.

_____ 9. The lost puppy wondered around the neighborhood for hours before its worried owner finally found him playing near the woods.

_____ 10. Concerned students should be present at the student council meeting to voice their opinion on related issues.

When analyzing TOEFL questions, it is usually best to **eliminate phrases** from your consideration. They usually have nothing to do with the error but complicate the sentence and make it confusing. By "throwing away" the phrases, it's easier to find the error.

However, we must be careful with one particular type of phrase. It's called a **verbal phrase** and could very well cause an error. Follow this rule: when you begin a sentence with a verbal phrase, make sure you have logical agreement with the subject of the main clause that follows. For example, it would be incorrect to say: **After *finishing* lunch, the *football game* started**. We don't have logical agreement between the verbal *finishing* and the subject *football game*. It's not logical because a football game can't finish lunch! *Las frases verbales tienen implicado el sujeto, y siempre debe de corresponder con el sujeto de la oración principal.*

Correcting sentences like this one is a little more complicated than simply changing a word or two. You can do one of two things to correct it:

1) Change the verbal phrase to a subordinate clause. For example: *After we finished lunch*, the football game started.

2) Change the subject of the main clause so that it agrees with the verbal phrase. For example: After finishing lunch, *we* watched the football game.

When you're taking the TOEFL exam and you find a sentence that begins with a verbal phrase, check to be sure that there is logical agreement with the subject of the main clause. Of course the difficulty here might be recognizing the verbal phrase. The following exercise should help you recognize verbal phrases. We will practice reducing subordinate clauses to verbal phrases just to have some practice in formulating, and hopefully, recognizing them.

All of the sentences in the following exercise are correct. And all of the subordinate clauses can be reduced to verbal phrases while maintaining logical agreement between the phrase and the subject of the main clause. One tip: when reducing subordinate clauses to verbal phrases, keep the introductory time words, but omit the introductory cause words. *Cuando se reducen oraciones subordinadas a frases verbales, se mantiene el indicador de tiempo, pero se quita el indicador de causa.*

VERBALS

Examine the following examples:

Subordinate Clause: While he was cooking dinner, the chef burned his hand.

Verbal Phrase: While cooking dinner, the chef burned his hand.

Subordinate Clause: Because she is sick, the girl didn't go to school.

Verbal Phrase: Being sick, the girl didn't go to school.

EXERCISE SWE-47

Directions: Rewrite the following sentences. Change the subordinate clauses to verbal phrases.

1. While he was driving to work, the man listened to the radio.

                 While driving to work, the man listened to the radio.

2. Because he had won the election, the politician gave a press conference.

   _____

3. After he ran all the way home, the little boy was exhausted.

   _____

4. Because it has a high caffeine content, coffee is avoided by insomniacs.

   _____

5. After he had graduated from college, Miguel was offered a good job.

   _____

6. Because they require little water, cacti grow well in the desert.

_____

7. Because it is easy to grow, tomatoes are a popular back yard vegetable.

_____

8. After it had been checked, the computer's phone modem functioned perfectly.

_____

9. When it is consumed frequently in large amounts, alcohol can cause liver problems.

_____

10. Since they are high in calories, regular soft drinks are often substituted by diet soft drinks.

_____

Now you should be able to recognize verbal phrases. Again, when taking the TOEFL, if your sentence begins with a verbal adjective phrase, check the subject of the main clause that follows to make sure you have logical agreement. Let's conclude our study of verbal adjective phrases with the following exercise. All of the sentences begin with verbal phrases, so check the subject of the main clause.

VERBALS

EXERCISE SWE-48

Directions: Underline the verbal in the verbal phrase and the subject of the main clause. Write OK if the sentence is correct and an (**X**) if it is wrong.

  X 1. <u>Hoping</u> to generate more education funds, a <u>lottery</u> might be approved by the legislature.

_____2. When applying for admission to an American university, the TOEFL exam is often required of students.

_____3. While cleaning the house, the maid listened to the radio.

_____4. After eating too much candy, a stomach ache caused discomfort to the little boy.

_____5. Standing in a long line, the sun burned the faces of the movie goers.

_____6. Made of fresh berries, the piping hot pie smelled delicious.

_____7. Arriving to her office late, Cristina missed the important staff meeting.

_____8. Running quickly around the track, his blood pressure began to rise.

_____9. Living in Los Angeles, the couple was accustomed to heavy traffic.

_____10. Loving the opera, the performance of Carmen was a treat for Alejandro.

_____11. Considering herself to be homely, parties were rarely attended by Jennifer.

_____12. Considered by many to be the greatest author of all time, the works of Charles Dickens are still enjoyed by many readers.

_____13. Offering discounts of up to 25%, the store recorded record sales.

_____14. Located in southern Mexico, Huatulco has a very hot climate.

_____15. Powered by batteries, electric cars do not pollute the air.

_____16. After practicing hard for several hours every day, the difficult routine was perfected by the young gymnast.

_____17. After being carried for several hours in the hot sun with no water, the beautiful arrangement of flowers began to wilt.

Here's a verb you might not know. *Wilt* means *marchitar*.

131

_____18. After working all day on his computer, Manuel's eyes were very tired.

_____19. When plugging in the TV with wet hands, an electrical shock was felt by the repairman.

_____20. Having already spent too much money using her credit cards, the shopper decided it was time to leave the mall.

That concludes our study of verbal adjectives and adjective phrases. Before we continue with the verbal (**VBL**) section, let's do a Mini TOEFL practice exercise.

MINI TOEFL-13

Directions: In questions 1-5, choose the one word or phrase that best completes the sentence. In questions 6-10, identify the underlined word(s) that should be changed to make the sentence correct.

TIME: 6 minutes

_____1. _____ only one hundred dollars, the couple was able to save several thousand in two years.

(A) Began with   (B) Beginning with   (C) Had begun with   (D) To begin with

_____2. Though known more for amusement parks and movies, _____.

(A) Broadway musicals have recently been produced by the Walt Disney company.

(B) produced recently by the Walt Disney company have been Broadway musicals.

(C) there have been Broadway musicals produced recently by the Walt Disney company.

(D) the Walt Disney company has recently produced Broadway musicals.

_____3 _____ by the researcher's report, the students asked many questions.

(A) Stimulated   (B) Stimulating   (C) Were stimulated   (D) They were stimulated

VERBALS

_____4. Having performed in public only once, _____ about giving the recital.

   (A) the violinist she was nervous   (B) the violinist was nervous

   (C) nervousness was felt by the violinist   (D) felt nervous the violinist

_____5. _____ in a tiny pueblo all her life, Irma was unaccustomed to the traffic and contamination of Mexico City.

   (A) Lived   (B) Having lived   (C) Had lived   (D) She lived

_____6. Located <u>between</u> Birmingham and Mobile, <u>the history of</u> the city <u>of</u>
                A   B   C

Montgomery, Alabama <u>is interesting</u>.
                      D

_____7. While skiing down the <u>steep mountain</u> in <u>freezing</u> weather <u>the nose of</u>
                            A   B   C

the skier became very cold and decided <u>to stop for a rest.</u>
                                           D

_____8. <u>After looked</u> all day for the perfect, new furniture,<u> the couple</u> still <u>could</u>
        A   B   C

not find exactly what they were looking <u>for</u> .
                               D

_____9. After finishing dinner, the <u>doorbell chimed and</u> doctor went<u> to see</u> who
                                    A   B

<u>was</u> at the door <u>at such a late hour</u>.
 C   D

_____10. <u>Flied through</u> the air with the <u>greatest of ease</u>, the trapeze <u>artist</u>
         A   B   C

suddenly fell <u>from the air</u> onto the safety net below.
               D

TOEFL PREP for Spanish Speakers

WF

STEP THREE

QUICK CHECK   Grammar Problem Areas

STEP ONE

    MC   (Main Clause)

    SC   (Subordinate Clause)

STEP TWO

    S=V   (Subject-Verb Agreement)

    S=P   (Subject-Pronoun Agreement)

    VTF   (Verb Tense or Form)

    PFR   (Pronoun Form or Reference)

STEP THREE

    VBL   (Verbal)

   >WF   (Word Form)

- Derived Forms
- Suffixes
- Comparative / Superlative Forms

WORD FORM

STEP FOUR

    WO   (Word Order)

    PS   (Parallel Structure)

    UR   (Unnecessary Repetition)

STEP FIVE

    CU   (Correct Usage)

WORD FORM

EXERCISE SWE-49

Directions: Using the abbreviations that identify each type of error, classify the following ten errors, then try to correct the errors. Only ten of the twelve types of errors are listed.

__SC__ 1. Insect repellents are available in sprays or lotions provide an effective solution to the mosquito problem.

__PFR__ 2. The stories whom appeared in the book were accompanied by beautiful illustrations.

__S=V__ 3. The elephant, along with most of the other animals in the circus, are poorly cared for.

__WO__ 4. I love having lunch with Tania because she always has funny something to tell me.

__S=P__ 5. The teacher along with all of the kindergarten children is eating their lunch.

__VBL__ 6. While looking at the garden through the window, it started to rain.

__MC__ 7. The church group back yesterday from its trip to Europe.

__PS__ 8. The art teacher asked the students to paint their pictures slowly, carefully, and using a lot of imagination.

__WF__ 9. Emotion problems can cause a variety of other problems, such as depression, alcoholism, and paranoia.

__UR__ 10. During the sale, the department store reduced its prices up to 50% less.

We finish STEP THREE with a study of word form (**WF**). In this section, we will see that sometimes a sentence on the TOEFL exam might have a word that is not exactly the wrong word, but not in the correct form. For example, perhaps we have a noun that should be in the adjective form. Refer to number nine in the above exercise. Notice that *emotion* should be *emotional*. We need the adjective form, not the noun form, to describe the noun *problem*.

Examine the following sentences. This should give you a good idea of what we mean by **WF** errors.

Omar wants to study *chemical*. (chemistry)

It is *danger* to ride a motorcycle without a helmet. (dangerous)

The teacher might not accept my paper with this ugly *erasing*.  (erasure)

I don't feel *well* today. I have a headache. (good)

In my opinion, María is the *most pretty* girl in the world. (prettiest)

In this section, we'll study derived words—words which are formed from other words—and their relationship (how a noun is formed from a verb, an adverb from an adjective, etc.) Knowing how a word functions is a very important skill—especially for the TOEFL exam. Maybe you won't always know exactly what the words means, but it will help to at least know how it functions.

Be familiar with the following suffixes that can be added to verbs to make derived nouns: **y, al, ure, ence, ance, ment, ation, sion**. When a word ends in one of these suffixes, you should recognize it as a noun. *Even if you have no idea what the word means!* Studying these suffixes will also help you later when we examine gerunds vs. derived nouns. *Estos son algunos de los sufijos más usados para crear sustantivos derivados de verbos.*

Erasure is a rather unusual word that you'll probably not use too often. In Spanish it means *borrón*. And what exactly is an erasure? In the box below, scribble for a couple of seconds with a pencil. Now lightly erase it. The mark that is left behind is an erasure!

It might help you to remember this word by thinking about the famous British pop group. Can you think of a song that this band made famous?

WORD FORM

EXERCISE SWE50

Directions: Using the previously listed suffixes, try to form derived nouns using the following verbs. Write the derived nouns in the spaces.

1. fail _____failure_____   11. refuse _____
2. deliver _____   12. advertise _____
3. try _____   13. observe _____
4. withdraw _____   14. judge _____
5. accept _____   15. exist _____
6. move _____   16. press _____
7. examine _____   17. recover _____
8. discover _____   18. correspond _____
9. please _____   19. form _____
10. erase _____   20. oblige _____

EXERCISE SWE-51

Directions: Examine the following sentences and try to find the nouns that are derived from verbs. Underline them and write in the blanks the verbs from which they were derived.

___propose___ 1. Your book proposal will be reviewed by our chief editor.

_____ 2. Flattery will get you nowhere.

_____ 3. Do you believe in the existence of ghosts?

_____ 4. His mastery of the violin represents many years of study.

_____ 5. You should try a classified advertisement to sell your car.

Withdrawal means *disposición* or *retiro*. The next time you go to an ATM (automated teller machine), or *cajero automático*, you might notice this word if there are English instructions.

WORD FORM

_____ 6. We need more help with the decorations for the prom.

_____ 7. Don't jump to conclusions without examining the facts.

_____ 8. The cat's refusal to eat is a sure sign of sickness.

_____ 9. Please forward all correspondence to my attention.

_____ 10. Although the death penalty is highly controversial, executions still occur in the U.S.

_____ 11. Fortunately, we have a great deal of coherence among our staff.

_____ 12. Books provide one of life's simple pleasures.

_____ 13. The man was charged with concealment of a weapon.

_____ 14. All personnel are required to take a medical examination.

_____ 15. Thank you for your thoughtful words of encouragement.

It is also sometimes possible to use a gerund as a derived noun. However, this type of derived noun can only be used if no other noun form exists. In other words, in formal English, you shouldn't use *preferring* as a noun because *preference* exists. *Sólo cuando no exista un sustantivo derivado se puede usar el gerundio como sustantivo.*

This little situation can cause some problems. How do you know if a verb has a derived form or if the use of the gerund form is permissible? Unfortunately, there are no rules that can be applied—there is no way to look at a verb and know if it has a derived form or not. This is simply a matter of practice and experience-- of vocabulary skills. The best method of improving this skill is to be as familiar as possible with the common suffixes (listed previously) that are used to formulate a derived noun from a verb.

We'll continue with a couple of exercises designed to give you practice with this.

EXERCISE SWE-52

Directions: Examine the gerunds. If the gerund can be used as a noun write (**OK**) in the blank. But if another derived noun form exists, write the correct form in the blank. Remember: you can only use gerunds if another derived form does *not* exist.

agreement 1. agreeing

_____ 2. deciding

_____ 3. preferring

_____ 4. resigning

_____ 5. refusing

_____ 6. learning

_____ 7. recovering

_____ 8. abandoning

_____ 9. installing

_____ 10. erasing

_____ 11. exciting

_____ 12. leaving

_____ 13. existing

_____ 14. implying

_____ 15. transforming

_____ 16. dividing

_____ 17. pressing

_____ 18. automating

_____ 19. departing

_____ 20. arranging

EXERCISE SWE-53

Directions: The following sentences contain at least one gerund. If all gerunds are used correctly write (**OK**) in the blank. But if it is incorrect, underline it and write the derived noun that should be used instead in the blank.

departure 1. The <u>departing</u> of flight 2356 is scheduled for 4:00 PM.

_____ 2. New linguistic studies show that learning a language is not easier for children than adults, as many had thought.

_____ 3. The resigning of the college president came as a shock to the faculty and students.

WORD FORM

_____ 4. The couple went to months of counseling before they agreed on a separation.

_____ 5. Your failing to improve your test score might suggest you need to prepare more.

_____ 6. The arranging of books in our library is consistent with the guidelines of the Dewey Decimal system.

_____ 7. The developing of new curriculum is one of the most challenging aspects of the teacher's job.

_____ 8. Please go to the front desk for informing on local tourist sites.

_____ 9. Although actually illegal, jay-walking is ignored by police in Mexico City.

_____ 10. On the Listening Comprehension section of the TOEFL, you must pay attention not only to the meaning but also to the implying of the words you hear.

_____ 11. You must be careful when making cash withdrawings in large cities as many people are robbed everyday at ATMs.

_____ 12. Check your pronouns and verbs for correct agreeing with the subject.

_____ 13. Alexander Bell had originally been credited with the discovering of the telephone.

_____ 14. The majority of the world's population believes in the existing of some higher being or god.

_____ 15. Perhaps because of his urban upbringing, Marco found life in the rural town boring.

And that brings us to our next **Mini TOEFL** practice exercise.

WORD FORM

MINI TOEFL-14

Directions: In questions 1-5, choose the one word or phrase that best completes the sentence. In questions 6-10, identify the underlined word(s) that should be changed to make the sentence correct.

TIME: 6 minutes

_____1. The _____ in the banquet hall should accommodate 500 people.

    (A) seat arranging   (B) arranging of seats

    (C) seating arranging   (D) arrangement of seats

_____2. The rapid _____ is changing the face of our city.

 (A) developing of new neighborhoods   (B) development of new neighborhoods

(C) neighborhood's new developing   (D) neighboring developing

_____3. The _____ has not been met with unanimous support.

       (A) president's recommendation   (B) recommending of the president

       (C) president's recommending   (D) presidential recommending

_____4. _____ is a highly controversial issue in the United States.

       (A) Desegregating of schools   (B) School desegregation

       (C) School desegregating   (D) Scholarly desegregating

_____5. _____ it started to rain.

       (A) While finishing dinner   (B) Having finished dinner

       (C) After we finished dinner   (D) After finishing dinner

WORD FORM

_____ 6. The <u>company's</u> <u>expanding into</u> Latin American <u>countries is</u>

              A   B   C

responsible for a 25% increase <u>in</u> gross revenue.

                               D

_____ 7. <u>Severe bleeding</u> can be <u>controlled for</u> applying <u>pressure</u> to the injury

            A   B   C

for <u>several minutes</u>.

     D

_____ 8. It's not <u>so much</u> what you said that <u>bothers me</u> as the <u>implying</u>

                  A   B   C

hidden <u>between the lines</u> of your letter.

         D

_____ 9. The <u>departing of</u> the next <u>flight to</u> France <u>will be delayed</u> until

              A   B   C

tomorrow <u>due to</u> severe weather in the Paris area.

     D

_____ 10. Many are becoming <u>disgruntled</u> with the <u>failing of</u> the U.S. Congress

                           A   B

<u>to pass</u> legislation that reduces taxes for <u>the</u> working class.

 C   D

We continue with our study of **WF** with more suffixes. Remember, knowing how a word functions, even when you don't know what the word means, is an important skill that will be very useful when taking the TOEFL exam. We're now going to see suffixes that indicate that a word is a noun that refers to people and suffixes that indicate that a word is an adjective.

The following are examples of some common suffixes that refer to people: *ist, er, ian, ant, ster, tor, ic, ite, eer, ee.* As you can see, there are quite a few. Especially compared with Spanish, where the more common ones include: *o, a,* and *ista (carpintero, estilista, electricista).*

EXERCISE SWE-54

Directions: Using the list of abstract nouns (nouns which refer to intangible things) try to formulate nouns that refer to people. Use the suffixes listed above (try to use each one only once) and write the nouns referring to people by the abstract form.

1. employment   employee   6. youth   _____
2. alcoholism   _____   7. service   _____
3. invention   _____   8. carpentry   _____
4. sociability   _____   9. racket   _____
5. magic   _____   10. biology   _____

Some of the suffixes that are used to derive an adjective from a noun include: *ful, esque, en, an, some, ish, ic, able, less, al, ly, ary, ive, ous, proof, ory,* and *y.* Again, in Spanish, there aren't as many. Some common ones include: *ico (metálico), osa (sedosa),* and *al (musical).*

WORD FORM

EXERCISE SWE-55

Directions: Try to formulate adjectives using the following list of nouns. Use the suffixes listed previously to help you.

1. peace	_peaceful_		9. impression	_____
2. penny	_____		10. picture	_____
3. gold	_____		11. fanatic	_____
4. Nebraska	_____		12. ghost	_____
5. introduction	_____		13. awe	_____
6. self	_____		14. action	_____
7. fire	_____		15. glamour	_____
8. majesty	_____		16. chill	_____

It's a good idea to study the derived words in the two exercises above—**pay attention to the suffixes**. They should help you recognize nouns that refer to people and adjectives—even when the word is not familiar to you. For a little extra practice, try formulating sentences using the above words using the two forms.

Next, we'll learn to distinguish between adjectives and adverbs that end in *ly*. It's always important to know in what form a word is functioning, but this could be particularly important here in identifying errors in parallel structure. Imagine that you have a sentence with what appears to be several *ly* adjectives separated by commas. It seems the parallel structure is OK. But one of the words you assumed to be an *ly* adjective is really an *ly* adverb. So the parallel structure is not good.

It's easy to tell the difference between an *ly* adjective and an *ly* adverb. Just take away the *ly* and examine the base word that is left. If you are left with a noun, you have an *ly* adjective. If you are left with an adjective, you have an *ly* adverb. *El sufijo* ly *puede ser añadido a sustantivos para hacer adjetivos o a adjetivos para hacer adverbios.*

WORD FORM

This process is illustrated in the box below. For example, *costly* is an adjective because *cost* is a noun, while *beautifully* is an adverb because *beautiful* is an adjective.

```
┌─────────────────────────────────────────────────────────┐
│              LY ADJECTIVES AND ADVERBS                  │
│                                                         │
│                 DROP LY AND CHECK BASE                  │
│                          ↓                              │
│                                                         │
│        NOUN                              ADJECTIVE      │
│         ↓                                    ↓          │
│                                                         │
│     LY ADJECTIVE                         LY ADVERB      │
└─────────────────────────────────────────────────────────┘
```

Try the following exercise for practice with this.

EXERCISE SWE-56

Directions: Indicate if the following words are adjectives or adverbs by writing (**ADJ**) or (**ADV**).

1. seriously   ___ADV___   11. beautifully   _____
2. shapely   _____   12. imaginatively _____
3. neighborly   _____   13. friendly   _____
4. patiently   _____   14. miraculously   _____
5. amazingly   _____   15. stately   _____
6. foolishly   _____   16. worldly   _____
7. elegantly   _____   17. amusingly   _____
8. monthly   _____   18. candidly   _____
9. sincerely   _____   19. costly   _____
10. perfectly   _____   20. legally   _____

Studying the relationship between word forms can be helpful. Knowing one form might help you figure out another form. Try to fill in the blanks in the following chart. After it is completed, study the relationship among the various forms. Note: you might find more than one possible option for some forms.

EXERCISE SWE-57

NOUN	VERB	ADJECTIVE	ADVERB
1. excellence			
2.		satisfactory	
3.			confidentially
4.	succeed		
5. decision			
6.		energetic	
7.			excessively
8.	repeat		
9. category			
10.		imaginative	

Now we'll practice identifying word form errors in the context of the TOEFL exam with the following Mini TOEFL practice exercise.

MINI TOEFL-15

Directions: In questions 1-5, choose the one word or phrase that best completes the sentence. In questions 6-10, identify the underlined word(s) that should be changed to make the sentence correct.

TIME: 6 minutes

_____1. I hope to take several courses in _____ before finishing my degree.

(A) comparison linguistics (B) comparative linguistics

(C) comparatively linguistic (D) linguistic comparative

_____2. Water, perhaps our most important _____, is often wasted and polluted.

(A) naturally resource (B) resourceful of nature

(C) naturally resourceful (D) natural resource

_____3. To operate a small business that is a _____, a person must be willing to work extremely long hours.

(A) success   (B) successfully   (C) successful   (D) succeeding

_____4. Mark and Bill _____ planned their three days in New York city to include a Broadway show, lunch in Chinatown, and a Mets game.

(A) careful   (B) care   (C) carefully   D) had a carefully

_____5. The small town of Canoe, Alabama _____ the Indians who once lived there.

(A) got its name from (B) its name got from

(C) got it's name from (D) it got the name from

_____6. Because our focus is on creative writing, higher grades will be given
                                        A   B

to those students who write the most imagination essays.
                     C   D

_____7. The flight attendant's decision action helped keep the situation under
                                  A   B

control when the airplane was flying through turbulent weather.
        C   D

_____8. The chemicals plant has been accused of dumping toxic wastes and
         A   B   C

could be forced to pay penalties that reach millions of dollars.
                                  D

_____9. The head of the English departmental is planning to include TOEFL
                          A   B

preparation courses as part of the newly developed curriculum.
                    C   D

_____10. Last month a Boston research laboratory developers a new
                              A   B

medication that might be used in the treatment of baldness in men.
                  C   D

Most of the time adjectives are used to modify nouns and adverbs are used to modify verbs. But sometimes it is necessary to use an adjective to modify a verb—when that verb falls under one of three categories: 1) adjective-verb combinations, 2) sense verbs, 3) linking verbs.

You should not have much difficulty with the first two categories of verbs. The 1) **adjective-verb combination** category includes verbs such as: *keep quiet, open wide, break loose, stand still, etc.* Notice that the adjective becomes part of the verb.

2) **Sense verbs** include words such as: *smell, taste, look, feel,* etc. Just make sure the verb is actually acting as a sense verb and not an action verb, in which case the normal adverb would be used. For example: The soup **smells** *good.* With my cold I can't **smell** *well.* In the first sentence *to smell* functions as a sense verb so an adjective is used to modify it. In the second sentence *to smell* functions as an action verb so an adverb is used to modify it. This is also logical. **Soup can't smell *well* because soup doesn't have a nose!**

Try to imagine a bowl of soup...   ...with a nose!

3) **Linking verbs** might be a little difficult for you. A linking verb connects the subject of a sentence to a complement. This complement could be an adjective which describes the subject it refers to. For example: *Felipe* **is** *nice.* The verb *to be* functions as a linking verb. Other linking verbs include: *appear, become, grow, get, remain, prove,* and *turn.*

149

Linking verbs might describe a transformation in attitude, appearance, emotional state, etc. You can usually substitute the verb *to become* or *convertir* without changing the meaning. Some verbs have active and linking verb meanings. If they function as an active verb, the adverb, not the adjective, is used to modify it. For example: The tree **grew** *quickly*. Tania **grew** *angry*. In the first sentence *to grow* functions as an action verb so an adverb is used to modify it. In the second sentence *to grow* functions as a linking verb so an adjective is used to modify it.

Los adverbios se usan con todos los verbos excepto con aquellos que caen en cualquiera de las siguientes categorías:

1) combinaciones especiales en las que el adjetivo es parte de la combinación

2) verbos que se usan como verbos sensitivos

3) verbos usados como verbos de unión

En estos tres casos el verbo va seguido de un adjetivo.

EXERCISE SWE-58

Directions: Examine the verbs in the following sentences and circle the correct adverb or adjective forms. Choose the adjective only if the verb falls into one of the three categories mentioned above.

1. Jorge felt (**sleepy**, sleepily) after driving all night.

2. The crowd got (quiet, quietly) when the curtain went up.

3.. The coach screamed (angry, angrily) at the basketball players.

4. A few days at the beach sounds (wonderful, wonderfully).

5. The lady looked (careful, carefully) in her desk for her wallet.

6. Please keep (quiet, quietly) while we're in the library.

7. When she heard the news, Jane turned (pale, palely).

8. We felt (sad, sadly) after seeing the movie.

9. The barbecued chicken smells really (good, well).

10. The kids go (crazy, crazily) when they're stuck inside on rainy days.

11. She sipped the hot soup very (careful, carefully).

12. The dentist asked the patient to open (wide, widely).

13. I trusted the woman because she looked (honest, honestly).

14. The sun was shining (bright, brightly) when the picnic began.

15. Tom grew (angry, angrily) when he heard the news.

16. The students were almost asleep when the bell (final, finally) sounded.

17. After two weeks without a bath, the dog didn't smell (good, well).

18. The audience laughed (uncontrollable, uncontrollably) at the comedian.

19. The bouquet of flowers smells (sweet, sweetly).

20. We all felt (happy, happily) after winning the game.

Remember that adjectives modify nouns, and in special cases, verbs. Adverbs, however, can modify adjectives, other adverbs, as well as verbs. Adverbs are often used to intensify the meaning of adjectives or other adverbs. Here, they have the meaning of *extremely*.

*Los adjetivos modifican sustantivos, y los adverbios pueden modifcar verbos, adjetivos o incluso otros adverbios. Los adverbios pueden ser utilizados para intensificar el significado de un adjetivo o de otro adverbio. Estos intensificadores tienen el significado de **muy**.*

For example: *very   interesting   book*

    Notice an adverb is used to intensify an adjective that modifies a noun.

        ate   extremely   quickly

Notice the adverb is used to intensify another adverb that modifies a verb.

WORD FORM

Keeping this in mind will help you make decisions between tricky adjective-adverb pairs, such as *real* and *really*, *high* and *highly*, *considerable* and *considerably*, and *extreme* and *extremely*.

EXERCISE SWE-59

Directions: Analyze the following phrases and circle the correct adjective or adverb form.

1. appeared (extreme, (extremely)) beneficial
2. was (high, highly) amused
3. seemed (extreme, extremely) happy
4. 🔍 (extreme, extremely) heat
5. is (high, highly) recommended
6. (real, really) wonderful book
7. a (real, really) diamond
8. (extreme, extremely) amusing movie
9. very (original, originally) idea
10. felt (extreme, extremely) pleasure

As you try to improve your writing skills, you might want to keep the above structures in mind. Especially the **adverb-adjective-noun** structure. You see, using this easy structure it is possible to create some rather interesting combinations that are difficult to express using only adjectives. For example, let's say you want to describe some aspect of a restaurant, maybe the dining room. You might come up with something like *the **warmly noisy** dining room*. That creates a special feeling: there's a certain comfortable level of activity. You can get pretty complicated here also, like *the **unobtrusively grandiloquent** dining room!* Try to include some of these structures in your written essay on the TOEFL exam. They're really not difficult. Can you come up with a few interesting combinations?

🔍 Compare the following: *extreme heat* but *extremely hot*. Notice an adjective modifies a noun while an adverb modifies an adjective. This works the same in Spanish: *calor extremo* but *extremadamente caliente*.

We'll finish the **WF** section and STEP THREE with a brief study of comparative and superlative forms. Every adjective has three forms: a base, comparative, and superlative form. The comparative is used to compare two people or things while the superlative is used with three or more. *Los adjetivos pueden tener tres formas: base, comparativa que se usa para señalar las diferencias entre dos personas o cosas, y superlativa que se usa cuando tres o más personas o cosas están involucradas.*

There are a few irregular comparative and superlative forms, such as *good, better, best* and *little, less, least*. Most adjectives, however, follow the following patterns in the comparative and superlative form.

	ONE SYLLABLE	TWO SYLLABLES OR MORE	TWO SYLLABLES ENDING WITH Y
ADJECTIVE	long	interesting	funny
COMPARATIVE	longer	more interesting	funnier
SUPERLATIVE	longest	most interesting	funniest

Note: some adjectives are "absolute" in meaning and should not be used in comparative or superlative forms. These include words such as *dead, perfect,* and *wrong*.

WORD FORM

EXERCISE SWE-60

Directions: Fill in the blanks with correct comparative and superlative forms.

	COMPARATIVE	SUPERLATIVE
1. happy		
2. obscure		
3. wise		
4. generous		
5. messy		
6. good		
7. long		
8. funny		
9. interesting		
10. green		
11. bad		
12. beautiful		
13. fast		
14. comfortable		
15. great		
16. strange		
17. irregular		
18. careful		
19. lazy		
20. crazy		

Remember, the **comparative form** is used only for *two*, the **superlative** for *three or more*.

EXERCISE SWE-61

Directions: Choose and circle the correct comparative or superlative form.

1. This dessert is the (more delicious, **most delicious**) I've ever eaten.
2. Of the two pairs of shoes, I like this one (more, the most).
3. Melissa's understanding of computers is (better, best) than mine.
4. Of her two gymnastic routines, the latter was the (better, best).
5. Eric is the (taller, tallest) child in the kindergarten.
6. The longer she waited the (more, most) she cried.
7. This exercise is (less, least) difficult than the first one.
8. A beam of light travels much (faster, fastest) than a speeding bullet.
9. English was my (easier, easiest) subject in elementary school.
10. Compared (to, with) most other students, Rafael is extremely smart.
11. The longer he skied the (more exhausted, most exhausted) he became.
12. Even though you didn't study, try to do your (better, best) on the test.
13. My brother is the (taller, tallest) person in our family.
14. Nick wanted to buy the (better, best) stereo he could find.
15. This paperback edition is (less, least) expensive than that hardback one.

Notice that *compared to* is used to show equality or similarity while *compared with* is used to point out difference. It might help you remember by studying the following. Notice that the equal sign, which represents similarity or equality has two marks, while the word *to* has two letters. *With*, of course has more than two letters, like the unequal sign. It is often useful to formulate a mental association such as this one to help you remember details.

| compared *to* | = |
| compared *with* | ≠ |

WORD FORM

Let's finish this section with a Mini-TOEFL practice exercise.

MINI TOEFL-16

Directions: In questions 1-5, choose the one word or phrase that best completes the sentence. In questions 6-10, identify the underlined word(s) that should be changed to make the sentence correct.

TIME: 6 minutes

_____1. Of the two books written on the subject, this one is the _____.

(A) best   (B) worst   (C) most complete   (D) better

_____2. Of all the many babies in the nursery, ours is the _____.

(A) prettiest   (B) more pretty   (C) prettier   (D) most pretty

_____3. Mrs. Goodman was on the floor looking _____ for her diamond ring.

(A) careful   (B) carefully   (C) for carefully   (D) searching

_____4. This book of short stories contains several _____

(A) real interesting tales   (B) interesting really tales

(C) really interesting tales   (D) really interested tales

_____5. Of all the piano students, Beatriz is _____ advanced.

(A) the more   (B) most   (C) more   (D) the most

_____6. Most teachers and researchers regular visit university libraries to stay
            A   B   C

abreast of new developments within their particular fields of study.
                                                                           D

_____ 7. Although he has comparative few contacts in the music industry,
              A   B

Rogelio is hoping his rock band will find a producer for a new CD.
            C   D

_____ 8. Although the teacher agreed that the thesis was written in a concise
              A

and succinct format she was not convinced that the subject had been
    B   C

adequately covered.
       D

_____ 9. The sweet, elderly couple strolled lazy, hand-in-hand through the
                         A   B

gardens as they had done for some fifty years.
                   C   D

_____ 10. The head of the English departmental will make a decision on
               A   B   C

including the TOEFL exam as a requirement for completion of language studies.
                              D

POP QUIZ

Why can't soup smell *well*?

What's the difference between *compared to* and *compared with*?

How do you tell the difference between *ly* adjectives and *ly* adverbs?

What British pop group recorded *A Little Respect* and *Chains of Love*?

TOEFL PREP for Spanish Speakers

WO

STEP FOUR

QUICK CHECK   Grammar Problem Areas

STEP ONE

    MC   (Main Clause)

    SC   (Subordinate Clause)

STEP TWO

    S=V   (Subject-Verb Agreement)

    S=P   (Subject-Pronoun Agreement)

    VTF   (Verb Tense or Form)

    PFR   (Pronoun Form or Reference)

STEP THREE

    VBL   (Verbal)

    WF   (Word Form)

- **Subject-Verb inversion**

WORD ORDER

STEP FOUR

    >WO   (Word Order)

    PS   (Parallel Structure)

    UR   (Unnecessary Repetition)

STEP FIVE

    CU   (Correct Usage)

- Direct vs. Indirect Questions

WORD ORDER

EXERCISE SWE-62

Directions: Using the abbreviations that identify each type of error, classify the following ten errors, then try to correct the errors. Only ten of the twelve types of errors are listed.

__CU__ 1. The caged birds begin chirping when the sun raises.

__WO__ 2. Under the house the old furniture is stored.

__UR__ 3. Cherry trees are trees that fill Washington D.C. with flowers in April.

__SC__ 4. The pie which was cooked by Jan who loves to cook.

__S=P__ 5. Everyone should help themselves to drinks and hors d'oeuvres.

__PFR__ 6. The surgeon which did the operation was highly recommended.

__VBL__ 7. Cindy cut her foot on the breaking glass on the kitchen floor.

__S=V__ 8. Five million dollars were a lot of money to win in the lottery.

__WF__ 9. School desegregating remains a complicated issue for politicians.

__PS__ 10. Swimming, jogging, and to play tennis are good forms of exercise.

Most of our study of **WO** errors will involve subject-verb inversion. Keep in mind that in normal word order we have: **SUBJECT + VERB + OBJECT**

For example, **Nick ate a hamburger.** However, sometimes it is necessary to put the verb (sometimes an auxiliary verb) before the subject. This is what we mean by subject-verb inversion. For example, **Down came the rain.** Notice that the verb *came* is placed before the subject *rain*.

To chirp means *piar*. This is called onomatopoeia—using words that imitate a sound. Did you know that the animals make different sounds in English than in Spanish? Of course, they really make the same sound. It is our interpretation of the sound that varies. For example, in English the rooster says, "Cocka-Doodle-Doo", while in Spanish it says, "Ki-Ki-Ri-Ki". What are some other animals whose sounds are expressed differently?

For many students, inverted word order is very difficult. When we learn a second language we usually learn *one* way to express an idea. It is unusual that we go back and look for several **alternative ways** of expressing the same idea. There will always be an easier, non-inverted way to express the idea, and most of us like to stick with this easier way because we're more accustomed to it.

In fact, using inverted order might feel somewhat strange to some. Try to learn to express ideas in an inverted form and include them more often in your **normal speech patterns**. You will sound much more fluent in English—a native speaker will use these inversions without even thinking about it. Try to apply the seven rules that follow for subject-verb inversion.

RULES FOR SUBJECT-VERB INVERSION

1. If you begin a sentence with a **negative word** (or expression) or ***only* with a time expression**, you must use inverted order. *Cuando una oración comienza con una palabra (o expresión) negativa o con* only *y una expresión de tiempo, primero va el verbo y después el sujeto.*

Negatives include words and phrases such as: *never, hardly, seldom, at no time, not only, nowhere, etc.* Some examples of *only* with a time expression include: *only once, only after he graduated from college, only on Saturdays.*

If you begin a sentence with any of these words or phrases, they must be followed by: **AUX. VERB + SUBJECT + MAIN VERB**. For example, **Never has air pollution reached such dangerous levels** and **Only once have I skied**. Can you read these sentences, changing them to their non-inverted forms? It's easy—just start with the subject. They mean exactly the same in their inverted forms.

Perhaps the word order is not so difficult here as recognizing the negative word or phrase. Many negatives don't look so obviously negative as *never*. If you're not sure if you have a negative or not, try applying the question *How frequently?* Negatives (as well as "only" expressions of time) will answer this question (with a few possible exceptions, such as *nowhere*, which should appear obviously negative because of the word *no*). Also, be aware that the time expression after *only* might be only one word or a long phrase. Make sure you get all the way to the end of the time expression before you begin the inversion of the subject and verb in the main clause

NOTE: With the verb *to be* an auxiliary verb is not necessary. Just put the verb *to be* before the subject. Before continuing with the subject-verb inversion rules, let's work with negatives.

EXERCISE SWE-63

Directions: The following sentences, which are incorrect, begin with negative words or phrases or *only* with a time expression. Write them again, making corrections in the word order (don't change the first word or phrase).

1. Never the temperature has been so high in the month of April.

    Never has the temperature been so high in the month of April.

2. Only once Juan has forgotten to do his English homework.

3. Scarcely I had sat down for dinner when the phone rang.

4. Only after he passed the TOEFL he did begin to study Japanese.

_____

5. Only once I have gone to a college football game.

_____

6. Never before I have seen so much pollution in the city.

_____

7. Nowhere the price of beef is more expensive than in Japan.

_____

8. Not only we went to the picnic but we also stayed for the baseball game.

_____

9. Only in the morning the doctor does see patients.

_____

10. Rarely it snows in Atlanta.

_____

11. Only after doing extensive research the doctoral candidate began writing his dissertation on language acquisition.

_____

12. At no time the concert goers were allowed to stand in their chairs.

_____

13. Nowhere I have enjoyed shopping as much as in New York City.

_____

14. Only after practicing for hours she could play the Bach prelude.

_____

15. Only on Sunday the museums are free of charge in Mexico City.

_____

SUBJECT-VERB INVERSION RULES CONTINUED

2. If you've already studied the **S=V** (subject-verb agreement) section, you might recall that the words *there, here,* and *where* do not function as subjects. When you begin sentences with these words you should put the subject after the verb. For example: *Here* are the **books** that you ordered.

Cuando una oración comienza con there, here, *o* where, *primero va el verbo y después el sujeto.*

Inversion is also required if you begin a sentence with *little, such, so,* or *few,* unless they modify a noun (in which case the noun will immediately follow). For example: *Little* did **we** *know that a war had been declared,* but *Such* **behavior** *is not allowed.* In the second example, *such* modifies **behavior**, a noun.

Cuando una oración comenza con little, such, so *o* few, *primero va el verbo y después el sujeto (excepto cuando está modificando un sustantivo).*

You must also invert your subject and verb if you begin a sentence with an adverb such as *up, down, in,* or *out.* For example: *Down* came the **rain.**

Cuando una oración comienza con un adverbio como down, in, out, *o* up, *primero va el verbo y después el sujeto.*

In review, subject-verb inversion is required when you begin sentences with: 1) *there, here,* or *where,* 2) *little, such, so,* or *few,* or 3) *down, in, out, up,* etc.

EXERCISE SWE-64

Directions: The following sentences, which are incorrect, begin with special words found in Rule 2. Write them again, making corrections in the word order (don't change the first word or phrase).

1. Up the flowers came after several weeks of rain.

   _____Up came the flowers after several weeks of rain._____

2. So hungry the children were that they could hardly wait for dinner.

   _____

3. There many important reasons are for learning English well.

   _____

You might recall when you were a child learning a little song about a spider. The English version of this song, "Itsy Bitsy Spider", has quite a few inversions of this type. Hand motions are used to describe actions such as: *"Down came the rain", "Out came the sun",* and *"Up came the flowers".*

WORD ORDER

4. Here the answers are to the last quiz.

_____

5. Little the boy does know that he has a very serious medical problem.

_____

6. In the judge walked as everyone in the courtroom rose.

_____

7. Such is a desire to win not healthy.

_____

8. Few include literary works such details as those of James Joyce.

_____

9. Up the smoke rose from the burning building.

_____

10. Out the children ran from the school when the bell sounded.

_____

11. So clever the thief was that the police never found him.

_____

12. Such are animals common in Africa.

_____

13. Here the books are that you asked me to find in the library.

_____

14. So was she talented that she was invited to perform at Carnegie Hall.

_____

15. Few the nights were that she didn't have a migraine headache.

_____

Before we continue with the rules for subject-verb inversion, let's do a Mini TOEFL practice exercise.

MINI TOEFL-17

Directions: In questions 1-5, choose the one word or phrase that best completes the sentence. In questions 6-10, identify the word(s) that should be changed to make the sentence correct.

TIME: 6 minutes

_____1. Not until Gilberto finished his degree _____ to study Japanese.

   (A) did he begin (B) he began (C) does he begin (D) he did begin

_____2. Only after many weeks of gradually lowering his nicotine consumption _____ stop smoking for good.

   (A) James could   (B) James did   (C) did James   (D) he did

_____3. Down _____ the moment we realized that we had forgotten our umbrella.

  (A) the rain came (B) the rain comes (C) was the rain (D) came the rain

WORD ORDER

_____ 4. So _____ that he collapsed at the end of the race.

    (A) tired was the runner   (B) was the runner tired

    (C) the runner was tired   (D) tired the runner was

_____ 5. Here _____ that you asked me to find.

(A) the file is (B) the files are (C) is the file (D) did the file is

_____ 6. Here <u>the tools are</u> that <u>we will</u> need <u>to plant</u> our new <u>flower garden</u>.

            A   B   C   D

_____ 7. Only after the businessman <u>could provide</u> <u>sufficient identification</u> to

                                      A   B

embassy <u>staff members</u> <u>he was</u> issued a new passport.

            C   D

_____ 8. So heavy <u>the boxes of books were</u> that <u>it took</u> two men to carry

                        A   B

<u>them from</u> the delivery truck <u>to the</u> library office.

    C   D

_____ 9. Not until <u>recent</u> <u>has the use</u> of debit cards <u>become popular</u> among

               A   B   C

consumers who feel they are safer and <u>more practical</u> than cash.

                                               D

_____ 10. Only after you <u>have taken</u> a practice TOEFL exam <u>we can</u>

                       A   B

determine your level and decide if <u>you're ready</u> to begin <u>preparation classes</u>.

                                C   D

SUBJECT-VERB INVERSION RULES CONTINUED

3. Invert the subject and verb when beginning a sentence with **the main verb of a passive verb structure**. For example: *The bank robbers **were seen** running away* could also be written as ***Seen** running away **were** the bank robbers.* You often hear this type of word structure in news reporting. It puts more emphasis on the action.

Cuando un verbo pasivo es separado y el verbo principal comienza la oración, el sujeto va después del verbo.

4. Invert the subject and verb in **conditional sentences that do not begin with the words *if* or *unless***. For example: ***If** he had known, he would have come* could also be written as ***Had** he known, he would have come.* The meaning in both sentences in exactly the same.

En oraciones condicionales omitiendo if *o* unless, *primero va el verbo y después el sujeto.*

5. Invert the subject and verb if you begin a sentence with **a phrase which describes a location**. For example: *Several books are in the box* could also be written as *In the box **are** several books.*

EXERCISE SWE-65

Directions: The following sentences, which are incorrect, begin with special words found in Rules 3, 4, and 5. Write them again, making corrections in the word order (maintain the first word or phrase).

1. Had known he about the party he would have come.

   _____Had he known about the party he would have come._____

2. Under the table my shoes are.

   _____

WORD ORDER

3. Seen at the awards presentation several movie stars were.

_____

4. Somewhere over the rainbow a pot of gold is.

_____

5. Discovered in the basket a kitten was.

_____

6. Should go he, Mark will certainly enjoy the concert.

_____

7. Around the corner my grandmother lives.

_____

8. Engaged to be married the happy couple was.

_____

9. Had read he the newspaper, he would have known about the fire.

_____

10. At the top of the mountain the skiers waited.

_____

11. Accused of the crime three teenagers were.

_____

12. Stored in the big trunk the little boy's toys are.

_____

13. In the trunk of the car the spare tire is.

_____

14. Should see you it, please buy it for me.

_____

15. Placed at the top of the Christmas tree the star was.

_____

On the TOEFL exam you might find a structure that *should be* inverted and is *not*, but you might also find a structure that *is inverted* and *should not be*. Be especially careful with direct and indirect questions. In a direct question, such as *What is your name?*, inversion is required. However, inversion is not used in indirect questions, such as *I don't know **what your name is***.

Notice that in a direct question you are actually asking a question and expecting an answer, while in an indirect question you only give reference to the fact—you're not asking for an answer. The next exercise will give you some practice with direct and indirect questions. Remember that in a direct question you invert, in an indirect question you do not invert.

WORD ORDER

EXERCISE SWE-66

Directions: Examine the word order in the following sentences. In the blanks put (**D?**) for **direct questions** and (**I?**) for **indirect questions**.

_D?_ 1. where did you go

_____ 2. what did you say

_____ 3. where Jaime has been

_____ 4. how long does it last

_____ 5. what time it is

_____ 6. why Ana is on the floor

_____ 7. where he should turn

_____ 8. which he will choose

_____ 9. where Jaime and Ana are

_____ 10. how do you feel

_____ 11. what color the walls are

_____ 12. why Monica didn't come home

_____ 13. where the bank is

_____ 14. why is she here

_____ 15. why she left

_____ 16. are you sick

_____ 17. when they are arriving

_____ 18. how long will the movie last

_____ 19. which book he read

_____ 20. why Jaime, Ana, and Monica are laughing.

Now let's practice with some complete sentences that contain indirect questions that are incorrectly written as direct questions (they use inverted order when they should not).

EXERCISE SWE-67

Directions: Rewrite the following incorrect sentences, correcting the word order in the underlined part

1. The student asked <u>how did he do on the exam</u>.

   _____The student asked how he did on the exam._____

2. Do you know what kind of weather <u>will we have tomorrow</u>?

   _____

171

WORD ORDER

3. We are not sure when will we return from our trip to Europe.

_____

4. Please tell me how much money can I borrow.

_____

5. No one knew why was the alarm sounded.

_____

6. Don't tell me how did the movie end.

_____

7. I'm not sure how much postage does the letter need.

_____

8. The report never said where did the event take place.

_____

9. I must find out how much does the book cost.

_____

10. I can't predict what will the final score be.

_____

We need to review just a couple of small details to finish the **WO** section.

First, put adjectives *after* words that end in *one, body,* or *thing* (adjectives normally proceed nouns in English). For example: *something **wonderful***, not ***wonderful** something*.

Second, put nouns *after* the word *enough* (all other parts of speech precede this word). For example: ***tall** enough*, but *enough **money***.

We'll end the **WO** section with a Mini TOEFL practice exercise.

MINI TOEFL-18

Directions: In questions 1-5, choose the one word or phrase that best completes the sentence. In questions 6-10, identify the word(s) that should be changed to make the sentence correct.

TIME: 6 minutes

_____1. There _____ for us to continue waiting if the tickets are sold out.

   (A) no reason is (B) reason no is (C) is no reason (D) are no reason

_____2. At the end of the avenue _____ which serves great sandwiches.

      (A) a nice restaurant is   (B) be a nice restaurant

      (C) was a nice restaurant   (D) is a nice restaurant

_____3. _____ about the meeting I'm sure he would have come.

   (A) Had he known (B) He had know (C) Known had he (D) If he had

_____4. Only after getting her driver's license _____.

      (A) she was allowed to drive   (B) was allowed to drive

      (C) was she allowed to drive   (D) was allowed she to drive

WORD ORDER

_____ 5. Never _____ such rainy weather in February.

    (A) have we experienced   (B) experienced have we

    (C) we have experienced   (D) have been experienced

_____ 6. Only after <u>raising funds</u> for nearly two years <u>the club was</u> <u>capable</u> of
                                A   B   C

<u>financing</u> the expensive project.
  D

_____ 7. <u>At the edge</u> of the coral reef <u>a small shark was,</u> <u>although</u> none of the lifeguards noticed <u>it</u>.
               A   B   C   D

_____ 8. Down <u>came the rain</u> so <u>heavy</u> that it caused <u>severe flooding</u> in
                      A   B   C

several parts of the city and stranded <u>numerous motorists</u>.
                                                D

_____ 9. So good <u>her memory was</u> that Jane <u>almost never forgot</u> <u>someone's</u>
                        A   B   C

name <u>or</u> telephone number.
      D

_____ 10. <u>Bored</u> with trying <u>to meet</u> <u>new someone</u> at a nightclub, Bob decided
               A   B   C

<u>to try</u> the Internet chat lines.
  D

TOEFL PREP for Spanish Speakers

PS

STEP FOUR

QUICK CHECK   Grammar Problem Areas

STEP ONE

    MC   (Main Clause)

    SC   (Subordinate Clause)

STEP TWO

    S=V   (Subject-Verb Agreement)

    S=P   (Subject-Pronoun Agreement)

    VTF   (Verb Tense or Form)

    PFR   (Pronoun Form or Reference)

STEP THREE

    VBL   (Verbal)

    WF   (Word Form)

STEP FOUR

- Gerunds-Infinitives
- Clauses-Phrases
- Series
- Comparisons

PARALLEL STRUCTURE

    WO   (Word Order)

    >PS   (Parallel Structure)

    UR   (Unnecessary Repetition)

STEP FIVE

    CU   (Correct Usage)

PARALLEL STRUCTURE

EXERCISE SWE-68

Directions: Using the abbreviations that identify each type of error, classify the following ten errors, then try to correct the errors. Only ten of the twelve types of errors are listed.

WF   1. Mathematics was my easier subject in high school.

PFR 2. Me receiving a perfect score came as a surprise.

VBL 3. Steamed vegetables retain more nutrients than boiling ones.

VTF 4. By the end of the week, we will finished our final projects.

SC   5. The snack bar is closed for a few days so that can be remodeled.

CU   6. Most generic brands have much of the same characteristics as name brands.

PS   7. Included among his bad habits are smoking, drinking, and to eat excessively.

UR   8. The students prefer the new computer registration because it is fast and rapid.

S=V 9. *The Mexico City Times* run the book review from *The New York Times* every Wednesday.

MC   10. Although illegal in Mexico, abortion it is practiced in the United States.

Let's begin the parallel structure (**PS**) section of our study. Remember that we must maintain a certain balance in formal English sentences. This will often be tested by presenting a series. All parts of the series, which is almost always separated by commas, should use the same grammatical structure. In other words, don't mix parts of speech that are included in a series.

GOOD PS: He likes to paint, to sing, and to play the piano.

BAD PS: He likes to paint, to sing, and playing the piano.

GOOD PS: She is young, intelligent, and beautiful.

BAD PS: She is young, intelligent, and she looks beautiful.

GOOD PS: Please do your work quietly, carefully, and quickly.

BAD PS: Please do your work quietly, in a careful manner, and quickly.

When all of the elements of a series are in the same grammatical form, we have good **parallel structure**. When some part is different we do not. This is one of the easiest errors to find on the TOEFL (and it is fairly frequently tested!) When you notice the commas separating elements of your sentence, always check the **PS** to make sure everything is in the same form. Avoid mixing structures. You might find a **PS** error that incorrectly mixes phrases with clauses, adjectives with adverbs, gerunds with infinitives, etc.

Muchas oraciones presentan una serie de enunciados, frases, gerundios, infinitivos, adjetivos, adverbios, verbos, etc. Todas las partes de una serie deben tener la misma estructura gramatical para tener una buena estructura paralela.

EXERCISE SWE-69

Directions: All of the following sentences contain errors in parallel structure. Find the part of the sentence that is not parallel and underline it. Then write the correct form above it.

                                            to receive

1. Do you believe it is better to give than <u>receiving</u>?

2. I can offer you a glass of water, a wine, or a cup of coffee.

3. Most New York City tourists like attending Broadway shows, to eat in China Town, and shopping at Saks Fifth.

4. She is extremely successful because of her intelligence, because of her integrity, and because she works very hard.

5. You should check all the verbs for correct tense, agree, and form.

6. The household chores I hate the most are vacuuming the carpet, to wash the dishes, and dusting the furniture.

7. At our university you can study pharmacology, medical, or dentistry.

8. You may choose to make your payments in two, sixth, or twelve monthly payments.

9. Most new college quarterbacks are conscious of, interested, but frightened by their duties as the team leader.

10. The couple bought the new furniture because it was on sale, because they liked the style, and because of its comfort.

11. Good students study frequent, carefully, and consistently.

12. The kindergarten children are learning to read, to write, and doing simple math problems.

13. The meal was simple, sophisticated, and enjoyably.

14. At the football camp the players were taught to kick, to pass, and tackling.

15. Santa Clause does not reward children who cry, pout, or misbehaving.

We must also pay attention to the parallel structure when sentences contain correlative conjunctions. These include structures such as: *either...or, neither...nor,* and *not only...but also.* The words that follow both parts of the correlative conjunction should be in the same grammatical form. For example, if you have an adjective after *not only* you should also have an adjective after *but also.*

Cuando un enunciado contiene conjunciones correlativas lo que está de un lado debe ser paralelo a lo del otro lado.

PARALLEL STRUCTURE

EXERCISE SWE-70

Directions: Each of the following sentences contain correlative conjunctions. Check the parallel structure and write OK if the sentence is correct and an (**X**) if it is wrong.

__OK__ 1. Books are generally classified as either fiction or non-fiction.

_____ 2. She not only plays the trumpet but also the trombone.

_____ 3. Neither rain nor snow will delay the delivery of the mail.

_____ 4. The water in the Dead Sea is not only salty but also contains concentrations of other minerals.

_____ 5. When appraising the value of a diamond one should consider not only the cut but also the clarity and color.

_____ 6. The Banyan tree, a member of the mulberry family, commonly grows in either eastern India or near Malaysia.

_____ 7. The lucky winner not only receives a new car but also a motorcycle.

_____ 8. The psychiatric patient was not only paranoid but also felt nervous.

_____ 9. For fastest service you can make an appointment to take the TOEFL exam either by calling or faxing.

_____ 10. We hope to spend our summer vacation either in Paris or Rome.

We'll finish this **PS** section with a discussion of three types of errors in parallel structure that commonly occur when making **comparisons**.

1. To maintain good parallel structure, try to compare things that are actually comparable. For example:

GOOD PS: The books used in the fifth grade class are much more difficult than *those* in the third grade class.

BAD PS: The books used in the fifth grade class are much more difficult than the third grade class. (You can't compare the books with the class).

179

GOOD PS: The director's salary is higher than his secretary's.

BAD PS: The director's salary is higher than his secretary. (You can't compare the salary with the secretary).

Try to make sure that you are comparing the right things and things that are actually comparable. *Para tener una buena estructura paralela se deben comparar sólo cosas que son parecidas.*

2. When you compare a member of a group with the other members of the group, it is necessary to include words such as *any other* or *anyone else* (otherwise the sentence will not be logical). For example:

GOOD PS: Eduardo is smarter than anyone *else* in his family.

BAD PS: Eduardo is smarter than anyone in his family. (Eduardo is a member of the group *family* and he is not smarter than *himself*).

GOOD PS: The library is taller than any *other* building on campus.

BAD PS: The library is taller than any building on campus. (The library is a member of the group *buildings on campus* and it is not taller than *itself*).

Notice this works the same for people or objects. *Cuando un miembro de un grupo es comparado con los otros miembros del grupo se tiene que separar del grupo usando* anyone else *o* any other.

PARALLEL STRUCTURE

3. Do not eliminate words (even if they appear unimportant) when combining two comparisons in one sentence. Notice in the following example how two comparisons are correctly and incorrectly combined in one sentence.

First comparison: Ana's grades might be *better than* Juan's.
Second comparison: Ana's grades are *as good as* Juan's.

GOOD PS: Ana's grades are as good as if not better than Juan's.
BAD PS: Ana's grades are as good if not better than Juan's. (Notice that the word *as* from the second comparison has been incorrectly eliminated).

When combining two comparisons in one sentence, don't eliminate any words from either comparison. *Cuando dos comparaciones son combinadas, no se puede eliminar ninguna palabra de las dos comparaciones.*

EXERCISE SWE-71

Directions: Each of the following sentences contain comparisons. Check the parallel structure and write OK if the sentence is correct and an (**X**) if it is wrong.

__X__ 1. The books on this shelf are priced much lower than that shelf.

_____ 2. Disposable contact lenses are just as expensive if not more expensive than permanent lenses.

_____ 3. Carlos can play the trumpet better than anyone else in the marching band.

_____ 4. The population of Mexico City is larger than that of New York City.

_____ 5. Dick can run as fast if not faster than Jane.

_____ 6. The administration building is taller than any building on campus.

_____ 7. The operas of Mozart are more popular than Verdi.

PARALLEL STRUCTURE

_____8. I can type just as well if not better than my sister.

_____9. Alberto, the school's star player, is taller than anyone on the basketball team.

_____10. Tickets for this concert are more expensive than next week's.

_____11. Many argue that low tar cigarettes are just as dangerous as if not more dangerous than regular cigarettes.

_____12. The Braves are better than any baseball team in the world.

_____13. The rate for our suites is higher than that of our single rooms.

_____14. Apples are just as nutritious as if not more nutritious than bananas.

_____15. Tania is a better writer than anyone else in her journalism class.

Now let's do an exercise that will provide a good review of all the **PS** points we have studied.

EXERCISE SWE-72

Directions: All of the following sentences are incorrect because they contain some type of **PS** error. Identify the errors and rewrite the sentences correctly in the blanks.

1. A good typist works quick, accurately, and carefully.

   _____A good typist works quickly, accurately, and carefully._____

2. The apples on this tree are much redder than that tree.

   _____

3. My blue jeans look much older than you.

   _____

4. You should not only pick up a registration form but also a course list.

   _____

PARALLEL STRUCTURE

5. Hawaii is more expensive to live in than any state in the U.S.

6. We must decide where we will go and where to stay.

7. This book is just as exciting if not more exciting than the author's first one.

8. The damage caused by hurricane Camille was greater than Eloise.

9. Among her New Year's resolutions are to quit drinking, smoking, and to eat chocolate every day.

10. The team lost because of inexperience and because it made many mistakes.

11. The family not only swam but also playing tennis.

12. Antique furniture is as expensive if not more expensive than modern furniture.

13. To drop a course you must talk either to your counselor or your department head.

PARALLEL STRUCTURE

14. The band marches on the field, played several songs, and returned to their place in the stadium.

_____

15. More musical productions are staged in New York City than in any city in the world.

_____

Let's finish the **PS** section of our study with a Mini TOEFL practice exercise.

MINI TOEFL-19

Directions: In questions 1-5, choose the one word or phrase that best completes the sentence. In questions 6-10, identify the word(s) that should be changed to make the sentence correct. **TIME: 6 minutes**

_____1. The delay was caused either by mechanical problems _____ bad weather.

    (A) or caused by   (B) or   (C) or by   (D) nor by

_____2. Students may choose from among several elective courses, including many art related courses such as _____.

    (A) painting, drawing, and sculpture

    (B) to paint, drawing, and sculpture

    (C) how to paint, how to draw, and sculpture

    (D) techniques of painting, basics of drawing, and to sculpt.

_____3. This year's summer was _____ if not hotter than last year's.

    (A) hot   (B) as hot   (C) hottest   (D) as hot as

PARALLEL STRUCTURE

_____4. During the vacation, I want to ski, _____, and to snow board.

(A) ice skating   (B) to ice skate   (C) to go ice skating   (D) ice skate

_____5. She was hired because of her experience and _____.

(A) because she is a hard worker   (B) because she works hard

(C) she works hard   (D) because of her hard work

_____6. The country's currency was devalued because of an unstable Asian
        A   B   C

market and because investors reacted nervously.
                   D

_____7. The political candidate promised voters that he would fight against
           A   B

criminal, poverty, and drugs if elected.
   C   D

_____8. Compared to most schools, the military academy that I attended is
                 A   B

more disciplined, regimented, and difficult.
  C   D

Remember, *because of* is followed by a phrase (no verb) while *because* is followed by a subordinate clause (complete subject and verb). In this sentence, that rule affects what you can and can not change. **Sometimes what is *not* underlined is just as important as what *is* underlined—what you *can't* change affects what you *must* change**

_____9. The <u>coach's assistant</u> is responsible not only <u>for making</u> sure the team
                              A   B

uniforms <u>are ready</u> but also <u>keeps track</u> of the equipment.
           C   D

_____10. Wooden floors are just as <u>pretty</u> if not <u>prettier</u> than <u>carpeted</u>
                                             A   B   C

or <u>tiled</u> floors.
    D

TOEFL PREP for Spanish Speakers

UR

STEP FOUR

QUICK CHECK   Grammar Problem Areas

STEP ONE

    MC   (Main Clause)

    SC   (Subordinate Clause)

STEP TWO

    S=V   (Subject-Verb Agreement)

    S=P   (Subject-Pronoun Agreement)

    VTF   (Verb Tense or Form)

    PFR   (Pronoun Form or Reference)

STEP THREE

    VBL   (Verbal)

    WF   (Word Form)

- Synonyms

- Implication of More or Less

UNNECESSARY REPETITION

STEP FOUR

    WO   (Word Order)

    PS   (Parallel Structure)

    >UR   (Unnecessary Repetition)

STEP FIVE

    CU   (Correct Usage)

EXERCISE SWE-73

Directions: Using the abbreviations that identify each type of error, classify the following ten errors, then try to correct the errors. Only ten of the twelve types of errors are listed.

__MC__ 1. Is the constant horn blowing that bothers me most about being in a big city.

__S=P__ 2. The football crowd was so large that it took us half an hour to work through them and reach our seats on the top row of the stadium.

__PS__ 3. The misbehaved puppy chewed up my slippers, goes to the bathroom on the floor, and ran out the door and down the street.

__VTF__ 4. Yesterday Bobby swang on the rope and dropped into the creek at least fifty times.

__S=V__ 5. Everything, including the furniture, have been removed from the dilapidated house.

__CU__ 6. The mayor, city officials, and citizen representatives are discussing the issue between themselves.

__VBL__ 7. Although many still prefer importing wines, domestic varieties have been slowly increasing in popularity.

__WO__ 8. Why did he choose to live so far from home was never understood by his friends and family.

__UR__ 9. Quite often the university offers courses on various computer programs frequently.

__SC__ 10. The book is on the top shelf belongs to my sister.

We'll finish STEP FOUR with a study of unnecessary repetition. Don't confuse **UR** errors for repeated subjects (discussed in the **MC** section). When you have an **UR** error, it means that words which have the same meaning have been repeated within the same sentence. Obviously, the better your vocabulary skills the easier it will be to avoid using words that have the same meaning. We'll start our study with a review of some common words with multiple meanings. Avoid using these words repetitively.

Una oración que contiene dos o más palabras que expresan el mismo significado no es aceptable en inglés formal. Para evitar esto debemos reconocer las palabras que tienen el mismo significado.

UNNECESSARY REPETITION

EXERCISE SWE-74

Directions: After each of the following words, try to write at least two (more if possible) words which have the same meaning and would be repetitive if used together. A dictionary or thesaurus might be useful.

1. easy _____ simple, basic, uncomplicated _____

2. correct _____

3. pretty _____

4. large _____

5. total _____

6. initiate _____

7. fast _____

8. colorful _____

9. fancy _____

10. leap _____

11. moist _____

UNNECESSARY REPETITION

12. car _____

13. publicity _____

14. look _____

15. seldom _____

Some verbs in English have an implicit meaning of **more** or **less**. We should avoid using these verbs with the words *more* or *less*, as this would be considered unnecessary repetition. For example: *The store increased its prices by 15% more.* The word *more* is repetitive because *increase* has an implication of more. *Muchos verbos expresan la idea de* more *o* less—*en estos casos no debemos usar* more *o* less.

EXERCISE SWE-75

Directions: Study the following list of verbs. If the verb has an implicit meaning of *more*, write (↑) in the blank. If the verb has an implicit meaning of *less*, write (↓) in the blank. If the verb has neither an implicit meaning of more nor an implicit meaning of less, write (=) in the blank.

↑ 1. increase	_____ 6. enlarge	_____ 11. research
_____ 2. improve	_____ 7. regulate	_____ 12. diminish
_____ 3. report	_____ 8. devalue	_____ 13. expand
_____ 4. shrink	_____ 9. regress	_____ 14. deplete
_____ 5. surpass	_____ 10. reduce	_____ 15. inflate

190

UNNECESSARY REPETITION

EXERCISE SWE-76

Directions: Check the following sentences for unnecessary repetition. If the sentences are correct, write OK in the blank. If they are incorrect put an (**X**) in the blank.

__X__ 1. You must repeat the lesson again.

_____ 2. The concise and succinct report was well received.

_____ 3. Columbus discovered and explored the new land.

_____ 4. A car that is white in color stays cooler in the summer heat.

_____ 5. Simultaneously, the students began protesting at the same time.

_____ 6. The brief and impressive report revealed many new figures.

_____ 7. We annually release our study every year.

_____ 8. I won't guess or speculate about the outcome of the game.

_____ 9. Law requires that you wear a motorcycle helmet on your head.

_____ 10. You should thoroughly read the instruction booklet in a complete manner.

_____ 11. We have installed an alarm system in the house and in the yard.

_____ 12. An eagle is the emblem and symbol of the Mexican flag.

_____ 13. Contaminated water has killed many fish and caused them to die.

_____ 14. Please select and examine five slides under the microscope.

_____ 15. Oak trees are trees that grow in old, hardwood forests.

As you have probably noticed, this is the shortest point of our five step study of grammar—we've almost finished. Just keep in mind that English is a much more concise language than Spanish. Avoid translating. Many expressions in Spanish will be quite repetitive in English. After the following **Mini TOEFL**, we'll be finished with STEP FOUR and begin the final STEP FIVE, which includes correct usage (**CU**) errors.

UNNECESSARY REPETITION

MINI TOEFL-20

Directions: In questions 1-5, choose the one word or phrase that best completes the sentence. In questions 6-10, identify the word(s) that should be changed to make the sentence correct.

TIME: 6 minutes

_____1. After the annual sale the department store planned to increase its prices _____.

    (A) at 20 %   (B) by 20% more   (C) by 20%   (D) higher

_____2. The well documented report was written in a short, _____ format.

    (A) concise   (B) but complete   (C) succinct   (D) brief

_____3. Chocolate chip cookies are especially tasty _____ freshly baked.

    (A) when   (B) and delicious if they are

    (C) and yummy when   (D) after

_____4. United States citizens have the _____ to "bear arms".

    (A) constitutional right   (B) right constitution

    (C) constitution right   (D) rightly constitution

_____5. The ducks in the park generally _____ near the edge of the lake where people often throw food to them.

    (A) staying   (B) they are staying   (C) to stay   (D) stay

_____6. After swimming <u>for several</u> days with <u>minimum</u> sleep, she became
                            A   B

<u>fatigued and</u> exhausted and <u>eventually developed</u> leg cramps.
      C   D

_____ 7. Even though it is a law in most states for motorcycle riders to wear
           A   B

helmets on their heads, some still do not seem to take the law seriously.
        C   D

_____ 8. Sheep are extremely valuable to raise and profitable to sell in that its
                   A   B   C

provide people with meat to eat and wool to wear.
             D

_____ 9. The moisture and humidity in the greenhouse is carefully maintained
             A   B

at the proper level all year to insure maximum growth potential of all the plants.
   C   D

_____ 10. Although the English professor found the student's short story
                     A   B   C

fascinating and intriguing, he did not feel it met the required criteria.
            D

POP QUIZ

Can you think of three words that mean *húmedo,* three words that mean *rápido,* and three words that mean *amable*?

TOEFL PREP for Spanish Speakers

STEP FIVE

QUICK CHECK   Grammar Problem Areas

STEP ONE

    MC   (Main Clause)

    SC   (Subordinate Clause)

STEP TWO

    S=V   (Subject-Verb Agreement)

    S=P   (Subject-Pronoun Agreement)

    VTF   (Verb Tense or Form)

    PFR   (Pronoun Form or Reference)

STEP THREE

    VBL   (Verbal)

    WF   (Word Form)

- *A* vs. *An*
- Count vs. Non-Count nouns
- Definite / Indefinite Articles
- *Make* vs. *Do*
- Problematic Verbs

CORRECT USAGE

STEP FOUR

    WO   (Word Order)

    PS   (Parallel Structure)

    UR   (Unnecessary Repetition)

STEP FIVE

    >CU   (Correct Usage)

CORRECT USAGE

EXERCISE SWE-77

Directions: Using the abbreviations that identify each type of error, classify the following ten errors, then try to correct the errors. Only ten of the twelve types of errors are listed.

VBL 1. Growing up near the sea, surfing was Mark's favorite sport.

_PS_ 2. Roberto not only studies the violin but also the cello.

_WO_ 3. Only after finishing her dissertation Rebecca did receive her doctor's degree.

_CU_ 4. I traveled to Paris, Rome, and London, but the latter place was my favorite.

VTF 5. Houdini, who died on Halloween, performs remarkable acts of escape.

PFR 6. The person who I spoke with earlier suggested I call you.

_SC_ 7. If walk two miles south you'll find the lake is a perfect spot for fishing.

_S=P_ 8. Everyone, including the senior students, must apply for their parking permit before the end of this week.

_S=V_ 9. Both the lion and the tiger is in their house.

_WF_ 10. The poor girl has serious emotion problems as a result of many years of heavy drug use.

We're now ready to begin the final STEP FIVE of the grammar section. This is an interesting point to study. Instead of a long, intensive study of one particular grammar point, we'll take a quick look at a variety of usage errors. The **CU** section will cover common idiomatic problems, problematic verbs, count and non-count words, make vs. do, etc. It's also a good idea to carefully study Appendix F, Common Usage Errors, found on page 257. If you're looking for material to review just days before taking the TOEFL exam, these are good areas to study. You can often pick up a few quick points by reviewing a variety of usage errors.

CORRECT USAGE

We begin with something fairly elementary—the use of **a** vs. **an**. In general this is just a matter of using **a** with a word which begins with a consonant sound, such as **book**, and **an** with a word which begins with a vowel sound, such as **apple**.

However, we must give special consideration to words beginning with three particular letters, as they can cause confusion. Those three letters are: **h**, **u**, and **o**.

Use **a** with all **h** words unless the **h** is silent, in which case you should use **an**. For example: a hurricane, a home, a horn, but an honor, an honest face, an herb.

Use **a** with all **u** words that have a long **u** sound (such as the one heard in tune), but **an** with **u** words that have a short **u** sound (such as the one heard in bug). For example: a unicorn, a university, a union, but an umbrella, an unusual story, an umpire.

Use **an** with all **o** words (short or long sound as found in octopus or ozone, respectively) but **a** with **o** words that have a **w** sound. For example, an orange, an odor, an original poem, but a one-story building, a once-familiar subject, a onetime event. Notice all the words with a **w** sound are formed with the word *one* or *once*.

Obviously, the correct use of these letters depends on correct pronunciation—even if you're not speaking aloud, you must hear an internal pronunciation. We'll continue with an exercise that will give you some practice in pronouncing words and choosing between **a** and **an**.

EXERCISE SWE-78

Directions: Fill in the blanks with **a** or **an**.

1. _an_ orthopedic surgeon
2. _____ honorary degree
3. _____ one-eyed monster
4. _____ university degree
5. _____ house call
6. _____ half cup
7. _____ universal rule
8. _____ one-piece bathing suit
9. _____ one-sided argument
10. _____ honor student
11. _____ usual routine
12. _____ honest face
13. _____ only child
14. _____ unbelievable story
15. _____ herb garden
16. _____ union leader
17. _____ used car
18. _____ orange bicycle
19. _____ horror movie
20. _____ house boat

NOTE: **a** and **an** are called indefinite articles, while **the** is a definite article. Let's take a look at a few rules for the use of definite and indefinite articles.

RULES FOR INDEFINITE ARTICLES A/AN

1. The indefinite article **a** or **an** is used before singular count nouns (never with non-count nouns) to mean "one". For example, a book, an offer, an umbrella. *El artículo indefinido se usa delante de un sustantivo contable para expresar "un" o "una".*

2. The indefinite article is used with certain numerical expressions. For example: a few, a lot, a hundred, a couple, a dozen, a pound, etc. *El artículo indefinido se usa delante de una expresión numérica.*

3. The indefinite article is used before time expressions to mean "per". For example: an apple a day, a mile a minute, $5. an hour. *El artículo indefinido se usa delante de una cifra y significa "por".*

4. The indefinite article is used before names of professions. For example: My mother is a doctor.

The correct use of the definite article *the* is also often tested on the TOEFL exam. The rules for the definite article are a bit more complex than those for the indefinite article. Plus, you'll need to pay attention to when *not* to use it.

RULES FOR THE DEFINITE ARTICLE *THE*

1. A definite article is used when both the speaker and the listener know what is being referred to. For example: Could you please close the window. (It is obvious which window).

2. A definite article is used before expressions of time or position. For example: the morning, the present, the back, the top, the end.

3. A definite article is used with singular nouns that represent larger classes of animals, parts of the body, musical instruments, etc. For example: The violin is a stringed instrument. The lungs are damaged by smoking.

4. A definite article is used with ordinal numbers, but *not* with cardinal numbers. For example: The First World War, but World War Two. The fifth chapter, but Chapter Five.

 Note that in Spanish, the article is not used before names of professions: *Mi madre es enfermera.*

5. A definite article is used with decades, centuries, and general periods of time. For example: the 1930's, the fifties, the 20th century, the ages of rock and roll.

6. A definite article is used with the superlative form of adjectives. For example: the tallest building, the most important decision.

7. A definite article is used with the name of a nationality, but *not* before the name of a language. For example: The English love tea. English is spoken in Australia.

8. A definite article is used with an adjective such as *poor, young, rich,* etc. to mean "people who are…". For example: Robin Hood stole from the rich and gave to the poor.

9. A definite article is used when speaking about a specific noun, but it is *not* used when speaking in general terms. For example: I like pizza. I like the pizza at Pizza Hut.

10. A definite article is used with official names of nations, states, and cities, but *not* with common names. It is also used before plural geographic names of lakes, mountains, and islands, but *not* before individual ones. For example: The United States of America, but America. The State of Texas, but Texas. The Rocky Mountains, but Mount Rushmore.

 Careful here! In Spanish we put the article before the language: *el inglés.*

Se usa el artículo definido: 1) cuando el objeto en referencia es obvio, 2) con expresiones de tiempo o posición, 3) con sustantivos singulares si son nombres de clases más grandes, 4) con números ordinales—no con números cardinales, 5) con décadas, siglos y tiempos generales, 6) con un adjetivo en forma superlativa, 7) con el nombre de una nacionalidad—pero no con idiomas, 8) con adjetivos como pobre *o* joven *para significar "gente que es...", 9) con sustantivos específicos—no con sustantivos generales, 10) nombres oficiales—no con nombres comunes, nombres plurales de lugares geográficos—no con lugares individuales.*

Actually, there are even more rules for the use of the definite article, but these general rules should be enough for our purposes of TOEFL preparation. For a more detailed explanation you might consult an advanced English grammar handbook.

On the TOEFL exam you might find three types of errors involving definite and indefinite articles: 1. An incorrect use of a definite vs. an indefinite article (*a* instead of *an*, or *the* instead of *a* or *an*). 2. An incorrect inclusion or omission of an article—an article is included when it's not needed or omitted when it is needed. 3. An article used instead of a possessive—such as *the* instead of *its*.
Keep these types of errors in mind as you work through the following exercise and Mini TOEFL practice.

EXERCISE SWE-79

Directions: Practice using the correct articles by examining the choices in parenthesis and circling the correct one.

1. Spanish is ((the most), most) widely spoken Romance language.
2. Sequoia, (a Cherokee, Cherokee) leader, created (the, a) first written form of North American Indian language.

CORRECT USAGE

3. Tongan is spoken (in, in the) Tongan Islands, (a, an) kingdom just west (of, of the) International Date Line.

4. (A, The) Semitic languages, including Amharic, were introduced into Ethiopia from (a, the) Arabian Peninsula in (the, a) first millennium B.C.

5. Kalmyk is spoken in (a, the) Russian Republic of Kalmykia, located just to (the west, west) of the Volga River, northwest (of, of the) Caspian Sea.

6. The term "artificial language" refers to those, such as Esperanto, that have been created in (the hope, hope) that they might become (a, an) universal tongue.

7. The spectacular advance (of, of the) English across (a, the) face of the world is (a, an) phenomenon without parallel in (the, a) history of language.

8. Romany (is, is the) language (of a, of the) Gypsies who originally came from India.

9. (Chinese, The Chinese) is spoken by more people than any other language in (a, the) world.

10. Swedish is (most, the most) widely spoken of (a, the) Scandinavian languages, one branch of (a, the) Germanic languages.

MINI TOEFL-21

Directions: In questions 1-5, choose the one word or phrase that best completes the sentence. In questions 6-10, identify the word(s) that should be changed to make the sentence correct. **TIME: 6 minutes**

_____1. _____ desserts on our menu are extremely high in calories and not recommended for people that are on diets.

    (A) The most   (B) None of the   (C) No   (D) Most

_____2. Witch doctors are famous for _____ mysterious herbal remedies.

    (A) their   (B) the   (C) a   (D) an

201

CORRECT USAGE

_____3. The giant anaconda snake of South America can reach _____ of nearly 30 feet.

    (A) length   (B) long   (C) a length   (D) an length

_____4. Although Orville Wright is known as _____ man to fly an airplane, his first flight flew only 12 feet off the ground and lasted only 12 seconds.

    (A) a first   (B) first   (C) the first   (D) an first

_____5. _____ mountain in the North Carolina Blue Ridge mountain range is called Grandfather Mountain.

    (A) The highest   (B) A highest   (C) The higher   (C) An higher

_____6. A eclipse of the sun can be dangerous if viewed with the naked eye.
       A   B   C   D

_____7. New Year's Day, a first day of a new year, is celebrated on various
                          A   B   C   D

days around the world.

_____8. The trapeze artist slowly climbed to top of the rope and up to the
              A   B

platform where she would begin her spectacular performance of mid-air flips.
                         C   D

_____9. The last chapter of the book was such a disappointment that I
        A   B

regretted having spent so many time reading the 300 pages.
        C   D

CORRECT USAGE

_____10. It is not difficult to see the <u>solid</u> waste that is being dumped <u>into the</u>

                                              A   B

river by <u>the paper company</u> because <u>it floats to</u> surface of the water.

                        C   D

Let's continue with something that gives many people problems—especially Spanish speakers. In Spanish, we have the verb *hacer*, while in English we have two verbs—**make** and **do**. To make matters even more confusing we use *do* as a normal verb and also as an auxiliary verb. For our purposes here, however, we will only be considering *do* as a normal verb as we try to distinguish between the two.

Deciding between which verb—*make* or *do*—to use is somewhat difficult. Most grammar books or TOEFL preparation programs don't offer any rules. That's because their use is idiomatic—they don't really follow rules but must be learned by example, through experience. The use of these verbs does not always seem logical: why *make* the bed and then *do* the dishes?

What follows are not hard-fast rules, rather **guidelines** for the use of *make* and *do* which should help you make decisions most of the time. You might find an occasional exception, or a case that does not seem to fit neatly under any of the following guidelines.

Also keep in mind that *make* is used somewhat more frequently than *do*. If forced to guess, your chances are better with *make*! And like many points in **STEP FIVE**, you might see this on the TOEFL in the correct, not always the incorrect, form. Don't assume, in other words, that every time you see *make* or *do* (as well as other words in this section which commonly cause errors) that it is the error. Perhaps it is actually correct and the error is hidden somewhere else in the sentence.

We continue with guidelines that describe situations that normally require the use of *make* or *do*.

GUIDELINES FOR *MAKE*

1. The first category of activities that normally requires the use of *make* relates to **sound**. You *make* a sound, a noise; a musical instrument *makes* a tone.

2. The next category involves **verbal communication**—ideas that are spoken or in some other way communicated (perhaps written). You *make* a comment, a remark, a speech, a comparison, a suggestion, an announcement.

3. Use *make* for activities related to **planning**. You *make* plans, arrangements, and reservations.

4. *Make* is often used with a noun to replace a related verb. For example:

    discover = make a discovery

    offer = make an offer

    stop = make a stop

    turn = make a turn

    profit = make a profit

5. Use *make* with activities related to **achievement**—the result of work. You *make* progress, advances, a good effort, a deal.

6. The final category of activities that will normally be used with *make* involves **creative construction**—to create, produce, or change something, often involving an element of creativity or imagination. You *make* a cake, a sculpture, a fire, a mistake.

GUIDELINES FOR *DO*

1. Use *do* for activities that are **habitual**—routine activities that you do over and over in the same way. We often use *do* as a substitute for other verbs, especially those referring to household chores. You *do* the dishes, the housework, the laundry, the ironing, the cleaning.

2. Use *do* for activities that are **academic** by nature. You *do* research, homework, exercises (the academic or physical type).

3. Use *do* for activities directly related to the routine of **work**. You *do* your work, a good job, business, your best.

4. Be aware that many phrasal verbs formed with *do* have special meanings (refer to the Appendix of Common Phrasal Verbs). Notice the following examples: A vacation will *do* you good (improve your sense of well being or health). The picture does not *do* you justice (show you as attractive as you really are). The school decided to *do* away with the old computers (dispose of them).

5. You probably won't see this on the TOEFL, because it's extremely informal and not grammatically correct. But just in case you hear it in a movie or on the street, we'll mention it. *Do* is sometimes used in special ways and might be considered sophisticated or snobbish. For example, you might hear: " Let's *do* lunch tomorrow." "Let's *do* Acapulco this weekend." Again, this is not correct, but you might hear it!

Study these guidelines and remember that in general we use *do* to focus on an activity and *make* on the result of that activity. Make *y* do *significan hacer. Frecuentemente,* make *es más como fabricar. De manera general,* do *enfoca más la actividad en sí, y* make *el resultado.*

EXERCISE SWE-80

Directions: Examine the words in the box and then list them below in the *make* or *do* column.

an appointment	friends	homework
arrangements	a turn	money
the dishes	plans	the laundry
a tone	your best	research
a comparison	a speech	housework
an effort	a discovery	business
the bed	a proposal	a recommendation

MAKE	**DO**

PROBLEMATIC VERBS

We continue with what many grammar books call *problematic* verbs. Indeed, they are problematic—even for native speakers. These verbs include: *lie* and *lay, sit* and *set, rise* and *raise.*

Why are these verbs so difficult? They are difficult for several reasons. First of all, the **conjugation** is confusing. Study the table that follows carefully. Obviously, it will not help to learn all of the rules for correct usage if you don't know the correct conjugation. Notice that the present tense form *lay* is the same as the past tense form of *lie*. Notice the subtle difference between *lain* and *laid, lying* and *laying,* and *rising* and *raising*. These small differences in spelling make big differences in meaning.

The second reason they are difficult involves the **pronunciation**. It is true that you don't have to speak aloud when taking the TOEFL exam. However, we still "hear" an internal pronunciation when we read words. "Hearing" them wrong can lead to making wrong decisions on their usage. For example, if you pronounce *raise* with just a bit of a Spanish accent, you might hear something like RAH-EEZ, which sounds more closely to *rise*.

The final difficulty is in **usage**. These verbs, while they follow certain patterns, can be confusing. It is necessary to practice with as many example situations as possible. Luckily, the use of these verbs is not frequently tested on the TOEFL. And again, don't assume that every time you see one of these words that it is automatically the error. It might be a decoy to cover up another error in the sentence.

It will help as you study the conjugations below if you think of these verbs in groups of *transitive* and *intransitive*. Transitive verbs take a complement, intransitive verbs do not.

INTRANSITIVE VERBS

SIMPLE	PAST	PAST PARTICIPLE	PRESENT PARTICIPLE
sit	sat	sat	sitting
lie	lay	lain	lying
rise	rose	risen	rising

TRANSITIVE VERBS

SIMPLE	PAST	PAST PARTICIPLE	PRESENT PARTICIPLE
set	set	set	setting
lay	laid	laid	laying
raise	raised	raised	raising

We will examine each of these individually, but keep in mind that *lie* and *sit* are similar in the same way that *lay* and *set* are similar. *Lay* and *set* have the idea, in Spanish, of **poner** and will always have a direct object (you have to put *something*). *Lie* and *sit* have the idea, in Spanish, of **estar**— a reference to position (or assuming that position).

Raise in general means to elevate (always with a direct object), while *rise*, in general, means to increase. But you'll need to study these more carefully and keep in mind that *raise* is used to describe action that is forced or voluntary while *rise* is used to describe action that is natural or involuntary.

You can study **sit** and **lie** together. They are probably the easiest to use. Again, they are intransitive and usually mean *estar o ponerse*, the difference being *estar o ponerse en una posición sentado o reclinado*. *Lie* can also have the meaning of *mentir*, although the conjugations are different and there should never be much confusion between the two forms because they are so different in meaning.

Set and **lay** can also be studied together. They are transitive and always take a direct object. They have the meaning of **poner**—you use these meaning to put or place something. They can often be used interchangeably (you could *set* or *lay* a book on the table). However, there are quite a few idiomatic differences where we must use one or the other.

set	lay
a watch or clock	your head on the pillow
a table	a baby on the bed
broken bones	"lay to rest"
"set out" plants	"lay off" employees
a medical condition "sets in"	bricks

Rise and **raise** can be studied together. Remember that *rise* is intransitive and never has a direct object. It means *increase* or *move up without help*. It is used for action that is *natural* or *involuntary*. *Raise* is transitive and always has a direct object. It means to *elevate* or *increase something*. It is used for action that is *forced* or *voluntary*.

The use of *rise* and *raise* does not always seem logical. For example, you *raise* your hand or leg, but if you stand up you *rise*. Be especially careful with anything related to money—inflation, prices, rent, etc. You might use *rise* or *raise*, depending on whether or not the action is natural or forced.

Note: *Raise* also has the meaning of *criar* in reference to people or animals or *cultivar* in reference to plants. The conjugations are the same.

raise	rise
the flag	the sun
your hand	to stand up
a question	smoke
your voice	wake up
$ (see above)	$ infaltion, taxes, etc.

EXERCISE SWE-81

Directions: Circle the correct form of the verb in parenthesis.

1. Make sure you (**set**, sit) out the bulbs well before the arrival of spring.
2. The delivery boy (lay, laid) the pizza on the table.
3. If you're so tired, why don't you (lay, lie) down for a while?
4. Hot air balloons work because hot air (raises, rises).
5. The construction workers plan to (lay, lie) the bricks this afternoon.
6. The court will come to order. All (raise, rise) for the honorable judge.
7. The owner of the small candy store was forced to (rise, raise) her prices.
8. Prices often (raise, rise) as a result of increasing unemployment levels.
9. Gerardo was (raised, risen) in the Methodist church in a small town.
10. The vice president was forced to (raise, rise) the question at the meeting.
11. Her fear of cancer was (lay, laid) to rest by the doctor's kind words.
12. Your broken arm will have to be (sit, set) in a cast.
13. Avoid (sitting, setting) in the sun too long or you might burn your skin.
14. The box has been (lying, laying) in the attic for many years.
15. Students who work hard are able to (rise, raise) their TOEFL scores.

It is necessary in English to pay attention to words that are **countable** or **non-countable**, as well as countable words that refer to only two or to three or more people or things. In Spanish you do not have to concern yourself with these distinctions. For example, you use *entre* for 2 or 2,000. But in English we must use *between* for two and *among* for three or more.

210

CORRECT USAGE

The following exercise will give you some practice with words that must be used only to refer to two or to three or more.

Note: some of the forms below are comparative and superlative forms. Remember that comparative forms always refer to two, while superlative forms always refer to three or more.

EXERCISE SWE-82

Directions: Examine the following list of words. If they refer to two, write (**2**) in the blank. If they refer to three or more, write (**3+**).

<u> 3+ </u> 1. all

_____ 2. inferior

_____ 3. both

_____ 4. neither

_____ 5. greater

_____ 6. among

_____ 7. latter

_____ 8. nicest

_____ 9. none

_____ 10. worse

_____ 11. either

_____ 12. better

_____ 13. least

_____ 14. more

_____ 15. between

_____ 16. former

_____ 17. worst

_____ 18. superior

_____ 19. most

_____ 20. best

 Be careful not to confuse **latter**, *la segunda de dos,* with **later**, *más tarde.*

211

Now let's move a little closer to the format of the TOEFL exam. Try to think logically--picture what you're describing. Also, watch out for traps (unrelated errors in sentences where one of these words is used correctly).

EXERCISE SWE-83

Directions: Examine the following sentences and try to identify the error. Write the letter (**A**) or (**B**) which corresponds to the error.

___A___ 1. <u>All</u> of the tires on the bicycle <u>are</u> flat.
          A   B

_____ 2. Of <u>all</u> the homes in this neighborhood, mine has the <u>more</u> beautiful lawn.
        A   B

_____ 3. <u>Neither</u> of the five <u>best</u> pieces will be on public display.
        A   B

_____ 4. French and Arabic are spoken in Morocco but the <u>former</u> is used <u>most</u>
                                                      A   B

by the upper classes of society.

_____ 5. <u>Between</u> the waiters, chefs, and managers the lunch shift is <u>more</u>
          A   B

popular than the dinner shift.

_____6. The fifth chapter of the book contained the <u>most</u> important information

                                                                   A

but was also the <u>more</u> boring.

                 B

_____7. The poor cat was blind in <u>both</u> of its eyes and deaf in <u>all</u> of its ears.

                                      A   B

_____8. Of the five problems addressed today, the <u>latter</u> is by far the <u>most</u> serious.

                                                     A   B

_____9. The bilingual child spoke Spanish and English, <u>both</u> of which <u>was</u>

                                                                 A   B

learned from a very early age.

_____10. Of the two puppies, the <u>oldest</u> was the <u>more</u> active.

                                       A   B

Just as we must be concerned with words that refer to only two or to three or more, it is necessary to concentrate on countable and non-countable nouns and words used to refer to count, non-count, or to both count and non-count nouns.

Remember that a count noun, by definition, has a plural form. You can put a number in front of it. For example, you can say *5 books* but not *5 water.* A non-count noun has no plural form.

CORRECT USAGE

EXERCISE SWE-84

Directions: In the blanks write (**C**) for countable nouns and (**NC**) for non-countable nouns.

<u>NC</u> 1. accounting   _____ 11. withdrawal

_____ 2. lumber   _____ 12. circumstance

_____ 3. information   _____ 13. sophistication

_____ 4. shelf   _____ 14. moisture

_____ 5. 🔍 money   _____ 15. arrangement

_____ 6. respect   _____ 16. vote

_____ 7. age   _____ 17. art

_____ 8. tooth   _____ 18. electricity

_____ 9. innocence   _____ 19. strawberry

_____ 10. employment   _____ 20. job

Now let's examine the differences in the use of words used with only count nouns and words used with only non-count nouns. For example, in English we say *between* two people or things, but *among* three or more. In Spanish we can use *entre* for two or two thousand. Limited words, however, work the same in both languages. *Both* and *ambos* are used to refer only to two.

As you work through the following exercise, think of something countable such as "cookies" and something non-countable such as "milk"—for both count and non-count, think of "cookies and milk".

🔍 Some students have a hard time understanding why *money* is considered non-countable. *Money* is conceptual. What you actually count are the *monedas* and *billetes*.

CORRECT USAGE

EXERCISE SWE-85

Directions: In the blanks write (C) for words used only with countable nouns, write (NC) for words used with only non-countable nouns, and write (B) for words used with both countable and non-countable nouns.

   _B_ 1. some   _____6. quantity   _____11. neither/either

_____2. one, two, three…   _____7. few   _____12. any

_____3. amount   _____8. less   _____13. several

_____4. the   _____9. both of   _____14. much

_____5. many   _____10. little   _____15. none

Now we'll see how these words might be tested in a format closer to the TOEFL exam. Again, watch out for tricks! Don't assume that the error involves a countable or non-countable noun.

EXERCISE SWE-86

Directions: Examine the following sentences and try to identify the error. Write the letter (**A**) or (**B**) which corresponds to the error.

   _B_ 1. <u>All</u> of the rain that <u>fall</u> at the laboratory site is measured.
           A   B

_____2. The <u>amount</u> of books in the library is more important than the <u>number</u>
               A   B

of periodicals.

_____3. There are <u>little</u> cookies and even <u>fewer</u> sandwiches left for the guests.
                A   B

_____4. <u>A</u> water in the pool is so <u>heavily</u> chlorinated that it burns my eyes.
        A   B

_____5. Some of the book contain material that might be considered offensive

          A   B

to some readers.

_____6. Much plants are poisonous even though they appear lovely to the eye.

          A   B

_____7. All of the lifeguards are required to swim no less than 3 miles as a

          A   B

part of their intensive training.

_____8. Many of my work was done in the research library.

          A   B

_____9. If you are concerned about the quantity of sugar in your diet you

                                A

should consider drinking artificially sweetened beverages.

                              B

_____10. The researcher use many tests to draw their conclusions.

           A   B

We've almost finished with **STEP FIVE** and the Structure and Written Expression section of this program. Before you work through the next exercise and the final Mini TOEFL practice exercise, it is advised that you first study carefully Appendix F, Common Usage Errors, found on page 257. Here, you'll find explanations to several errors that are found in this exercise.

CORRECT USAGE

EXERCISE SWE-87

Directions: Examine the following sentences and write OK in the blank if they are correct. If they have a usage error, put an (**X**) in the blank and underline and correct the error.

(further)

__X__ 1. <u>Farther</u> research is still needed to solve the mysteries of the AIDS virus.

_____2. The counties effected by the hurricane were visited by the governor.

_____3. We are all ready to jump out of the airplane.

_____4. There seems to be a conflict among the doctors, nurses, and hospital administrators.

_____5. I often talk to my priest when I feel that I need sound advice.

_____6. There maybe a problem with your computer's phone modem.

_____7. Please set down at the table so that dinner can be served.

_____8. We must be concerned with the amount of prisoners in our overcrowded jails.

_____9. Fruits like oranges, grapefruits, and lemons are a good source of vitamin C.

_____10. The president will give his address from the front steps of the capitol.

_____11. Its already time to make reservations for our beach vacation.

_____12. These kind of books are difficult to find and very expensive.

_____13. We have to decide weather we'll go to the game or we'll just watch it on TV.

_____14. The student who's car was towed away will be very upset.

_____15. The weather today is pretty chilly and a little windy.

MINI TOEFL-22

Directions: In questions 1-5, choose the one word or phrase that best completes the sentence. In questions 6-10, identify the word(s) that should be changed to make the sentence correct. **TIME: 6 minutes**

_____1. _____ many factors to consider when choosing the right university.

   (A) Their are   (B) There is   (C) They're   (D) There are

_____2. The little boy told his mother that he _____ watch TV than practice the violin.

   (A) should   (B) would rather   (C) might   (D) had better

_____3. _____ of books were written for second year pre-med students.

   (A) This kind   (B) These kinds   (C) That kind   (D) This sort

_____4. Small dogs _____ Pekinese, Poodles, and Chihuahuas make good pets for people with limited space.

   (A) such as   (B) as such   (C) like   (D) as if

_____5. _____ will be necessary before conclusions can be drawn.

        (A) Further informations   (B) Farther information

        (C) Farther research   (D) Further information

_____6. It is better to <u>have less</u> students in a class <u>so that</u> each student <u>might</u>
                        A   B   C

get the individual attention from the teacher that <u>he needs</u>.
                                                        D

_____7. The university <u>intends</u> to conduct a <u>thorough search</u> involving several
                               A   B

candidates before <u>reaching a</u> agreement <u>on the</u> new president.
                          C   D

_____8. The students <u>who's names</u> are called <u>are requested</u> to <u>make</u> an
                          A   B   C

appointment this week with their faculty <u>advisor</u>.
                                                     D

_____9. <u>Whether might</u> be described as any combination <u>of</u> various <u>amounts</u>
                 A   B   C

of heat, <u>moisture,</u> and motion in the air.
      D

_____10. Compared <u>to the</u> last twenty winning seasons, <u>this year's</u> losing
                     A   B

season <u>was an</u> <u>enormous</u> disappointment.
        C   D

 **POP QUIZ**

Do you *rise* or *raise* a question?

Do you *make* or *do* exercises?

What three letters might cause problems with the use of *a* and *an*?

Is *quantity* used with count or non-count nouns?

TOEFL PREP for Spanish Speakers

WRITTEN ESSAY

PART THREE — Structure and Written Expression

Before the computer-based TOEFL, you only had to worry about the **written essay** if you were taking the TWE **(Test of Written English)**. It was a separate test with a separate score, although it was given in conjunction with the normal TOEFL. It could be avoided by taking the TOEFL on a date when it was not offered.

Well, things have changed! A **mandatory written essay** was first included in the computer-based TOEFL. And it's still included on the PBT version too—but not on ITP. The iBT now includes 2 essays—an independent and integrated writing task. It can no longer be avoided (unless you take the Institutional exam).

The good news is that by taking time to study the organization and requirements of a good essay, you can greatly improve your ability to write an essay with limited practice. It is fairly **easy to improve** by following the advice in this program and writing a few practice essays before the actual exam. Careful study of the previous grammar section will also greatly improve your writing skills.

The first question most students have regarding this essay is: **How long should it be?** Really, the length of this essay is much less important than how well you take and support a position and write a well organized essay that demonstrates skill in writing correctly in English. Generally speaking, however, this is a rather short essay. Probably a page and a half to two pages in length or a minimum of three to five strong paragraphs consisting of three to five sentences.

- Taking a Position
- Organization of Essay
- General Advice
- Score Explanation

• Sample Topics

TAKING A POSITION

Again, what you write is more important than how much you write. The first thing you should do is **choose your position**. Once you have done this, stick with it. Don't go back and forth on the issue unless you've specifically been asked to compare and contrast ideas. Remember, the people who grade your essay don't really care so much what your opinion is as how well you support it.

For example, suppose you've been asked the following question: **Do you prefer living in a big city or a small town?** Take a couple of minutes (the essay will be timed for 30 minutes) and make a decision—choose your position. Most likely you could think of reasons to support either side of this issue, but you must make a decision at this point.

WRITTEN ESSAY

ORGANIZING YOUR ESSAY

Once you're sure of your position, **choose at least three reasons** to support your position. Go ahead and try! Choose at least three reasons to support your position that you'd prefer to live in a big city or a small town. List them in the blanks below. Be brief—just 2 or 3 words should identify the reason. It's also possible to choose 4 or 5 reasons, depending on the complexity of the topic—try to limit your reasons to 5.

1. _____
2. _____
3. _____

That is perhaps the hardest part of writing an essay: choosing a position and supporting it with reasons. Now, you can easily organize your essay. If, however, you were not able to come up with at least three reasons to support your position, you really don't have much of a position to support! **You should reconsider your position.** It will be very difficult to write an acceptable essay if your position is not strong enough to be supported by three reasons.

ESSAY ORGANIZATION
Your essay should have three clearly defined parts:

I   Introduction Paragraph
II Body (1 to 3 paragraphs, minimum)
III Conclusion Paragraph

As you write your essay, think of the shape of an hour glass. You want to start in broad, general terms. Then you squeeze the middle into more specific information as you support your general ideas with reasons and examples. Then, just as the hour glass once again grows broader at the base, you want to conclude your essay in broad, general terms, once again briefly stating the main points you have used to support your position. The introduction and the conclusion are nearly identical. Again: **begin broadly, get more specific in the body, and conclude broadly.**

You should **start with the body** of your essay. Remember those three points that support your position? These points should be strong enough to turn them into **topic sentences** that will begin the paragraphs of the body of your essay. Of course, every sentence that follows a topic sentence should be directly linked to it and be supportive of it—don't include any sentences in this paragraph that are unrelated to your topic sentence. Go ahead. Take the three points above and write out complete topic sentences.

1. _____
   _____
2. _____
   _____
3. _____
   _____

Once you have your topic sentences ready to expand into paragraphs, take just a second and put them in the **best possible order**. Often a couple of your points may be stronger or weaker than the others—especially if you have more than three. You want to begin with what you feel is the strongest point—it's always good to start as convincingly as possible. Then save your second strongest point for last—it's also good to end strongly. Tuck the weaker point(s) in between.

After you write out the body paragraphs, go back and write your **introduction** paragraph. The first sentence, the topic sentence, should state your position. Clearly state your position, avoiding phrases like "In my opinion…", "After careful thought, it is clear to see…" In other words **avoid saying what you're going to say** and just say it! After the topic sentence, briefly state the reasons to support it—the same reasons that are used for the topic sentences in the body.

The **conclusion** is basically a repetition of your introduction. Again, restate the position you've taken and supported, perhaps by beginning with a word like "clearly" or "obviously". Then, once again briefly restate your main points. In the very last sentence, find one more way to state again the main position. You might use a clever quotation or rephrase the position in the form of a question. You could describe a conditional situation in which you choose an option…"If I had to choose between living in a city or a small town, I would not hesitate to…"

GENERAL ADVICE
The most important thing to remember when writing this essay, or anything for that matter, is your reader. **ALWAYS REMEMBER YOUR READER!** Don't make it difficult for your reader to understand what you've written. Don't assume any previous intelligence or expertise on the reader's part. Don't assume that the reader knows what you're thinking but never wrote. In short, take your reader by the hand and carefully walk him through your essay. Never let him fall into the "deep water" of your unintelligible writing and "drown." Keep your sentences short and simple, even if you feel like you're writing on a third-grade level. You won't get extra points for complexity, but you'll certainly lose points if the reader can't understand what you're trying to say. This is the biggest problem most students have with this essay. **Short, concise sentences are better than long, complicated ones.**

SPANISH SPEAKERS, BEWARE! Judging by the way many journalists write in leading Spanish language newspapers, it must be considered a sign of a talented writer to write very lengthy sentences, with several transitions and numerous ideas. This is **not** considered a good writing style in English. It will keep the reader's attention if you mix really short sentences with longer ones, but avoid very long sentences completely. Try to use one idea per sentence. Don't go on and on and on and… Better, put a period, let the reader "breathe", and start a new sentence! Using a short sentence style will make it easier for you to organize and express your ideas in an understandable format, which will certainly be easier for the reader to follow.

Remember, with just **limited practice** you can substantially improve your ability to write a good essay. Don't be afraid to pick up your pen and paper and try a few! Try to write at least three complete essays before the actual exam.

On the actual exam, you can choose to write your essay with the **computer keyboard or with pen and paper**. Most students will probably find it easier to use the computer keyboard. If, however, you are not familiar with using a keyboard, feel free to write it by hand. If you take the Institutional version, you do not have to write an essay.

Some **sample writing topics** follow—your teacher might assign a few of these to you to write outside of class. You can find more sample topics in the official TOEFL Bulletin. The following are quite typical of what you'll encounter on the real exam. Remember, the ETS writers tend to be "politically correct". You probably won't find any topics that are overly controversial. Don't expect to find questions about euthanasia, abortion, capital punishment, legalization of drugs, etc.

WRITTEN ESSAY

SAMPLE WRITING TOPICS

Let's begin with a topic you're already familiar with. Use the notes you made earlier and write out a complete essay for the following question number one. Don't worry about time on the first couple of essays. Once you get the structure right, then try to write future essays timed at 30 minutes, just like the real exam.

QUESTION NUMBER ONE

Do you prefer to live in a big city or a small town? Why? Support your opinion with specific reasons.

QUESTION NUMBER TWO

If you had to choose one thing to represent your country and *send* to an international symposium on culture, what would you choose. Why?

QUESTION NUMBER THREE

You must choose how your university should use a large grant of money. Would you use it: A) to buy computer equipment and software, B) to buy books for the library, or C) for general use in the athletic department? Choose only one and support your answer with specific reasons.

QUESTION NUMBER FOUR

Do you think it's preferable for college students to live at home or on their own? Support your opinion with detailed reasons.

QUESTION NUMBER FIVE

Do you agree or disagree with the following statement: Zoos play no useful role in society. Why or why not?

SCORING

Your PBT essay will be rated by two judges and given a score of 0 to 6. This score will ultimately represent 50% of your Structure and Written Expression score.

A score of 6 is given to an essay that effectively answers the question, takes and supports a position, demonstrates ability to write in an organized format, includes supporting details, displays good use of English with appropriate word choice.

A score of 5 is given to an essay that addresses all of the above points, but less effectively, with minimum errors. **A score of 4**: addresses the above points but with some errors that sometimes hide clarity of meaning. **A score of 3**: reveals inadequate organization, lack of supporting details, incorrect word choice, or structure or usage errors. **A score of 2**: demonstrates serious disorganization, little appropriate detail, serious structure or usage errors, serious lack of focus. **A score of 1**: is not complete, not understandable, with constant errors. **A score of 0**: nothing was written, the question was just copied, another language other than English was used.

Similar criteria is used to score your iBT essays, but a different grading scale is used. The highest possible score is 30 (out of a maximum of 120) points.

TOEFL PREP for Spanish Speakers

LISTENING

PART FOUR LISTENING COMPREHENSION

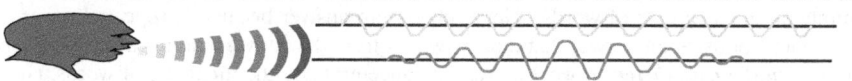

As stated earlier in this book, it is quite difficult to improve listening (and reading) skills in a short time. This is an ability that takes years to develop and also takes a long time to improve. That's why this program does not focus on the **Listening Comprehension** section of the TOEFL—it is more focused on the Structure and Written section because it's easier (and more time efficient) to improve this area.

· Focus on Meaning

Again, to improve your listening skills, you must *listen*. Try to expose yourself to as much spoken English as possible. Watch TV, see movies, listen to recorded cassettes. While this program alone may not really be able to improve your listening skills, we can at least try to improve your score by improving your *ability to take the Listening section*.

· Inflection of Voice and Implied Information

· Sound Confusions

Until the new computer-based test was introduced, most agreed that the best strategic tips for this section involved **anticipation.** Well, you can still (and should) anticipate what the question will be before you hear it, but you can no longer use time between questions to look ahead at the next set of answers. This, unfortunately, is no longer possible with the computerized format. If, however, you can take the Institutional TOEFL (pencil and paper version), this is still a very useful strategy.

· Opposite structures

TIPS and STRATEGIES

PART A—SHORT CONVERSATIONS

In this section of the test you hear a short conversation between **two speakers**, usually a man and a woman to make their voices easily distinguishable. Then, a third speaker asks a question based on this conversation.

Remember, **the question is almost always based on what the second speaker said.** Keeping this in mind, you should anticipate what the question will be before you hear it. This will help you answer quickly and efficiently.

PARTS B & C—LONGER TALKS

For many, these sections are more difficult because they require that you **understand and remember** more information. Try this: instead of just hearing the conversation, *try to see it*. That's right, use your imagination to picture the conversation taking place. This will help you recall details from your memory. What your mind's "eye" sees will probably be much more helpful than simply staring at a frozen computer image that will appear on the screen during the test.

GENERAL STRATEGY

Always concentrate on the **meaning** of words. Never choose an answer because it repeated a word or phrase that you heard. In fact, choosing an answer that repeats words from the conversation is a poor strategy because the *correct answer usually uses different words*. Again, concentrate on the **meaning** of words, not on the actual words.

Most of the incorrect answers have been designed to sound correct in some way. That makes it hard to eliminate obviously incorrect answers. Wrong answers are **disguised** to seem correct by repeating words you heard, or words that *sound* like words you heard. Sometimes an incorrect answer will sound perfect but actually has an *opposite meaning*. All of these traps can be avoided with practice (we'll review examples of each one).

Also, pay close attention to the **inflection** of the speaker's voice. Often, the way we say something can greatly affect the meaning of what we say. For example, by changing our inflection we can easily express feelings of surprise, sadness, disbelief, happiness, etc. Try to say the following phrase, inflecting each of the mentioned emotions:

"The day has arrived".

Be aware of this because you will often be asked about **implied information**. This is information that is not specifically stated, but implied. Often, the implication is expressed through inflection of the voice.

In addition to these tips, it is important to remain **concentrated**. During this section of the test, if you begin to think about problems at school or weekend plans, it's likely you'll lose the question, and **nothing will be repeated**. If this happens, don't panic! Put your guessing letter (*never* leave blanks) and refocus for the next question. You might miss one question but don't allow a quick loss of concentration to cause you to miss several questions by trying to save the one that's lost. *Let it go and refocus.*

Also, remember that ETS tends to write "politically correct" testing material (as discussed in the Writing section of this book). You can eliminate fairly safely any answer that appears in any way controversial or offensive.

The exercises that follow will help you avoid some of the wrong answers that have been designed to sound correct. You'll be working with words that sound similar or the same, but have different meanings, and confusing "opposite structures". Remember that meaning and inflection are important. You'll also find frequent idiomatic expressions in the Listening section—study the Appendix E for practice (or a more complete book of idiomatic expression if this seems to be a big problem for you).

LISTENING

Before you work through the exercises, take a close look at this **example question** that demonstrates clearly the kinds of wrong answers we want to eliminate. In the context of the actual test, we will see how the right answer often uses different sounds, vocabulary, or grammar to make it sound different from the conversation we heard. The same "traps" are found in all of the Listening sections. The right answer might sound wrong--the wrong answers right.

You Hear:

        MAN: Did you finish this week's reading assignment?

        WOMAN: I finished it, but I couldn't make heads or tails of it.

Question: What does the woman mean?

In your test book you read: A) She can barely understand any of the material.

        B) She finished the tale ahead of schedule.

        C) She thought the book was stupid and an insult to her intelligence.

        D) She preferred not to accept the bet.

Now let's **examine** each of the four answers. Notice how the wrong answers are designed in various ways to seem correct--the correct answer is designed to seem incorrect.

Choice (A) is the **correct choice**., but notice how it uses an **"opposite structure"**. You heard, "...I couldn't..." and the correct answer uses "She can barely..." The *meaning* is the same although what you heard uses a negative structure while the answer choice uses an affirmative structure with a negative word. Sometimes, you'll have two opposite structures in the answer choices—you can be almost certain one of them is the correct answer!

Choice (B) is designed to sound correct because of **similar and alike sounds**. The word "finished" is repeated, "tale" sounds like "tails" and "ahead" sounds like "heads".

Choice (C) should be eliminated because it is a bit **controversial**. It is rare to find a correct answer that might be so offensive. It would be more common to find something like "She didn't agree completely with the book's proposal" The "...stupid..." and "..insult to her intelligence..." in the answer choice are just too offensive.

Choice (D) Here, the meaning of the **idiomatic expression** "...couldn't make heads or tails..." which means, "...could not understand..." is being twisted around. Never choose answers that seem to restate idiomatic expressions literally. "Heads or tails" might refer also to flipping a coin, or making a bet—that's what they want you to think. Even if you didn't know this idiom, her *inflection* might have helped you guess that she did not understand what she had read.

Now we're ready to work through three exercises that will give you some practice in recognizing these "traps".

EXERCISE L-1 (Similar Sounds)

Directions: You will hear 20 words spoken by your teacher (or study partner). Try to choose the one you heard and mark it with an (**X**).

1. _____ (A) pal
   _____ (B) pill

2. _____ (A) sheet
   _____ (B) sheep

3. _____ (A) bins
   _____ (B) beans

4. _____ (A) backs
   _____ (B) box

5. _____ (A) duck
   _____ (B) dock

6. _____ (A) rest
   _____ (B) wrist

7. _____ (A) chicks
   _____ (B) checks

8. _____ (A) worm
   _____ (B) warm

9. _____ (A) high
   _____ (B) hay

10. _____ (A) last
    _____ (B) lost

11. _____ (A) 60
    _____ (B) 16

12. _____ (A) hitting
    _____ (B) heating

13. _____ (A) chair
    _____ (B) Cher

14. _____ (A) cream
    _____ (B) scream

15. _____ (A) lung
    _____ (B) long

16. _____ (A) pen
    _____ (B) pan

17. _____ (A) fill
    _____ (B) fell

18. _____ (A) tray
    _____ (B) try

19. _____ (A) could
    _____ (B) couldn't

20. _____ (A) four
    _____ (B) floor

EXERCISE L-2 (Alike Sounds)

Directions: Complete the following sentences by choosing (**A**) or (**B**). Here, the sounds are the same, but the meanings are different

_____ 1. That was quite a _____.

    (A) feet   (B) feat

_____ 2. Read me the _____.

    (A) tale   (B) tail

_____ 3. The judge tries to be _____.

    (A) fare   (B) fair

_____ 4. We'll go in the _____.

    (A) mourning   (B) morning

_____ 5. Your argument is _____.

    (A) week   (B) weak

_____ 6. He _____ to Nicaragua.

    (A) flew   (B) flu

_____ 7. The fast chef cooks with _____.

    (A) time   (B) thyme

_____ 8. The farmer's wife is _____ a dress.

    (A) sowing   (B) sewing

_____ 9. We will fly over the _____.

    (A) plane   (B) plain

_____ 10. She _____ me clean my room.

    (A) maid   (B) made

_____ 11. I hit the pitch _____ left field.

    (A) through   (B) threw

_____ 12. What beautiful _____ of flowers!

    (A) rose   (B) rows

_____ 13. The broken glass caused my _____.

    (A) pain   (B) pane

_____ 14. You'll be _____ for losing the book.

    (A) find   (B) fined

_____ 15. Try to _____ correctly.

    (A) right   (B) write

EXERCISE L-3 (Opposite Structures)

Directions: Choose the answer that *means* the same (although it uses an opposite structure or different words) as the one you hear. Circle (**A**) or (**B**). Pay attention to *implied* information.

1. You Hear: Juan always goes to church on Sunday.

   (A) Juan hardly attends church on Sunday.

   (B) Juan never misses church on Sunday.

2. You Hear: I have a hard time with algebra.

   (A) I don't have time for my algebra homework.

   (B) I can't easily understand algebra.

3. You Hear: He's not crazy about football.

   (A) He's a football fanatic.

   (B) He likes other things more than football.

4. You Hear: I can't stand to ride a bus that long.

   (A) I prefer to ride the bus for shorter periods of time.

   (B) I love to take long bus rides.

5. You Hear: I never drink anything except diet soft drinks.

   (A) I always drink normal soft drinks.

   (B) I only drink diet soft drinks.

6. You Hear: I prefer industrial music to rap.

   (A) I think rap is better than industrial music.

   (B) I don't like rap better than industrial.

7. You Hear: The new *Star Wars* movie doesn't compare to the original.

   (A) The original is better.

   (B) The new one is just as good.

LISTENING

8. You Hear: A laser printer produces better results than a dot matrix.

(A) The dot matrix isn't as good as the laser.

(B) The laser is just as good as the dot matrix.

9. You Hear: I don't like contemporary designs as much as antiques.

(A) I like antiques better than contemporary designs.

(B) I prefer contemporary designs to antiques.

10. You Hear: I always take the subway home from work.

(A) I never drive home from work.

(B) I sometimes skip the subway ride.

11. You Hear: I have a poor understanding of grammatical rules.

(A) I understand nearly perfectly grammatical rules.

(B) I'm not an expert in grammatical rules.

12. You Hear: The little boy loves nothing more than hotdogs.

(A) The little boy is crazy about hotdogs.

(B) The little boy might prefer hamburgers.

13. You Hear: There is a 90% chance of rain tonight.

(A) Rain tonight is doubtful.

(B) You can plan on rain tonight.

14. You Hear: Tokyo is somewhat more populated than Mexico City.

(A) Mexico City is more populated than Tokyo.

(B) Tokyo has more people than Mexico City.

15. You Hear: The registration deadline is tomorrow.

(A) You could not register after yesterday.

(B) You can't register after tomorrow.

TOEFL PREP for Spanish Speakers

READING

READING COMPREHENSION & VOCABULARY

This is probably the **least time efficient** area of the test to try preparing for. It is especially difficult to try and improve one's vocabulary in a short time—even if you study good lists with thousands of words, there's no guarantee that any of these words will be tested when you take the TOEFL. Likewise, general reading skills can't really be improved quickly.

To improve your reading skills—**you must read**. As you prepare for the TOEFL, set up a reading schedule. Try to read an hour or two everyday. Obviously, a library with books in English will be very useful. **Read a variety of materials**: short passages from textbooks, magazines, encyclopedias, newspapers, etc. List especially difficult words to check later in the dictionary.

Just as in the Listening section of this book, we'll concentrate here on **strategies**—test-taking skills that help you understand how to answer as many correct answers as possible. As in all sections of the test, it is important here to be familiar with the directions (so you don't waste any time reading them when you take the test). Also, make sure you understand the format of the test—what types of questions you can expect to find. We'll discuss these in detail and offer some strategic advice on how to answer each question type.

In the Institutional TOEFL format (pencil and paper), only multiple choice questions are included. But in the newer **computer-based** TOEFL, we now have three distinct **formats for questions:**

QUESTION TYPES

- Computer Format

- Strategic Tips

PART FIVE

(1) Multiple Choice with four answer choices

(2) Point & Click—using a computer mouse to identify a word or group of words in the text

(3) Adding Text—placing a sentence within the context of a paragraph

Yes, we have a greater variety of question formats, but the types of questions haven't changed much. However, to insure that you feel comfortable with the computer-based format (and also to help you save precious seconds) it is highly recommended that you review the Reading section on the **TOEFL Sampler** CD-ROM (available free from ETS—see p. 2).

You will notice that on the (computer-based) test, you'll be asked to scroll down through a passage and click when you're finished reading it and ready to begin answering questions. But remember: **you won't get any points for careful reading—only for correct answers!** Don't start studying the passage--get to the questions!

Don't even begin reading the passage until you've reviewed the questions first. Don't worry—you will be able to go back to questions and even change answers. But your focus should be on the **questions**, not on memorizing the passage which contains a lot of useless information. With practice you'll get better at "pulling out" the answers you need without reading word for word. Instead, you'll quickly **skim for key words.**

Time is very important in this section—that's why we want to be as familiar as possible with the types of questions, the directions, and the general format. Remember, you can answer the questions in any order, so **answer easy questions first.** If you do run out of time before you answer the questions, don't panic. Instead, try the **Running out of Time Strategy** found after the explanations of question types that follows.

QUESTION TYPES

1. MAIN IDEA QUESTIONS

You will often find this question **first** but you want to answer it **last!** This will be a very general question. For example:

What is the main topic of the passage?

If you answer the other questions first, you will gather more information about the topic which will help you correctly answer this type of question.

2. VOCABULARY-IN-CONTEXT QUESTIONS

At one time there was a separate vocabulary section on the TOEFL. That has been eliminated, but **vocabulary skills** are still tested by asking questions about words within the reading passage. In a way, this is easier than before because now you have a little more context to work with. However, **all of the answer choices will fit correctly** in the context of the passage if substituted. They will be correct grammatically and logically. It's still a case of "you know the word or you don't know it" usually. Of course there is some **strategy** that can be used to improve your chances of getting a vocabulary-in-context question correct.

First, be able to recognize this type of question. It will be worded like this example:

The word "catastrophic" in line 12 is closest in meaning to... (followed by 4 choices)

Before you review the answer choices, go to line 12 and try to replace the word with another word or phrase that will retain the original meaning of the sentence. This will help you eliminate words that **sound** right, but have different meanings. Compare your substituted word with the answer choices.

3. KEY WORD QUESTIONS

Obviously, these are questions that are based on key words and are sometimes the easiest to answer. A key word question will be worded like this example:

According to the passage, photosynthesis occurs primarily as a result of...

Can you **identify the key word**? It is, of course, *photosynthesis*. Now, go back to the passage and look for this word. Read the sentence before the one with the key word and the sentence in which it appears. You should find the answer to your question, but if not, quickly **skim** to see if the key word appears again. If the key word appears frequently, maybe you've chosen the wrong word, or maybe the question is really a more general one—examine the question again.

4. REFERENCE QUESTIONS

Reference questions ask you to identify what a noun, pronoun, or phrase refers to. A reference question will be worded like this example:

In line 4, *they* refers to...(followed by 4 choices)

The best strategy here is **substitution**. Try substituting the word in question with your answer choices until you find the one that doesn't change the meaning of the sentence. Read the sentence in which the word in question appears as well as the sentence before. Remember, the reference is not always found with the closest words—they are often separated.

Read the following sentence and try to pick the correct reference from the answer choices that follow.

1 Recently, scientists questioned whether Pluto actually met the criteria of being classified
2 as a planet. Some even suggested that *it* be deleted from the list of planets in our ...

In line 2, *it* refers to...
(A) criterion
(B) the list
(C) planet
(D) Pluto

5. NEGATIVE QUESTIONS

These questions, which include words such as *except, not,* or *least likely*, ask you to identify what is **not mentioned** in the passage. A negative question will be worded like this example:

None of the animals in the zoo were infected with the disease EXCEPT... (followed by 4 choices)

Find the key word "animals", then go to the passage where animals are mentioned and begin **eliminating answers**. When you've eliminated 3 choices, you're left with the correct answer!

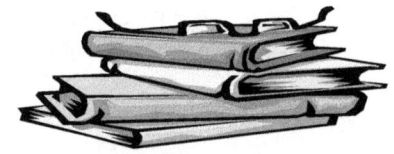

6. BEFORE & AFTER QUESTIONS

These are hypothetical questions that ask you to put lines logically within a text or to identify what might have been written immediately before or after a passage. A before and after question will be worded like this example:

The paragraph following this passage will most likely discuss what? (followed by 4 choices)

Here, use common sense—concentrate on the "cause and effect" or what was or will be a logical chain of events. For **"before" questions**, make sure your answer choice includes the same main subject. For **"after" questions**, concentrate on the final two sentences. In these last sentences you should find a quick summary of what was said with clues as to where the next paragraph will begin.

7. INFERENCE QUESTIONS

In inference questions you must literally **"read between the lines"**. These questions, similar to those in Listening Comprehension, will ask questions about information that is implied by not specifically stated. An inference question will be worded like this example:

It can be inferred from the passage that... (followed by 4 choices)

These are quite similar to main idea questions—**you'll need a general idea about the complete passage** to answer them correctly. These tend to be difficult and should be saved, along with main idea questions, until all other questions have been considered and answered. Answering the other questions will help you gather information to make logical, general inferences.

RUNNING OUT OF TIME STRATEGY

If the time has run down to **three minutes**, you should have no more than one unread passage. First, answer any question with line numbers—these could include "vocabulary in context" or "reference" questions. Then try to skim quickly through the passage and answer "key word" questions. By now, you should have a general idea of the passage and might be able to answer the "main idea" question (usually the first one) and maybe a "negative" or "inference" question. If you don't have time to study the more difficult types of questions, try to eliminate answers and guess with the answer that sounds most logical. With only **5 seconds** left, put a guessing letter for answers you could not study more carefully—never leave a blank.

Again, being familiar with the most common **types of questions** and how to answer them is your best strategy in this section. Always go to the questions **before reading** the passage. Answer the **easiest questions** first. Be careful with **time**.

Try to get **reading pract**ice—for extra practice see if you can formulate questions that are like the various types we've just seen. This will help you think like the people who actually write the questions. You might even try to write out some incorrect answers.

For most students, the Reading section will be their best. Remember, if you're a little weak in the Listening or Structure and Written Expression sections—this is your opportunity to pull up your overall score.

TOEFL PREP for Spanish Speakers

APPENDICES

PART SIX

		PAGE
A.	List of Irregular Verbs	237
B.	List of Prepositions	240
C.	Phrasal Verb Clusters	241
D.	Verbs Used with Infinitives or Gerunds	252
E.	100 Common Idiomatic Expressions	253
F.	50 Common Usage Errors	257
G.	25 False Cognates (English-Spanish)	262
H.	Verb Tense Models	263
I.	Preposition combinations	266
J.	Score Calculation Table	268
K.	Computer-Based Test Score Conversion	269
L.	Answer Key	270

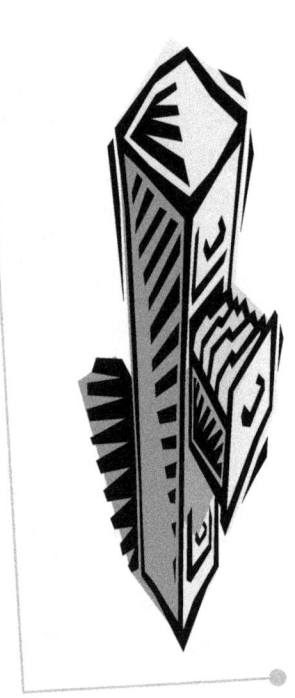

Table of Contents—Appendices

APPENDIX A
IRREGULAR VERBS

SIMPLE	PAST	PAST PARTICIPLE
be	was, were	been
become	became	become
begin	began	begun
bend	bent	bent
bite	bit	bitten
blow	blew	blown
break	broke	broken
bring	brought	brought
broadcast	broadcast	broadcast
build	built	built
buy	bought	bought
catch	caught	caught
come	came	come
cost	cost	cost
cut	cut	cut
dig	dug	dug
do	did	done
draw	drew	drawn
drink	drank	drunk
drive	drove	driven
eat	ate	eaten
fall	fell	fallen
feed	fed	fed
feel	felt	felt
fight	fought	fought
find	found	found
fit	fit	fit
fly	flew	flown
forget	forgot	forgotten
forgive	forgave	forgiven
freeze	froze	frozen
get	got	gotten
give	gave	given
go	went	gone
grow	grew	grown

IRREGULAR VERBS

hang	hung	hung
have	had	had
hear	heard	heard
hide	hid	hidden
hit	hit	hit
hold	held	held
hurt	hurt	hurt
keep	kept	kept
know	knew	known
lay	laid	laid
lead	led	led
leave	left	left
lend	lent	lent
let	let	let
lie	lay	lain
light	lit (lighted)	lit (lighted)
lose	lost	lost
make	made	made
mean	meant	meant
meet	met	met
pay	paid	paid
put	put	put
quit	quit	quit
read	read	read
ride	rode	ridden
ring	rang	rung
rise	rose	risen
run	ran	run
say	said	said
see	saw	seen
sell	sold	sold
send	sent	sent
set	set	set
shake	shook	shaken
shoot	shot	shot
shut	shut	shut
sing	sang	sung
sit	sat	sat
sleep	slept	slept
slide	slid	slid
speak	spoke	spoken
spend	spent	spent
spread	spread	spread
stand	stood	stood
steal	stole	stolen
stick	stuck	stuck
strike	struck	struck
swear	swore	sworn
sweep	swept	swept
swing	swung	swung
swim	swam	swum
take	took	taken
teach	taught	taught

IRREGULAR VERBS

tear	tore	torn
tell	told	told
think	thought	thought
throw	threw	thrown
understand	understood	understood
upset	upset	upset
wake	woke	waked (woken)
wear	wore	worn
win	won	won
withdraw	withdrew	withdrawn
write	wrote	written

 **POP QUIZ**

Can you work through the list and give a Spanish translation of each of the verbs?

APPENDIX B
PREPOSITIONS
(A Brief List with Spanish Translations)

About — *alrededor de, acerca de*
Above — *encima de, más de, superior a*
Across — *a través de, al otro lado de*
After — *después de, detrás de*
Against — *contra, junto a*
Along — *a lo largo de, por*
Among — *entre, en medio de*
Around — *alrededor de*
At — *en, a* (time or price)
Before — *delante de, antes de*
Behind — *detrás de*
Below — *bajo, debajo de*
Beneath — *bajo, debajo de* (same as *below*)
Beside — *cerca de, al lado de*
Besides — *además de, excepto*
Between — *entre*
Beyond — *más allá de, además de*

By — *por, según, junto a*
Despite — *a pesar de*
Down — *abajo*
During — *durante*
For — *para, por, a causa de*
From — *de*
In — *en, dentro de*
Into — *en, hacia el interior de*
Like — *como, igual que*
Near — *cerca de, junto a*
Of — *de*
On — *en, sobre, encima de*
Out — *fuera de*
Over — *(por) encima de*
Since — *desde, a partir de, después de*
Through — *por, a través de, hasta e incluso*
Toward — *hacia*
Under — *debajo de, de acuerdo con*
Until — *hasta*
Up — *en lo alto de, arriba*
With — *con, en compañía de, según*
Without — *sin, a falta de*

240

APPENDIX C
PHRASAL VERBS
(A Mini Dictionary of Common Clusters)

Phrasal verbs are idiomatic combinations of verbs and other parts of speech. Many are obvious in meaning—they're easily formed and understood. Others are more difficult—especially multiple forms using the same verb with varying meaning. Those are the focus of the following listing.

Act as — to play the role of
Act for — to represent someone
Act up — to misbehave or to become painful or problematic
Act up to — to live up to (expectations)
Act upon — to take action regarding

Add in — to put something in the middle
Add on — to put something extra at the end, to expand one's home
Add to — to increase, to make a sum
Add together — to total all parts
Add up — to make a total of numbers, or to make sense
Add up to — to amount to

Allow for — to take into consideration, to provide
Allow in — to permit to enter
Allow to — to give under law
Allow up — to release from bed (medical conditions)

Answer back — to respond to someone in a rude manner
Answer for — to account for, to answer in the place of someone else, to take the responsibility for
Answer to — to be called a name, to obey, to report to someone
Answer up — to respond clearly, without fear

Appear at — to arrive or perform at a certain place, to face a court of law
Appear before — to arrive before a certain time, to face a court of law
Appear for — to act as a lawyer for someone in a court of law
Appear in — to suddenly be seen, to perform in, to be published in
Appear on — to be displayed on
Appear under — to perform using a name

Ask about — to request information
Ask after — to inquire about someone's health
Ask back — to have back, to invite to return
Ask for — to request, to invite trouble
Ask in (or up) — to invite someone in your home
Ask of — to request, to expect from
Ask out — to invite out
Ask over — to invite over
Ask to — to invite someone to be a guest at an event

PHRASAL VERBS

Back away — to move away in fear
Back down — to accept defeat in an argument
Back into — to enter or to hit something when driving
Back off — to retreat from
Back onto — to be arranged in continuation (used with land and buildings)
Back out — to get out of a commitment
Back up — to support, to go backwards

NOTE: The number of phrasal verbs that can be formed with the verb **"to be"** is too great to address in the context of this list. Please consult a dictionary of phrasal verbs if you need to review this.

Break away — to escape, to come apart
Break down — to be defeated, to stop working (machines), to reduce or destroy
Break even — to show no gain and no loss
Break in — to enter by force, to interrupt, to wear new shoes for the first time
Break into — to divide into parts, to enter by force
Break loose — to escape, to become out of control
Break off — to come apart, to end a relationship
Break open — to open by force
Break out — to unwrap or open, to have an outbreak (medical)
Break up — to divide or destroy, to end a relationship

Bring about — to cause to happen
Bring along — to carry with
Bring around — to persuade someone to change their opinion
Bring back — to take something back to its original place
Bring down — to defeat, to reduce (prices)
Bring in — to bring indoors, to profit (financial), to gather (crops)
Bring on — to cause to appear
Bring out — to produce, to cause to be noticed

Call away — to cause a departure (usually for business purposes)
Call back — to ask someone to return, to return a telephone call
Call for — to need or deserve, to demand something, to arrive to collect
Call in — to ask someone to attend, to pay a short visit (ships)
Call off — to cancel, to cause to keep away (usually an animal)
Call on (upon) — to visit, on business or socially
Call out — to shout
Call over — to ask someone to come to where you are
Call up — to give someone a telephone call, to remember

Carry away — to take away, to excite or persuade
Carry forward — to move a figure to the next page (business)
Carry off — to succeed, to remove (usually by force)
Carry on — to take something with you (usually in an airplane), to continue in spite of difficulties
Carry over — to move to a later date, to move a figure to the next page (business)
Carry through — to help someone live through danger, to lift
Carry with — to take with you, to persuade someone to support you

Catch it — to be reprimanded
Catch on — to become popular, to understand
Catch up — to reach someone who is ahead, to be very busy with

Chop down — to make fall (usually a tree)
Chop off — to cut off, to remove with an axe
Chop up — to cut into smaller pieces

Come about — to happen
Come across — to travel a short distance, to find, to be understood
Come across as — to seem to be
Come after — to follow, to chase
Come along — to arrive with someone, to pass, to arrive by chance
Come apart — to break into parts
Come between — to happen between, to get in the way, to interrupt
Come by — to obtain or receive
Come clean — to admit
Come down — to move to a lower level, to get sick, to reduce, to pass along through family generations
Come forward — to move to the front, to offer your help
Come next — to follow
Come out — to move outside, to be removed
Come through — to pass through something, to do what is hoped for, to survive in spite of difficulty
Come to — to reach a point, to regain consciousness, to move near
Come up — to create, to rise, to grow

Do about — to take action about something
Do badly — to be in poor health, to be unsuccessful
Do for — to serve the purpose of
Do good — to help people, to improve
Do in — to murder, to ruin
Do over — to repeat, to improve the appearance of something
Do up — to make oneself more attractive, to wrap or tie in an arrangement
Do with — to be satisfied with, to control, to deal with
Do without — to survive without something you need

Drive at — to suggest something
Drive away — to work hard at something, to leave in a vehicle
Drive back — to force backwards
Drive crazy (or mad) — to annoy, to cause someone to go mad
Drive home — to make a point understood, to travel to one's home
Drive in — to teach with force, to force into position with a hammer
Drive off — to make go away, to cause to go back
Drive out — to make someone or something move away

Drop in — to arrive informally for a visit (usually unannounced)
Drop it — to stop doing something or talking about something
Drop off — to leave someone somewhere, to become worse, to fall asleep
Drop out — to choose to leave (usually school), to fall out of

Eat away — to gradually destroy
Eat into — to use part of, to harm or have a bad effect
Eat out — to eat in a restaurant, or out of the house
Eat up — to use a lot of, to defeat, to hurt emotionally

Enter by — to go into a place using a certain entrance
Enter in — to write something in a record
Enter into — to begin something, to begin to examine or work with, to write in a record
Enter upon (on) — to begin, to take responsibility for (formal)

Fall apart — to end in failure, to break into pieces without being forced
Fall back on — to use one's reserved resources or someone's help
Fall behind — to be behind schedule or late in paying money
Fall down — to tumble down (usually a building), to accidentally fall
Fall from — to loose one's high standing ("fall from grace"—to become immoral)
Fall in — to accidentally fall into, to get into formation, to be ruined
Fall into — to be divided among kinds, to begin a state of being
Fall off — to become worse, to become suddenly lower (geographical or financial)
Fall out — to have a dispute, to tumble out
Fall short — to be left with less than expected

Frighten away (off) — to scare someone into leaving
Frighten into — to force someone with fear to do something
Frighten out of — to prevent someone with fear from doing something

NOTE: The number of phrasal verbs that can be formed with the verbs **"to get"** and **"to go"** is too great to address in the context of this list. Please consult a dictionary of phrasal verbs if you need to review this.

Grow apart — to become separated
Grow away from — to become independent of
Grow back — to return to original length (often with hair)
Grow from — to develop from
Grow in — to develop or increase size in regard to a quality ("grow in number")
Grow into — to become accustomed to, to grow larger so as to fit (for clothing)
Grow on — to gradually like more, to become habit
Grow out — to become larger (in an outward direction)
Grow up — to become more mature, to develop

PHRASAL VERBS

Hang around — to stay near a certain place
Hang back (off) — to hesitate in acting, keep oneself in the background
Hang in — to keep trying in spite of difficulties
Hang on — to depend on something, to wait, to continue holding
Hang out — to spend leisure time at a particular place
Hang over — to threaten or surround with fear or doubt, to be in a state of suffering after drinking too much alcohol
Hang up — to put the telephone receiver down, to be stubborn about something, to delay

Hold back — to control (feelings), to delay
Hold dear — to value highly, to respect
Hold down — to keep food in the stomach, to control, to keep employed ("hold down a job"), keep at a lower level
Hold in — to control (feelings), to keep inward
Hold off — to cause delay
Hold on — to continue in spite of difficulties, to continue holding
Hold out — to last, to stretch forward (your hand)
Hold up — to delay, to rob, to wait for someone

Identify by — identify by means of something (or someone) else
Identify oneself — to reveal one's name
Identify with — to feel the same way, to feel sympathy for

Join in — to take part
Join in with — to take part with someone (or a group), to share the cost
Join with — to share the feelings of someone

Jump at — to eagerly accept an opportunity
Jump down — to spring downward ("jump down one's throat" means to be angry with)
Jump in — to be eager to participate, to spring into the middle
Jump off — to spring off of something
Jump out of — to leave suddenly ("jump out of one's skin" means to be very afraid)
Jump to — to go quickly to
Jump up — to rise suddenly

Keep abreast of — to stay completely informed
Keep after — to find fault, to continuously ask someone to do something, to continue chasing
Keep ahead — to remain in advance of
Keep apart — to maintain separate
Keep away from — to avoid, to keep at a distance from someone
Keep by — to maintain close to
Keep cool — to remain calm, to prevent from becoming warm
Keep from — to avoid, to stop or delay an action
Keep going — to continue an activity
Keep off — to cause to remain at a distance
Keep up — to continue, to keep prices high, to remain the same (usually weather), to maintain good condition

Kick back — to fire backwards (an engine), to keep a portion of a financial profit
Kick down — to make fall by kicking
Kick in — to damage by kicking, to add a share of money
Kick out — to make someone leave a place, to push outside with the foot
Kick up — to make noise or trouble

Knock down — to make fall by hitting, to destroy a building, to reduce the price
Knock off — to reduce the price, to stop working, to murder, to stop something that annoys someone
Knock on — to strike a hard object
Knock out — to hit someone and force a loss of consciousness, to cause to go to sleep (with medication), to remove with a hit
Knock over — to make something fall by hitting it, to easily defeat

Know about — to be informed about something
Know as — to be called by a name
Know best — to be the best judge
Know better — to have more sense
Know of — to have knowledge about

Lay away — to save for a customer to purchase
Lay before — to place in front of, to offer before an official government body
Lay down — to state firmly, to risk money
Lay low — to hide (usually from authorities)
Lay off — to rest, to stop doing something, to end employment
Lay out — to spread for use or viewing
Lay over — to make an overnight stop during a trip

Leave behind — to go away without taking
Leave in — to allow to remain inside or a part of
Leave out — to fail to include on a list, to fail to consider, to place something for someone, to ignore
Leave up — to allow someone to make the decision
Leave with — to give someone a responsibility, to remain in the care of someone

Let alone — to not have anything to do with, to not mention, to not bother
Let by — to allow to pass without comment
Let down — to fail to keep a promise, to lower
Let in — to admit, to allow to enter a place
Let loose — to allow freedom
Let off — to allow to leave, to excuse from punishment
Let on — to tell a secret, to pretend

Live down — to cause people to forget
Live for — to wish for, to have as a reason for living
Live off — to find sufficient income, to live at the cost of someone else
Live through — to remain alive in spite of difficulty, to experience
Live up — to enjoy life
Live up to — to behave in a manner worthy of

Look ahead — to think about the future, to see in front
Look alike — to have the same appearance
Look back — to think about the past, to see behind
Look down on — to have a poor opinion of someone
Look forward to — to expect and wait for
Look out — to be cautious, to have a view of
Look up to — to respect or to admire

Make away with — to steal or to destroy
Make certain — to be sure of the truth
Make good — to repay a debt, to live a successful life
Make light of — to make something seem less serious than it really is
Make out — to write, to see clearly, to understand, to reach an answer, to claim, to kiss passionately
Make over — to change the appearance of something or someone, to remake
Make up — to invent a story, to apply cosmetics to the face, to be part of, to take an exam outside of the normal schedule
Make up for — to repay, provide a balance for

Move away — to live somewhere else, to change one's opinion
Move forward — to advance or improve, to go ahead
Move in — to take control or to attack, to assume a place of residence
Move in on — to share a place without permission, to surround and attack
Move over — to yield one's position, to move to another place

Name after — to give someone the name of someone else
Name as — to give a title to someone

Note down — to record in writing
Note for — to be famous because of

Open into — to provide a view of
Open out — to spread out or become wide open
Open up — to bring within reach (usually a possibility), to open for business, to speak more freely

Pass by — to overlook or disregard, to pass by without pleasure (usually life), to grow later (time), to move past
Pass down — to send from person to person, to give to younger family members
Pass off — to make someone accept by deceit, to succeed in pretending to be something (or someone)
Pass up — to fail to take advantage of an opportunity, to give to someone on a higher level

Pick apart — to find fault in, to separate the pieces of
Pick at — to play with instead of eating food, to make fun of
Pick from — to choose from a group, to lift or remove
Pick out — to recognize in a crowd, to find a musical melody by ear, to choose
Pick up — to collect, to meet romantically, to give someone a ride, to lift, to tidy a room, to obtain cheaply, to improve (business)

Play along — to pretend to agree with, to keep waiting for an answer
Play back — to hear a recording again
Play out — to perform, to mark the end of, to finish playing a game
Play safe — to avoid risk and possibility of failure

Pull aside — to take one away for a private conversation
Pull for — to cheer for (usually a sports team)
Pull off — to succeed in spite of difficulty, to drive to the side of the road, to remove by force
Pull out — to move away, to stretch, to escape
Pull over — to drive to the side of the road
Pull through — to survive in spite of difficulty, to make pass through
Pull together — to work together on a common goal, to improve
Pull up — to come to a stop, to lift, to correct or to improve

Put across — to make understood, to place in a position crossing something
Put ahead — to move a clock forward, to advance
Put away — to store in a box or space, to eat a lot of food, to save money, to stop thinking about
Put back — to return, to regain weight, to cost money, to delay, to move a clock backwards
Put behind — to delay, to end a difficult situation
Put down — to record in writing, to criticize, to eat a lot of food, to lower, to pay part of a price
Put off — to delay, to discourage
Put up — to increase in cost, to provide funds, to provide overnight accommodations, to take something out of use
Put up with — to tolerate

PHRASAL VERBS

Rest against — to lean on for support
Rest in — to exist because of, to lie in comfort, sleep, or death ("rest in peace")
Rest on (upon) — to cause to lie safely or comfortably in sleep or death, to cause to touch or reach, to depend on
Rest up — to have a complete rest after an illness, to catch up on sleep

Run about — to use a vehicle for driving around, to run without direction
Run across — to pass over a space, to find or meet someone or something by chance
Run after — to chase, to flirt with, to attempt to achieve something
Run against — to compete with in an election
Run amuck — to behave out of control
Run away — to escape, to flow away, to leave by running
Run behind — to be behind schedule
Run down — to knock down and damage, to find by searching, to flow downward, to loose power
Run in — to enter quickly, to flow into, to arrest (by police)
Run through — to flow through something, to be a part of, to spend (money) fast, to read quickly, to repeat for practice
Run up — to raise (a flag), to allow to increase, to increase the price of

See about — to deal with or to attend to, to make arrangements
See after — to take care of or to take responsibility for
See ahead — to think about, to plan for, to see in the distance
See around — to see or meet someone regularly
See fit — to decide that it is correct to do something
See in — to show into a room or building, to have as a reason for liking
See over — to look around, to have sight over the top of something
See through — to work until finished, to look through something invisible

Set ahead — to move the hour of a clock to a later time, to change an event to an earlier date
Set apart — to place separately, to be or feel different from others
Set aside — to stop paying attention to (feelings), to discontinue, to place on one side
Set before — to offer for consideration or approval, to place in front of
Set beside — to place next to, to compare
Set in — to begin and seem likely to continue (weather and medical conditions), to put in something (such as a frame), to print with a certain kind of type, to provide with a setting in a particular place (such as a book)
Set off — to begin a trip, to start something working, to start happening
Set out — to begin a profession, to begin a trip, to spread for use, to make known, to start an activity
Set right — to correct, to make someone feel better (with medicine)
Set up — to start, to put in a certain position, to establish, to cause to receive the blame

Show around — to take on a tour of a place
Show for — to have as a result of
Show off (out) — to show pride in, to behave with a sense of self-importance, to accentuate the best qualities
Show up — to arrive, to accentuate, to lead upstairs, to make to look foolish, to win a competition

Sleep around — to have sexual relations with many people
Sleep in — to sleep late
Sleep over — to stay overnight at someone's home
Sleep through — to remain sleeping through an event (such as bad weather)

Stand aside — to take no action, to move to one side
Stand back — to maintain one's distance, to refuse to take part in
Stand between — to try to prevent an action, to be in a position between two other things or people
Stand by — to be loyal to someone, to be ready for action, to be near something
Stand for — to support, to represent, to believe in, to accept or to bear
Stand out — to be noticeable, to be of better quality
Stand up for — to demand, to support

Take after — to look like, to begin to chase, to swallow after a certain point (medicine)
Take apart — to separate into parts, to severely criticize
Take as — to understand or assume to be as
Take down — to record in writing, to remove from a higher position, to disassemble
Take off — to remove, to leave or go away, to rise from the ground (airplane), to reduce weight
Take on — to accept work, to employ, to accept as an opponent, to begin to show a quality, to become popular
Take out — to remove, to remove a stain, to take food outside a restaurant, to lead or carry outside
Take over — to win control of, to accept responsibility for

Talk about — to gossip about, to consider an idea, to have a conversation about
Talk back — to reply (often rudely)
Talk down — to speak to as if another person is less important, to criticize
Talk into — to persuade into doing something, to direct the voice into something (a telephone)
Talk out (over) — to consider completely, to settle by talking
Talk out of — to persuade someone against doing something

Throw away — to get rid of, to fail to take advantage of
Throw back — to delay the advance of, to return by throwing
Throw down — to defeat or to destroy, to direct with force to the ground
Throw in — to add as a gift, to stop attempting, to include or add, to direct with force into something
Throw off — to surprise ("throw off guard"), to release heat or smell, to remove quickly (clothing)
Throw open — to open quickly, to declare free to enter

Turn around — to improve after failing, to change one's opinion, to change a person's version of a story, to move the other way
Turn away — to refuse entry, to refuse, to move in a direction away from
Turn back — to stop moving forward, to cause to go backwards, to turn to a previous page in a book
Turn down — to fold backwards (the sheets of a bed), to refuse to accept
Turn in — to drive into a place, to give something back after use, to present (homework), to go to bed
Turn into — to change and cause to become something or someone else
Turn loose — to give someone freedom to act as he wishes, to free
Turn off — to stop with a control (water), to drive in a different direction, to cease to like
Turn on — to start with a control (water), to attack someone (a dog), to be attracted to
Turn out — to stop with a switch (the lights), to turn inside out, to result, to gather in large numbers
Turn over — to start an engine, to trade a sum of money, to leave one's place of employment
Turn to — to change into, to go to for help, to direct one's attention to
Turn up — to happen, to arrive unexpectedly, to find by chance, to increase the volume

Wait at — to stay in a place expecting something or someone
Wait for — to expect something or to stay in a place expecting something or someone
Wait on — to continue waiting, to attend to (a waiter in a restaurant)
Wait out — to wait for something to be over with (usually a storm)
Wait up — to delay going to bed until someone arrives, to delay to wait for another person

Walk away from — to leave unhurt (a crash), to defeat, to steal, to take away the attention
Walk in — to be able to secure a job easily, to enter without permission or appointment
Walk off — to leave suddenly, to reduce by walking (weight, pain, problem)
Walk on — to take a small role in a play, to be inconsiderate of
Walk out — to leave in opposition, to refuse to work in protest, to go outside
Walk out on — to desert someone, to fail to fulfil an agreement

Work at — to have one's job at a particular place, to put effort into something
Work for — to be employed by someone, to do a job in order to earn
Work in — to enter gradually, to be able to include in a written work
Work loose — to cause to become loose
Work off — to cause to end by working, to pay a debt with work instead of money, to cause with movement to become loose
Work out — to calculate, to force loose with movement, to invent or develop, to understand, to find an answer to, to exercise
Work up to — to excite and reach a state, to begin to reach a point, to prepare to say something, to gradually get near
Work with — to have the company and help of, to perform work with the aid of something, to have a cooperative spirit

APPENDIX D
VERBS USED WITH GERUNDS OR INFINITIVES

With most verbs it is OK to use a gerund or an infinitive as a complement:
I like swimming is the same as *I like to swim*. However, there are a few verbs that should only be used with a gerund or only with an infinitive. Those are included here.

VERBS USED WITH A GERUND

admit, anticipate, appreciate, avoid, complete, consider, delay, deny, discuss, dislike, enjoy, finish, keep, mention, miss, postpone, practice, quit, recall, recommend, regret, resent, resist, risk, stop, suggest, tolerate, understand

VERBS USED WITH AN INFINITIVE

afford, agree, appear, arrange, ask, beg, care, claim, consent, dare, decide, demand, deserve, encourage, expect, fail, forget, hesitate, hope, instruct, intend, learn, manage, mean, need, offer, order, permit, plan, prepare, pretend, promise, refuse, remind, require, seem, struggle, tend, threaten, volunteer, wait, want, wish

APPENDIX E

100 COMMON IDIOMATIC EXPRESSIONS

Here, we include a glossary of 100 common idioms. These are often heard in the Listening Comprehension section of the TOEFL. Some of them are quite similar to phrasal verbs. Some of them function as part of longer clichés or *dichos*. This is only a sample of the hundreds of idioms that exist in American English. Remember, on the TOEFL they often try to trick you with idioms by including answers that contain their literal, rather than implied meaning.

1. **all thumbs** — to be clumsy, not coordinated, especially with the hands

2. **ball of fire** — describes a person who has a lot of energy and ambition

3. **be on target** — to be exactly right in one's analysis of something

4. **be tied up** — to be very busy

5. **beat to the draw** — to win a race

6. **blow the whistle** — to reveal secret information

7. **blow one's own horn** — to promote oneself, to call attention to one's skills

8. **butt in** — to interrupt

9. **call the shots** — to be in charge, to give commands

10. **can of worms** — a complex problem, a whole new set of complications

11. **catch one's eye** — to attract one's attention

12. **clown around** — to be silly, to not be serious

13. **come out of one's shell** — to stop being shy and become more extraverted

14. **cry over spilled milk** — to be upset over something that has happened and can't be undone

14. **down in the dumps** — feeling low, in a bad mood or depressed

15. **eager beaver** — a person who is enthusiastic and hard-working

16. **end of one's rope** — the position whereby a person can no longer cope or try

17. **fed up with** — tired of dealing with—annoyed

18. **flat broke** — having no money

19. **get a word in edgewise** — successfully making a comment to a person who is controlling the conversation

20. **get off the ground** — to successfully begin, such as a business

21. **get one's goat** — to get on one's nerves, to make very angry

22. **get the message** — understand a subtle hint, understand what is meant

23. **get through one's head** — to convince

24. **give a hand** — to applaud or to help someone

25. **give a hard time** — to make problems for someone

26. **green thumb** — the ability to grow plants well, especially flowers

27. **hang up** — an unexpected delay, an unnatural feeling about a normal life occurrence, to break a phone line

28. **hard act to follow** — a great performance that will be hard to compete with

29. **have a hand in** — to be involved in

30. **have well in hand** — to have perfectly under control

31. **head over heels** — to be in love with

32. **heads or tails** — describes the action of flipping a coin or being completely ignorant of ("...can't make heads or tails")

33. **hit the jackpot** — to be extremely lucky, to win

34. **hit the nail on the head** — to get something exactly right, to completely understand

35. **horse of another color** — something completely different from something else

36. **hot under the collar** — really angry, agitated

37. **in a bind** — with a real problem or conflict

38. **in a stew** — in a state of anger

39. **in one's right mind** — to be sane

40. **in the doghouse** — in big trouble with someone

41. **jump on the bandwagon** — join a larger group of people by sharing their opinion

42. **keep one's cool** — to remain calm under pressure

43. **keep one's eyes peeled** — to keep close watch for

44. **keep one's fingers crossed** — to hope for good luck or for the desired result

45. **keep something to oneself** — to keep a secret

46. **keyed up** — nervous or excited

47. **knock oneself out** — to go out of one's way to do something, to work very hard

IDIOMATIC EXPRESSIONS

48. **(not to) know if one is coming or going** — to be undecided, in a state of confusion, often caused by overwork

49. **learn the ropes** — learn the art of or the details of performing an activity

50. **(a) load off one's mind** — good news that causes relief

51. **look on the bright side** — focus on the positive aspects

52. **lose one's temper** — to become very angry

53. **lose touch with** — to be out of contact

54. **lucky dog** — a person who is very fortunate

55. **make it** — to be successful

56. **make up** — to complete an activity at a time later than originally scheduled

57. **measure up** — to meet one's expectations

58. **miss the boat** — to let an opportunity slip away without taking advantage of it

59. **money to burn** — excess money

60. **monkey business** — comical or silly activities or dishonest acts

61. **name of the game** — the reason for doing something

62. **night owl** — a person who likes to stay out late at night

63. **not in your life** — never

64. **on sale** — marked down to a special price

65. **out on a limb** — in a position where one states his position openly at the risk of criticism or failure

66. **over one's head** —too difficult to understand

67. **play by ear** — to play music without written notes, or to perform in an unplanned, impromptu manner

68. **pooped out** — really tired

69. **pop the question** — ask a very important question, perhaps to propose marriage

70. **pull one's leg** — to joke with

71. **put the squeeze on** — to flirt with

72. **save for a rainy day** — to put away to enjoy in less profitable times (money)

73. **say a mouthful** — to say something of great importance or meaning

74. **see eye to eye** — to understand another person, to agree with

IDIOMATIC EXPRESSIONS

75. **(a) show of hands** — a way to count the number of people who agree or disagree with something

76. **skate on thin ice** — barely avoiding a big problem

77. **snake in the grass** — an evil, sneaky person

78. **something else** — really special

79. **something to crow about** — something outstanding that deserves to be bragged about

80. **stand one's ground** — to stay firm in one's belief or position

81. **steer clear of** — to avoid completely

82. **stick like glue** — to always be with someone

83. **stick one's neck out** — to express one's opinion even at the risk of being ridiculed

84. **straight from the horse's mouth** — said by the person directly involved in the event

85. **strike it rich** — to be very lucky and acquire a large amount of money

86. **sweat out (the details)** — to work through the hard part

87. **(a) sure thing** — something that is certain not to change

88. **take a break** — have a rest from work

89. **take it easy** — to relax

90. **take one up on something** — to accept an offer

91. **thumbs up (or down)** — to show approval (up) or disapproval (down)

92. **throw caution to the wind** — to act in a carefree manner, to do something dangerous or potentially harmful

93. **throw in the towel** — to give up on

94. **tide one over** — to last through a lean period (money or food)

95. **too big for one's britches** — with too much self assurance, an exaggerated feeling of self-worth

96. **tons** — a large quantity or amount

97. **turn one's cheek** — to accept rejection or criticism without reacting negatively

98. **up in the air** — undecided, not confirmed

99. **wash one's hands of** — to forget about a problem or situation

100. **wing it** — to do something with no practice, preparation, or experience

APPENDIX F
50 COMMON USAGE ERRORS

The following list contains words that often cause usage errors. They are confusing because they sound alike or have similar meanings or spellings so its easy to use the wrong word. This is a good list to review just before taking your TOEFL exam—you might be able to pick up a few extra points quickly by studying this carefully. Go over it completely a few times—once is probably not enough.

1. **A, AN (*UN, UNA*)** <u>A</u> is used before a word with a consonant sound, while <u>AN</u> is used before vowel sounds. Be careful with the letter *H, U,* and *O* (see the **CU**).
<u>A</u> hurricane, but <u>an</u> honor. <u>A</u> university, but <u>an</u> uncle. <u>A</u> once-familiar face, but <u>an</u> orange.

2. **ACCEPT** *(ACEPTAR)*, **EXCEPT** *(EXCEPTO)*
Please <u>accept</u> the award on my behalf.
Everyone <u>except</u> Ernesto is here.

3. **ACCESS** *(ACCESO)*, **EXCESS** *(EXCESO)*
The young children were denied <u>access</u> to the R-rated movie.
We were charged a fee by the airline for our <u>excess</u> baggage.

4. **ADVICE** *(CONSEJO)*, **ADVISE** *(ACONSEJAR)*
You should follow the <u>advice</u> of your parents.
Please <u>advise</u> me on how I might improve my TOEFL score.

5. **AFFECT** *(AFECTAR)*, **EFFECT** *(EFECTO)*
The pollution <u>affects</u> everyone in Mexico City.
The <u>effect</u> of the herbal remedy is still being studied.

6. **AGAIN** *(OTRA VEZ)*, **AGAINST** *(CONTRA)*
Please call me <u>again</u> next Monday.
The UNAM teachers are demonstrating <u>against</u> their low salaries.

7. **ALLUSION** *(ALUSIÓN)*, **ILLUSION** *(ILUSIÓN)* <u>ALLUSION</u> is an indirect reference, <u>ILLUSION</u> is something that appears real but isn't.
I accidentally made an <u>allusion</u> to his mother's death.
The <u>illusions</u> of magician David Copperfield are so outrageous as to be unbelievable.

8. **ALMOST** *(CASI)*, **MOST** *(LA MAYORÍA)*
<u>Almost</u> everyone will be present tonight.
<u>Most</u> people are afraid of snakes.

9. **ALREADY** *(YA)*, **ALL READY** *(TODO LISTO O PREPARADO)*
I have <u>already</u> called the fire department.
I plan to be <u>all ready</u> to take my exams.

257

10. **AMOUNT, NUMBER** *(CANTIDAD)* While no distinction is made in Spanish, <u>AMOUNT</u> is used with non-count nouns and <u>NUMBER</u> is used with count nouns.
The <u>number</u> of students, but the <u>amount</u> of time.

11. **BARELY, SCARCELY, HARDLY** *(APENAS, CASI NO)* These words all mean basically the same, but they are important because they are considered negative words. Avoid using them with other negative words. I can <u>barely</u> hear the teacher, NOT "I can <u>barely not</u>..." Also remember to use inverted word order if you begin a sentence with these words (see the **WO** section).

12. **BESIDE** *(AL LADO DE)*, **BESIDES** *(ADEMÁS DE)*
The little girl sleeps with her doll <u>beside</u> her.
<u>Besides</u> the TOEFL, I must also take the GMAT exam.

13. **BETWEEN, AMONG** *(ENTRE)* While no distinction is made in Spanish, <u>BETWEEN</u> is only for two, and <u>AMONG</u> is used with three or more.
<u>Between</u> you and me, I think that restaurant is too expensive.
There is a great deal of interaction <u>among</u> the various departments of the hotel.

14. **CAPITAL** *(CAPITAL)*, **CAPITOL** *(CAPITOLIO)*
Montgomery is the <u>capital</u> of Alabama. OR More <u>capital</u> will be required to finance the project.
There will be no tours of the <u>capitol</u> today because the Congress is in session.

15. **CLOTHES** *(ROPA)*, **CLOSE** *(CERRAR O CERCA)*
I need to buy new <u>clothes</u>.
Please <u>close</u> the door. OR The school is <u>close</u> to my home.

16. **COMPLEMENT** *(COMPLEMENTO)*, **COMPLIMENT** *(CUMPLIDO)* Both of these nouns can also be used as verbs (*complementar y felicitar*)
This orange and blue tie will make a nice <u>complement</u> for my new blue suit.
Thanks very much for your kind <u>compliments</u>.

17. **CONSIDERABLE** *(CONSIDERABLE)*, **CONSIDERATE** *(CONSIDERADO)*
The staff has gone to <u>considerable</u> lengths to make the new member feel welcomed.
It was very <u>considerate</u> of you to send the wedding gift.

18. **COSTUME** *(DISFRAZ)*, **CUSTOM** *(COSTUMBRE)*, **CUSTOMS** *(LA ADUANA)*
María won the prize for best Halloween <u>costume</u>.
Most countries have distinct <u>customs</u>.
I hope I can get my new computer system through <u>customs</u> without paying too much in taxes.

19. **COUNCIL** *(CONSEJO, JUNTA)*, **COUNSEL** *(CONSEJO O ACONSEJAR)*
Juan is running for an office on the city <u>council</u>.
Ricardo appreciated the <u>counsel</u> given to him by his student advisor.
His priest <u>counseled</u> him to go into drug rehabilitation.

20. **CREDIBLE** *(CREIBLE)*, **CREDITABLE** *(LOABLE)*
Her version of the apparent crime was quite <u>credible</u>.
His <u>creditable</u> status had to be proved before he could secure financing for the car.

21. DECENT *(DECENTE)*, DESCENT *(BAJADA)*
A <u>decent</u> person would never take advantage of the elderly.
The pilot began his final <u>descent</u> into New York as he approached La Guardia Airport.

22. DESERT *(DESIERTO)*, DESSERT *(POSTRE)*
It's always good to remember a mental association to help avoid confusing these words. Here, notice the word dessert has two letter "S"s. Remember the ice cream cone has a double scoop!
Many animals are adapted for living in the hot, dry <u>desert</u>.
For <u>dessert</u>, I'll have the hot fudge sundae with chocolate syrup and nuts.

23. DEVICE *(APARATO)*, DEVISE *(CREAR)*
The <u>device</u> uses only batteries.
Scientist struggled for years to <u>devise</u> a vaccine for the smallpox virus.

24. DIFFER *(DIFERIR)*, DIFFERENT *(DIFERENTE)*
The new Volkswagen sedan <u>differs</u> enormously from the original.
It's refreshing to know people whose taste are somewhat <u>different</u>.

25. ELICIT *(SACAR)*, ILLICIT *(ILEGAL)*
The letter to the editor <u>elicited</u> responses from numerous readers.
The use of <u>illicit</u> drugs is strictly prohibited on this campus.

26. EXAMPLE *(EJEMPLO)*, SAMPLE *(MUESTRA)*
Grape juice changing to wine is an <u>example</u> of fermentation.
Publishing houses usually require <u>sample</u> work before offering book contracts.

27. FARTHER *(MÁS LEJOS)*, FURTHER *(MÁS LEJOS O MÁS)*
<u>FARTHER</u> is only used with distance, <u>FURTHER</u> can be used for distance, but also for time, degree, and quantity.
Acapulco is a bit <u>farther</u> from Mexico City than Cuernavaca.
<u>Further</u> research is needed before conclusions can be drawn.

28. FEWER, LESS *(MENOS)*
While no distinction is made in Spanish, <u>FEWER</u> is used only with count nouns, while <u>LESS</u> is used only with non-count nouns.
<u>FEWER</u> coins, but <u>LESS</u> money. <u>FEWER</u> minutes, but <u>LESS</u> time.

29. FORMER, FIRST *(PRIMERO)*
While no distinction is made in Spanish, <u>FORMER</u> refers to the first of two, while <u>FIRST</u> refers to the first of three or more.
Both halves of the basketball game were exciting, but the <u>former</u> seemed faster.
Carlos was the <u>first</u> student from my class to be selected to receive a scholarship.

30. FORMERLY *(PREVIAMENTE)*, FORMALLY *(FORMALMENTE)*
He <u>formerly</u> served on the board of directors.
Everyone at the embassy reception was dressed extremely <u>formally</u>.

31. FORTH *(ADELANTE)*, FOURTH *(EL CUARTO)*
During the storm, the boat rocked back and <u>forth</u>.
Winning <u>fourth</u> place in the beauty contest was a disappointment for Refugio.

32. HAD BETTER *(DEBERÍAS)*, WOULD RATHER *(PREFERIRÍA)*
You <u>had better</u> study for your TOEFL exam!
I <u>would rather</u> go to the beach for the weekend.

33. IMAGINARY *(IMAGINARIO)*, IMAGINATIVE *(IMAGINATIVO)*
Alice in Wonderland is filled with imaginary characters.
Lewis Caroll's work was certainly imaginative.

34. IMMORTAL *(INMORTAL)*, IMMORAL *(INMORAL)*
The music of Mozart is immortal.
The immoral behavior of the child was a disappointment to her parents.

35. INDUSTRIAL *(INDUSTRIAL)*, INDUSTRIOUS *(DILIGENTE)*
The music major never planned on doing industrial work for a living.
Her success as a student is due to her industrious study habits.

36. INSPIRE *(INSPIRAR)*, ASPIRE *(ASPIRAR)*
The architect claims that his work was inspired by the music of Rachmaninoff.
She aspires to be a writer although her work has yet to be published.

37. INTELLIGENT *(INTELIGENTE)*, INTELLIGIBLE *(INTELIGIBLE)*
Trading my car for a bicycle proved to be an intelligent decision.
Her accent is so strong that her English is hardly intelligible.

38. ITS *(SU)*, IT'S *(ESTÁ O ES)*
The dog finally found its way home after being lost for three days.
It's time to leave or we'll miss our flight for sure.

39. KIND, SORT, TYPE *(CLASE O TIPO)*
These words have the same meanings, but rember they have plural forms that we often neglect to use.
One KIND, but those KINDS. A SORT, but two SORTS.

40. LATER *(MÁS TARDE)*, LATTER *(LA SEGUNDA DE DOS)*
Would you like to go to the grocery store now or wait until later?
I like both restaurants, but the latter might be better if we plan to take the children.

41. LIKE *(COMO)*, AS IF *(COMO SI)*, SUCH AS *(TALES COMO)*
Bernardo looks very much like his father.
The pies smell as if they are burning.
Woodwinds such as oboes, clarinets, and bassoons require the use of a reed.

42. LONELY *(SOLITARIO)*, ALONE *(SOLO)*
Martha has felt lonely since her children have all left home.
Sometimes it's nice to be alone.

43. LOOSE *(FLOJO)*, LOOSEN *(SOLTAR)*, LOSE *(PERDER)*, LOSS *(PÉRDIDA)*
The light bulb doesn't work because it's too loose.
Toward the end of the day the executives like to loosen their ties and roll up their sleeves.
Gambling is a good way to lose your money quickly.
The climb in interest rates caused the unexpected loss of money.

44. MAYBE *(TAL VEZ)*, MAY BE *(PUEDE SER O ESTAR)*
Maybe this rain will end soon and we can play football.
It may be time to have the car tuned up.

45. PASSED *(PASÓ)*, PAST *(PASANDO O PASADO)*
I easily passed my exam this morning.
The boy ran past the house and continued around the block.
Sometimes it's better to think of the future instead of dwelling on the past.

46. PERSONAL *(PRIVADO)*, PERSONNEL *(LOS EMPLEADOS DE UNA EMPRESA)*
Note that the Spanish word PERSONAL has both meanings.
Whom I voted for is personal.
We have a personnel meeting this afternoon.

47. QUIET *(QUIETO)*, QUITE *(BASTANTE)*, QUIT *(RENUNCIAR)*
You must remain quiet in the library.
It's quite cold today.
Juan decided to quit his job after 15 years.

48. THOROUGH *(COMPLETO)*, THROUGH *(A TRAVÉS DE)*
A thorough physical exam is a good idea if you plan to start training for the marathon.
My cat loves to spend hours looking through the window.

49. WEATHER *(EL CLIMA)*, WHETHER *(SI)*
We're expecting beautiful weather for the concert.
I haven't decided whether to buy a car now or wait for the new models.

50. WHO'S *(QUIÉN ES O ESTÁ)*, WHOSE *(DE QUIÉN O CUYO)*
Who's your English teacher this semester?
Does anyone know whose book this is?

APPENDIX G
25 FALSE COGNATES (ENGLISH-SPANISH)

We have many Spanish words that look similar to English words—and quite often they have the same meaning, which is useful. However, these words sometimes have different meanings, which can be especially confusing. Some of the most common "false cognates", words that look alike but have different meanings, are listed here.

1. **ACTUAL** means *de verdad, NOT del momento*

2. **ADVERTISEMENT** means *anuncio, NOT advertencia*

3. **ASSIST** means *ayudar, NOT asistir*

4. **ATTEND** means *asistir, NOT atender*

5. **CABINET** means *armario, NOT gabinete*

6. **COLLEGE** means *universidad, NOT colegio*

7. **CONFIDENCE** means *confianza, NOT confidencia*

8. **CORRESPONDING** means *correspondiente, NOT corrrespondencia*

9. **CUP** means *taza, NOT copa*

10. **DISGUST** means *aversión, NOT disgusto*

11. **EMBARRASSED** means *apenado, NOT embarazada*

12. **EXIT** means *salida, NOT éxito*

13. **FACILITIES** means *instalaciones NOT facilidades*

14. **INTRODUCE** means *presentar, NOT introducir*

15. **LECTURE** means *conferencia, NOT lectura*

16. **LIBRARY** means *biblioteca, NOT librería*

17. **LUXURY** means *lujo, NOT lujuria*

18. **MANNERS** means *modales, NOT maneras*

19. **NOTICE** means *aviso, NOT noticia*

20. **PARENTS** means *padres, NOT parientes*

21. **REALIZE** means *darse cuenta, NOT realizar*

22. **RELATIVES** means *parientes, NOT relativos*

23. **RESORT** means *lugar de vacaciones, NOT resorte*

24. **SENTENCE** means *oración, NOT sentencia*

25. **SUCCESS** means *éxito, NOT suceso*

APPENDIX H
VERB TENSE MODELS
WITH SPANISH EQUIVALENTS

SIMPLE PRESENT TENSE
Remember to add an "s" in the third person singular.

I walk *(Yo camino)*
You walk
He, she, it walks
We, you, they walk

PRESENT PERFECT TENSE
Remember to use "has" in the third person singular.

I have walked *(Yo he caminado)*
You have walked
He, she, it has walked
We, you, they have walked

PRESENT CONTINUOUS TENSE
Here, we conjugate the verb *to be* in the simple present tense.

I am walking *(Yo estoy caminando)*
You are walking
He, she, it is walking
We, you, they are walking

PRESENT PERFECT CONTINUOUS TENSE
Here, we conjugate the verb *to have* in the simple present tense and use "been".

I have been walking *(Yo he estado caminando)*
You have been walking
He, she, it has been walking
We, you, they have been walking

SIMPLE PAST TENSE
Here, we simply add "ed" to all conjugations, unless the verb is irregular, in which case we use the irregular form for all conjugations.

I walked *(Yo caminé)*
You walked
He, she, it walked
We, you, they walked

PAST PERFECT TENSE

Here, we use *had* with a past participle.

I had walked *(yo había caminado)*
You had walked
He, she, it had walked
We, you, they had walked

PAST CONTINUOUS TENSE

Here, we conjugate the verb *to be* in the past tense.

I was walking *(Yo estaba caminando)*
You were walking
He, she, it was walking
We, you, they were walking

PAST PERFECT CONTINUOUS TENSE

Here, we use *had been* in each conjugation.

I had been walking *(Yo había estado caminando)*
You had been walking
He, she, it had been walking
We, you, they had been walking

SIMPLE FUTURE TENSE (WITH WILL)

Here, we use the word *will* with the simple form of a verb.

I will walk *(Yo caminaré)*
You will walk
He, she, it will walk
We, you, they will walk

FUTURE WITH "GOING TO" TENSE

Here, we use a conjugated form of the verb *to be*, the words *going to*, and the simple form of a verb

I am going to walk *(Yo voy a caminar)*
You are going to walk
He, she, it is going to walk
We, you, they are going to walk

FUTURE PERFECT TENSE

Here, we use *will, have,* and a past participle

I will have walked *(Yo habré caminado)*
You will have walked
He, she, it will have walked
We, you, they will have walked

FUTURE CONTINUOUS TENSE

Here, we use *will be* with an *ing* from.

I will be walking *(Yo estaré caminando)*
You will be walking
He, she, it will be walking
We, you, they will be walking

FUTURE PERFECT CONTINUOUS TENSE

Here, we use *will, have, been,* and an *ing* form

I will have been walking *(Yo habré estado caminando)*
You will have been walking
He, she, it will have been walking
We, you, they will have been walking

APPENDIX I
PREPOSITION COMBINATIONS

Review these well, as they cause problems for many Spanish-speakers. They don't follow rules—they must be learned by example, and they often work differently in Spanish (so translating is not a good idea). For example, in English, you *think of*, while in Spanish you *pensar en*.

A *absent from, accustomed to, add to, acquainted with, admire for, afraid of, agree with/on/about something, angry at/with, apologize to, apply to, approve of, argue with, arrange to, arrive at/in, ask about/for, aware of*

B *bad for, believe in, belong to, bored with/by, borrow from*

C *capable of, clear to, command to, compared to/with, complain to/about, composed of, concentrate on, conscience of, consist of, crazy about, crowded with*

D *depend on/upon, decide to, devoted to, determined by, delighted by, differ in, different from, disagree with, disappointed in, discuss with, divide into, divorced from, done with, dream about/of*

E *enable to, encouraged by, engaged to, equal to, escape from, excited about, excited by, excuse for, excused from, exhausted from*

F *familiar with, forgive for, friendly to/with, frightened of/by, fulfilled by, full of*

G *get rid of, giggle at, gone from, good for, graduate from*

H *happen to, hear about/of, hear from, help with, hide from, hope for, humbled by, humiliated by, hungry for*

I *impressed by, informed of, insist on, instruct to, interested in, intrigued by, introduce to, invite to, involved in*

J *joke at/with, jot down, judge by/from, jump at, justified by*

K *kind to, know about/of, known as*

L *laugh at, listen to, loan to, look at, look for, look forward to*

M *mad at, made of, married to, matter to*

P *participate in, pay for, patient with, pleased with, point at, polite to, prepared for/to, protect from, proud of*

S *satisfied with, scared of/by, search for, separate from, similar to, sorry about/for, speak to/with, specialized in, stare at, subtract from, sure of, surprised by*

T take *care of, talk to/with/about, tell about/to, terrified of/by, thank for, thirsty for, threatened by, tolerant of, tired from/of, train in, travel to*

W *wait for/on, wish for, worried about*

APPENDIX J
SCORE CALCULATION TABLE

NOTE: Even though this edition does not include practice exams they are widely available and you should take a few before you take the actual TOEFL. This table will help give you an approximate score, based on the number of correct answers in each section. See the following appendix to convert this score to the iBT testing scale.

To get an overall score, take your three converted scores (one from each section), add them together, divide by three, then multiply by ten.

60	—	—	67
59	—	—	66
58	—	—	66
57	—	—	66
56	—	—	65
55	—	—	65
54	—	—	65
53	—	—	64
52	—	—	64
51	—	—	64
50	68	—	63
49	66	—	63
48	64	—	63
47	63	—	62
46	62	—	62
45	61	—	61
44	60	—	61
43	59	—	60
42	58	68	60
41	57	67	59
40	57	66	58
39	56	65	57
38	55	64	56
37	54	63	55
36	53	61	54
35	53	59	53
34	52	58	52
33	51	57	51
32	51	56	51
31	50	54	50
30	49	53	49
29	49	52	49
28	48	51	48
27	48	50	47
26	47	49	46
25	47	48	45
24	46	47	44
23	46	46	43
22	45	45	43
21	44	44	42
20	43	43	41
19	42	42	40
18	42	41	39
17	41	40	38

APPENDIX K

ITP/PBT—iBT SCORE CONVERSIONS

ITP/PBT	iBT
677	120
650	115
640	112
630	109
620	105
610	102
600	100
590	96
580	92
570	88
560	83
550	80
540	76
530	71
520	68
510	64
500	60
490	57
480	54
470	52
460	48
450	45
440	42
430	39
420	36
400	32

APPENDIX L

ANSWER KEY

SWE-2: 2. 3, Fishing 3. 2, This 4. 3, Breathing 5. 5, Whoever finds the lost puppy 6. 1, Tornadoes 7. 4, To drive 8. 1, Mumps 9. 1, Papyrus 10. 3, Falling 11. 5, That pigeons can find their way home 12. 1, Subjects 13. 4, To study 14. 1, Silk 15. 3, Advertising

SWE-3: 2. will begin blooming 3. should have been, was reached 4. is 5. are 6. is spoken 7. was sued 8. was, is considered 9. is done 10. will be 11. has seen 12. has given 13. are discouraged 14. is considered to be 15. are, score

MINI TOEFL-1: 1. C, 2. B, 3. A, 4. B, 5. C, 6. A, 7. D, 8. A, 9. B, 10. B

SWE-4: 2. B, 3. NV, 4. B, 5. B, 6. B, 7. AV, 8. B, 9. NV, 10. B, 11. B, 12. B, 13. B, 14. B, 15. B, 16. B, 17. B, 18. B, 19. AV, 20. B

SWE-5: 2. V, 3. V, 4. X, 5. V, 6. X, 7. V, 8. X, 9. X, 10. X, 11. V, 12. X, 13. X, 14. V, 15. V, 16. V, 17. V, 18. X, 19. X, 20. V

SWE-6: 2. P 3. P 4. C 5. C 6. C 7. C 8. C 9. P 10. P 11. C 12. P 13. P 14. C 15. C

SWE-7: 2. - 3. ✓ 4. + 5. - 6. ☐ 7. - 8. - 9. + 10. ✓ 11. ✓ 12. - 13. + 14. - 15. -

MINI TOEFL-2: 1. B, 2. C, 3. D, 4. A, 5. B, 6. A, 7. B, 8. A, 9. B, 10. C

SWE-9: 2. MC, 3. SC, 4. MC, 5. SC, 6. MC, 7. SC, 8. SC, 9. SC, 10. MC, 11. MC, 12. SC, 13. SC, 14. SC, 15. SC

SWE-10: 2. X, 3. SC, 4. SC, 5. X, 6. SC, 7. SC, 8. X, 9. X, 10. SC, 11. SC, 12. X, 13. SC, 14. SC, 15. SC

SWE-11: 2. X, 3. X, 4. SC, 5. X, 6. MC, 7. X, 8. X, 9. MC, 10. SC, 11. X, 12. SC, 13. X, 14. X, 15. SC

ANSWER KEY

MINI TOEFL-3: 1. C, 2. A, 3. B, 4. D, 5. C, 6. A, 7. C, 8. B, 9. A, 10. C

SWE-12: 2. X, 3. NC, that we won the game 4. NC, how children acquire a second language 5. NC, Where we shop for fresh vegetables 6. NC, that the Tooth Fairy really exists 7. NC, That it infrequently rains in the desert 8. X, 9. X, 10. NC, How much money the politician spent on his campaign 11. NC, That cigarettes cause cancer 12. NC, that about 95% of the population is right handed 13. NC, that no two fingerprints are the same 14. NC, how to operate the microwave oven 15. NC, How twins interact during childhood 16. NC, that the game had to be cancelled because of bad weather 17. NC, that his project is the best 18. NC, that dogs and cats are color blind 19. NC, How the brain functions 20. X

SWE-13: 2. he wanted to be a fireman 3. the man had run a red light 4. the congressman will loose the election 5. the patient was in stable condition 6. crystals have healing powers 7. the new law had been passed 8. we will score above 500 on the TOEFL 9. we will have a fire drill today 10. carbohydrates be limited

SWE-14: 2. which the skunk discharges 3. which are located near the base of the skunk's tail 4. which can be smelled from half a mile away 5. which can also sting the eyes 6. skunks eat 7. scientists have classified 8. skunks typically reach 9. the skunk must avoid 10. scientists have found in South America

MINI TOEFL-4: 1. D, 2. B, 3. B, 4. C, 5. A, 6. B, 7. B, 8. C, 9. A, 10. D

SWE-15: 2. (García...name), Chang...world 3. (Christmas...December 25), Even though...Jesus Christ 4. (the secret...men), Since...1886 5. (it...fly), Because...bird, although...hour 6. (he...school), Unless...bicycle, even though...time 7. (the flower...Asia), Although...tulips 8. (writers...typewriters) Until...invented, even though...tedious 9. (The university...week), so that...taken, before...begins 10. (Tickets...expensive), although...available, if...minute 11. (Please...staff), as soon as...know, if...planned 12. (we...game), Unless...Saturday 13. (you...discounts), If...early, although...penalized 14. (Antonio...sleeping), When...rang, although...wake up 15. (The light...rainbow), although...sun

ANSWER KEY

SWE-16: 2. SC, ADV 3. MC 4. SC, ADV 5. SC, ADJ 6. MC 7. SC, ADV 8. MC 9. SC, ADJ 10. X 11. SC, ADJ 12. SC, N 13. SC, ADV 14. SC, N 15. MC

SWE-17: 2. 3 3. 1 4. 3 5. 4 6. 1 7. 2 8. 4 9. 1 10. 3 11. 3 12. 2 13. 2 14. 4 15. 2

MINI TOEFL-5: 1. A 2. D 3. B 4. B 5. C 6. D 7. A 8. A 9. C 10. A

SWE-19: 2. team, are 3. Japanese, are 4. data, are 5. Deer, are 6. All, are 7. candles, are 8. pilots, are 9. Alumni, are 10. Ana, is 11. English, is 12. results, are 13. Some, are 14. police, is 15. All, are

MINI TOEFL-6: 1. A 2. D 3. C 4. A 5. C 6. C 7. B 8. A 9. C 10. A

SWE-20: 2. is 3. are 4. is 5. are 6. is 7. are 8. is 9. are 10. are 11. is 12. are 13. is 14. is 15. is

SWE-21: 2. history, is 3. cholera, is 4. Essential Spanish for Tourists, provides 5. Everyone, has 6. secretaries, have 7. players, referees, are 8. check, was 9. van, is 10. Some, has 11. attendant, usher (proceeded by every), is 12. crimes (proceeded by the number of), has 13. pair, is 14. school, was 15. It, was

MINI TOEFL-7: 1. D 2. A 3. B 4. C 5. C 6. A 7. A 8. B 9. B 10. B

SWE-23: 2. their 3. her 4. his 5. our 6. his 7. his 8. their 9. our 10. his

SWE-24: 2. its 3. their 4. its 5. their 6. its 7. their 8. their 9. its 10. her

SWE-25: 2. Every has to present his... 3. ...is going to order its new...4. The one million dollars was given...who won it... 5. ...are popular...because of their warm... 6. ...is available...students request it. 7. ...his pet...for his actions. 8. Everyone needs to take his...9. Many a man has...10. books have...they would disappear.

MINI TOEFL-8: 1. D 2. C 3. A 4. D 5. B 6. C 7. D 8. A 9. C 10. C

SWE-27: 2. X, for some time now, (is planning) 3. X, since the end of the football season, (is) 4. ✓, So far, (have been reached) 5. ✓, up until now, (has been found) 6. X, When she died, (has...been) 7. X, By the end of the class, (will had finished) 8. X, In the early seventies, (is recording) 9. ✓, since this morning, (has been dropping) 10. X, By the time we get home, (will had arrive)

ANSWER KEY

SWE-28: 2. hold/held 3. wrote/written 4. lived/live 5. became/become 6. discovering/discovered 7. wrote/written 8. made/make 9. have gave/have given 10. give/given 11. make/made 12. know/known 13. bit/bitten 14. sworn/swore 15. became/become

MINI TOEFL-9: 1. A 2. A 3. D 4. B 5. A 6. C 7. B 8. A 9. C 10. A

SWE-30: (top to bottom; line by line) my, yourself, his, her, its, our, yours, them, oneself, who

SWE-31: 2. O 3. PA 4. PP 5. R 6. S 7. PA 8. PP 9. PA 10. O 11. S 12. PA 13. PA 14. R 15. S

MINI TOEFL-10: 1. A 2. C 3. D 4. A 5. D 6. A 7. A 8. C 9. A 10. B

SWE-32: 2. X 3. ✓ 4. ✓ 5. X 6. X 7. ✓ 8. ✓ 9. ✓ 10. X

SWE-33: 2. X 3. ✓ 4. ✓ 5. X 6. X 7. ✓ 8. ✓ 9. ✓ 10. X

SWE-34: 2. ✓ 3. ✓ 4. X 5. X 6. ✓ 7. ✓ 8. X 9. ✓ 10. ✓

SWE-35: 2. ✓ 3. X 4. ✓ 5. X 6. ✓ 7. X 8. ✓ 9. ✓ 10. ✓

SWE-36: 2. X 3. ✓ 4. ✓ 5. ✓ 6. ✓ 7. ✓ 8. X 9. ✓ 10. X

MINI TOEFL-11: 1. A 2. C 3. D 4. A 5. D 6. A 7. A 8. C 9. A 10. B

SWE-37: 2. ✓ 3. X 4. ✓ 5. ✓ 6. ✓ 7. ✓ 8. X 9. ✓ 10. X 11. ✓ 12. ✓ 13. ✓ 14. ✓ 15. X

SWE-39: 2. PREP 3. INF 4. INF 5. INF 6. PREP 7. INF 8. INF 9. PREP 10. INF 11. INF 12. INF 13. INF 14. INF 15. INF 16. PREP 17. INF 18. PREP 19. PREP 20. PREP

ANSWER KEY

SWE-40: 2. S-We, V-go, I-to learn 3. IS-To drive, V-is 4. S-Jesus, V-wants, I-to drive 5. S-Doctors, V-need, I-to keep 6. S-She, V-went, I-to buy 7. IS-To control, V-spray 8. S-Researchers, V-hope, I-to find 9. IS-To eat, V-is 10. S-I, V-want, I-to see 11. S-band, V-is going, I-to perform 12. S-Giovanna, V-likes, I-to cook 13. S-We, V-plan, I-to put 14. S-We, V-need, I-to plan 15. S-I, V-hope, I-to make

SWE-41: 2. S-grandmother, V-is arriving 3. S-They, V-enjoy, G-playing 4. GS-Backpacking, V-requires 5. S-orchestra, V-is practicing 6. GS-Learning, V-is 7. S-He, V-is becoming, G-playing 8. GS-Flooding, V-was caised. G-breaking 9. GS-Mailing, V-insures 10. S-players, V-are becoming 11. S-She, V-thanked, G-baby-sitting 12. GS-Swimming, V-is 13. S-family, V-is going 14. GS-Roller-blading, V-is 15. S-Greg Louganis, V-perfected, G-diving

MINI TOEFL-12: 1. C 2. B 3. D 4. A 5. D 6. A 7. B 8. C 9. C 10. A

SWE-42: 2. (grown), (hanging) 3. (recruited), (scheduled) 4. (bubbling) 5. (showing), (aspiring) 6. (playing) 7. (Folding), (exhausted) 8. (swimming) 9. (accused), (coming) 10. (selling), (barking) 11. (torn), (experienced) 12. (Neglected), (abused) 13. (circulating), (polluted) 14. (reserved) 15. (tossed), (shredded), (sliced), (grated)

SWE-43: Active Verbs: is walking, are playing, were helping, looks, was put, will call, have been fed, drank, are studying, is cooking Verbal Adjectives: selling, speaking, eating, acting, participating, looking, remembering, reviewing, jumping, crying

SWE-44: 2. convincing, convinced 3. surprising, surprised 4. annoying, annoyed 5. exhausting, exhausted 6. entertaining, entertained 7. frightening, frightened 8. amusing, amused 9. entertaining, entertained 10. excting, excited

SWE-45: 2. A 3. B 4. A 5. B 6. B 7. A 8. A 9. B 10. B

SWE-46: 2. X 3. v 4. X 5. v 6. X 7. v 8. X 9. v 10. v

SWE-47: 2. Winning the election...or Having won the election...3. After running all the way home...4. Having a high caffeine content...5. After graduating from college...6. Requiring little water...7. Being easy to grow...8. After being checked...9. When consumed frequently...10. Being high in calories...

SWE-48: 2. applying, TOEFL exam, X 3. cleaning, maid, v 4. eating, stomach ache, X 5. Standing, sun, X 6. Made, pie, v 7. Arriving, Cristina, v 8. Running, blood pressure, X 9. Living, couple, v 10. Loving, performance, X 11. Considering, parties, X 12. Considered, works, X 13. Offering, store, v 14. Located, Huatulco, v 15. Powered, electric cars, v 16. practicing, routine, X 17. being carried, arrangement, v 18. working, Manuel's eyes, X 19. plugging, electrical shock, X 20. Having spent, shopper, v

MINI TOEFL-13: 1. B 2. D 3. A 4. B 5. B 6. B 7. C 8. A 9. A 10. A

SWE-50: 2. delivery 3. trial 4. withdrawal 5. acceptance 6. movement 7. examination 8. discovery 9. pleasure 10. erasure 11. refusal 12. advertisement 13. observation 14. judgement 15. existence 16. pressure 17. recovery 18. correspondence 19. formation 20. obligation

SWE-51: 2. Flattery, flatter 3. existence, exist 4. mastery, master, 5. advertisement, advertise 6. decorations, decorate 7. conclusions, conclude 8. refusal, refuse 9. correspondence, correspond 10. executions, execute 11. coherence, cohere 12. pleasures, please 13. concealment, conceal 14. examination, examine 15. encouragement, encourage

SWE-52: 2. decision 3. preference 4. resignation 5. refusal 6. OK 7. recovery 8. abandonment 9. installation 10. erasure 11. excitement 12. OK 13. existence 14. implication 15. transfer 16. division 17. pressure 18. automation 19. departure 20. arrangement

SWE-53: 2. OK 3. resigning, resignation 4. OK 5. failing, failure 6. arranging, arrangement 7. developing, development 8. informing, information 9. OK 10. implying, implication 11. withdrawings, withdrawals 12. agreeing, agreements 13. discovering, discovery 14. existing, existence 15. OK

MINI TOEFL-14: 1. D 2. B 3. A 4. B 5. C 6. B 7. B 8. C 9. A 10. B

SWE-54: 2. alcoholic 3. inventor 4. socialite 5. magician 6. youngster 7. servant 8. carpenter 9. racketeer 10. biologist

SWE-55: 2. penniless 3. golden 4. Nebraskan 5. introductory 6. selfish 7. fireproof 8. majestic 9. impressionable 10. picturesque 11. fanatical 12. ghostly 13. awesome 14. active 15. glamorous 16. chilly

ANSWER KEY

SWE-56: 2. ADJ 3. ADJ 4. ADV 5. ADV 6. ADV 7. ADV 8. ADJ 9. ADV 10. ADV 11. ADV 12. ADV 13. ADJ 14. ADV 15. ADJ 16. ADJ 17. ADV 18. ADV 19. ADJ 20. ADV

SWE-57: 1. excel, excellent, excellently 2. satisfaction, satisfy, satisfactorily 3. confidence, confide, confidential 4. success, successful, successfully 5. decide, decisive, decisively 6. energy, energize, energetically 7. excess, exceed, excessive 8. repetition, repetitive, repetitively 9. categorize, categorical categorically 10. imagination, imagine, imaginatively

MINI TOEFL-15: 1. B 2. D 3. A 4. C 5. A 6. D 7. A 8. A 9. A 10. B

SWE-58: 2. quiet 3. angrily 4. wonderful 5. carefully 6. quiet 7. pale 8. sad 9. good 10. crazy 11. carefully 12. wide 13. honest 14. brightly 15. angry 16. finally 17. good 18. uncontrollably 19. sweet 20. happy

SWE-59: 2. highly 3. extremely 4. extreme 5. highly 6. really 7. real 8. extremely 9. original 10. extreme

SWE-60: 1. happier, happiest 2. more/most 3. wiser, wisest 4. more/most 5. messier, messiest 6. better, best 7. longer, longest 8. funnier, funniest 9. more/most 10. greener, greenest 11. worse, worst 12. more/most 13. faster, fastest 14. more/most 15. more/most 16. stranger, strangest 17. more/most 18. more/most 19. lazier, laziest 20. crazier, craziest

SWE-61: 2. more 3. better 4. better 5. tallest 6. more 7. less 8. faster 9. easiest 10. with 11. more exhausted 12. best 13. tallest 14. best 15. less

MINI TOEFL-16: 1. D 2. A 3. B 4. C 5. D 6. B 7. B 8. B 9. B 10. B

SWE-63: 2. Only once has Juan forgotten... 3. Scarcely had I sat down... 4. Only after he passed the TOEFL did he begin... 5. Only once have I gone... 6. Never before have I seen... 7. Nowhere is the price... 8. Not only did we go... 9. Only in the morning does the doctor see... 10. Rarely does it snow... 11. Only after doing extensive research did the doctoral candidate begin... 12. At no time were the concert goers allowed... 13. Nowhere have I enjoyed... 14. Only after practicing for hours could she play... 15. Only on Sunday are the museums...

ANSWER KEY

SWE-64: 2. So hungry were the children... 3. There are many important reasons... 4. Here are the answers... 5. Little does the boy know... 6. In walked the judge... 7. Such a desire to win is not healthy... 8. Few literary works include such... 9. Up rose the smoke... 10. Out ran the children... 11. So clever was the thief... 12. Such animals are common... 13. Here are the books... 14. So talented was she... 15. Few were the nights...

MINI TOEFL-17: 1. A 2. C 3. D 4. A 5. C 6. A 7. D 8. A 9. A 10. B

SWE-65: 2. Under the table are... 3. Seen at the awards presentation were... OR At the awards presentation were seen... 4. Somewhere over the rainbow is... 5. Discovered in the basket was... OR In the basket was discovered... 6. Should he go... 7. Around the corner lives... 8. Engaged to be married was... 9. Had he read... 10. At the top of the mountain waited... 11. Accused of the crime were... 12. Stored in the big trunk are... 13. In the trunk of the car is... 14. Should you see it... 15. Placed at the top of the Christmas tree was...

SWE-66: 2. D? 3. I? 4. D? 5. I? 6. I? 7. I? 8. I? 9. I? 10. D? 11. I? 12. I? 13. I? 14. D? 15. I? 16. D? 17. I? 18. D? 19. I? 20. I?

SWE-67: 2. ...we will have tomorrow? 3. ...when we will return... 4. ...how much money I can borrow. 5. ...why the alarm was sounded. 6. how the movie ended. 7. ...how much postage the letter needs. 8. ...there the event took place. 9. ...how much the book costs. 10. ...what the final score will be.

MINI TOEFL-18: 1. C 2. D 3. A 4. C 5. A 6. B 7. B 8. B 9. A 10. C

SWE-69: 2. a glass of wine 3. eating 4. because of her hard work 5. agreement 6. washing the dishes 7. medicine 8. six 9. in 10. because it was comfortable 11. frequently 12. to do 13. enjoyable 14. to tackle 15. misbehave

SWE-70: 2. X 3. v 4. X 5. v 6. v 7. X 8. X 9. X 10. X

SWE-71: 2. X 3. v 4. v 5. X 6. X 7. X 8. X 9. X 10. X 11. v 12. X 13. v 14. v 15. v

ANSWER KEY

SWE-72: 2. ...much redder than those on that tree. 3. ...than yours. 4. You should pick up not only... 5. ...than any other state... 6. ...and where we will stay. 7. ...just as exciting as... 8. ...greater than that of... 9. ...and eating chocolate... 10. ...because of many mistakes. 11. ...played tennis. 12. ...as expensive as... 13. ... or to your department head. 14. The band marched... 15. ...than any other city...

MINI TOEFL-19: 1. C 2. A 3. D 4. B 5. D 6. D 7. C 8. A 9. D 10. A

SWE-74: (sample answers—many more could be used) 2. right, accurate 3. beautiful, cute 4. big, huge 5. complete, whole 6. start, begin 7. quick, rapid 8. bright, vivid 9. elegant, sophisticated 10. jump, spring 11. humid, damp 12. auto, vehicle 13. advertising, commercials 14. stare, watch 15. rarely, hardly ever

SWE-75: 2. ↑ 3. = 4. ↓ 5. ↑ 6. ↑ 7. = 8. ↓ 9. ↓ 10. ↓ 11. = 12. ↓ 13. ↑ 14. ↓ 15. ↑

SWE-76: 2. X 3. v 4. X 5. X 6. v 7. X 8. X 9. X 10. X 11. v 12. X 13. X 14. v 15. X

MINI TOEFL-20: 1. C 2. B 3. A 4. A 5. D 6. C 7. C 8. C 9. A 10. D

SWE-78: 2. an 3. a 4. a 5. a 6. a 7. a 8. a 9. a 10. an 11. a 12. an 13. an 14. an 15. an 16. a 17. a 18. an 19. a 20. a

SWE-79: 2. A Cherokee, the 3. in the, a, of the 4. The, the, the 5. the, the west, of the 6. the hope, a 7. of, the, a 8. is the, of the 9. Chinese, the 10. the most, the, the

MINI TOEFL-21: 1. D 2. A 3. C 4. C 5. A 6. A 7. A 8. B 9. D 10. D

SWE-80: MAKE: appointment, arrangements, tone, comparison, effort, friends, turn, plans, speech, discovery, proposal, money, recommendation DO: dishes, bed, best, homework, laundry, research, housework, business

SWE-81: 2. laid 3. lie 4. rises 5. lay 6. rise 7. raise 8. rise 9. raised 10. raise 11. laid 12. set 13. sitting 14. lying 15. raise

ANSWER KEY

SWE-82: 2. 2 3. 2 4. 2 5. 2 6. 3+ 7. 2 8. 3+ 9. 3+ 10. 2 11. 2 12. 2 13. 3+ 14. 2 15. 2 16. 2 17. 3+ 18. 2 19. 3+ 20. 3+

SWE-83: 2. B 3. A 4. B 5. A 6. B 7. B 8. A 9. B 10. A

SWE-84: 2. NC 3. NC 4. C 5. NC 6. NC 7. C 8. C 9. NC 10. NC 11. C 12. C 13. NC 14. NC 15. C 16. C 17. NC 18. NC 19. C 20. C

SWE-85: 2. C 3. NC 4. B 5. C 6. C 7. C 8. NC 9. C 10. NC 11. C 12. B 13. C 14. NC 15. B

SWE-86: 2. A 3. A 4. A 5. B 6. A 7. B 8. A 9. A 10. A

SWE-87: 2. X 3. v 4. v 5. v 6. X 7. X 8. X 9. X 10. v 11. X 12. X 13. X 14. X 15. v

MINI TOEFL-22: 1. D 2. B 3. B 4. A 5. D 6. A 7. C 8. A 9. A 10. A
L-2: 1. B 2. A 3. B 4. B 5. B 6. A 7. B 8. B 9. B 10. B 11. A 12. B 13. A 14. B 15. B
L-3: 1. B 2. B 3. B 4. A 5. B 6. B 7. A 8. A 9. A 10. A 11. B 12. A 13. B 14. B 15. B

CPSIA information can be obtained
at www.ICGtesting.com
Printed in the USA
LVHW10s0359300818
588631LV00006B/725/P